WE ARE A MUSLIM, PLEASE

Zaiba Malik is an award-winning investigative journalist who has worked on some of the BBC's and Channel 4's most acclaimed radio and TV documentaries, including *Sleepers: Undercover with the Racists*, *Dispatches: Trouble at the Mosque* and *Killing for Honour*. She writes for newspapers including the *Guardian* and *Independent*, and was recently named as one of the twenty most influential black and Asian women in the UK.

D1235398

Zaiba Malik

WE ARE A
MUSLIM,
PLEASE

WILLIAM HEINEMANN: LONDON

Published by William Heinemann 2010

2 4 6 8 10 9 7 5 3

Copyright © Zaiba Malik 2010

Zaiba Malik has asserted her right under the Copyright, Designs
and Patents Act, 1988, to be identified as the author of this work

This book is a work of non-fiction based on the life, experiences and recollections of
the author. In some limited cases names of people, places and dates, sequences or the
detail of events have been changed solely to protect the privacy of others. The author
has stated to the publishers that, except in such minor respects not affecting the
substantial accuracy of the work, the contents of this book are true.

First published in Great Britain in 2010 by
William Heinemann

Random House, 20 Vauxhall Bridge Road,
London SW1V 2SA

www.rbooks.co.uk

Addresses for companies within The Random House Group Limited can be found at:
www.randomhouse.co.uk/offices.htm

The Random House Group Limited Reg. No. 954009

Every effort has been made to contact all copyright holders. If notified, the publisher
will be pleased to rectify any errors or omissions at the earliest opportunity.

A CIP catalogue record for this book
is available from the British Library

ISBN 9780434018475

The Random House Group Limited supports The Forest Stewardship
Council (FSC), the leading international forest certification organisation. All our
titles that are printed on Greenpeace approved FSC certified paper carry the FSC logo.
Our paper procurement policy can be found at: www.rbooks.co.uk/environment

Mixed Sources
Product group from well-managed
forests and other controlled sources
www.fsc.org Cert no. TT-COC-2139
© 1996 Forest Stewardship Council

Typeset in Fournier MT by Palimpsest Book Production Limited,
Falkirk, Stirlingshire

Printed and bound in Great Britain by
CPI Mackays, Chatham ME5 8TD

For Umejee, of course, who I love very much.

'The Bradford years were the formative years . . . I was moulded and coloured, so to speak, by the West Riding, and more particularly by Bradford.' J.B. Priestley

Contents

Prologue

Interrogation (2002)

It was the first thing that I noticed. The dents in the wall. All at the same height, about five feet off the ground. It was an old colonial building. Of course there were going to be knocks and bruises in the decor. But there was something more sinister about these holes. They weren't just wear and tear. The whitish-yellow wooden panels had been forced through, revealing the brickwork underneath only at the epicentre where the impact had been the greatest.

The second thing I noticed was the stink. All the windows were shut, so of course the room was going to reek of sweat, but I could smell something else, something prickly, something electrical. Just thinking about it now makes the tip of my tongue feel as though it's been poked into a power socket. Like that time when I was at university at Nottingham and my flatmate dared me to touch the heated element of our electrical fire and I did it, and before I noticed the burns that left me able to analyse my singed fingerprints for weeks after, I felt that same metallic buzz on the tip of my tongue.

'Sit down,' the man ordered.

Where to sit? On the wooden benches lining the holey walls? On the spotlit black plastic seat standing alone in the middle of the room? On the tiled floor?

As he moved to sit behind a desk, I was prompted to sit opposite him on a worn rickety grey chair.

I'd been feeling nauseous for days, but now I was on the verge of vomiting. I scanned the room for a dustbin or a plant pot. No joy. I swallowed hard. The man was the Torturer. And I was in the Torture Room.

'I am thirty-eight years old,' he announced. 'I was born in Bangladesh. People in Bangladesh, they have nothing. You must have seen this while you have been here. We are a poor country but we are not weak. I have worked hard and it is because of this that I am now a senior officer. My intention and my path in life is to serve my motherland and my religion. For it is these two things that have given me everything that I have. I live by their rules. Rules must be obeyed or else there will be chaos. Rules make people strong. I am a strong man.'

That much was obvious. The Torturer wasn't scrawny, like most of the Bangladeshis I'd seen. He was fit, muscular – like he worked out. And the discipline I could see in his attire. Even though it was mid-afternoon and hot, the only creases on his beige shirt were the two running strictly down each sleeve. He sat perfectly still and perfectly straight.

'I have seen life outside of Bangladesh. I have travelled all over the world. I have seen what there is in the world. Rich countries like America where they have everything – house, car, food. For a while, I too wanted those things. But then I learnt that those are corrupt countries where they have no rules.

'Everything changed for me when I served with the UN in Bosnia, with the Peacekeeping Mission. There, I saw with my own eyes the persecution of my fellow Muslims. They raped our girls and our women. Do you know what a heinous crime that is in Islam? Our men were put in camps and starved. Thousands and thousands of Muslims were murdered and their bodies thrown into graves. They burnt down our houses and our mosques. This is what they call "ethnic cleansing". Those miscreants wanted to kill our people, but they could not kill our beliefs.

'And what did the world do? Do you know? Nothing! The world watched this and they did nothing. Why? Because it was Muslims suffering. The world hates Muslims. I know this.

'After Bosnia, I could not serve anywhere else. There was only one rule. To be a Muslim and to protect other Muslims. I returned to Bangladesh. I will never leave this country again. I am here to protect my people. The world thinks nothing of Bangladesh as it thinks nothing of Muslims. That we are a poor nothing country. That we are something on your shoe. That they can take what they want from us and spit at us. Because they think we are poor, they think also that we are stupid. We are not stupid. We are not weak. I am a strong man. I will protect my country and the people of my country. And you . . .'

He gestured at me. His face, which until now had been ordered and rational, became sharp and pointed.

'. . . you will not stop us.'

Now I wanted to vomit and wet myself at the same time. If I wet myself, I wondered, would he say or do anything? Or would he just ignore it? Like that time when I was at university and I saw a middle-aged punk kick a car that hadn't stopped at a zebra crossing and three black men got out and pulled a knife on him and he fell on to the pavement and pissed himself. Passers-by just passed by, ignoring

3

him and the pool of urine that was slowly trickling from his black jeans down towards Radford Road.

'But I'm a Muslim,' I pleaded. 'I have no intention of hurting other Muslims.'

'No, you are not a true Muslim,' the Torturer replied.

That was the only time I ever went into the Torture Room, my one and only visit.

I wasn't strapped to that black plastic chair and given electric shocks.

I didn't have my head smashed against that whitish-yellow wall.

I wasn't hauled on to those benches and whipped with a long wooden stick.

I wasn't forced to squat for hours on that tiled floor or pinned down on it as nails were hammered into my feet.

All forms of torture that were routinely used against Bangladeshi prisoners.

No, I didn't have to suffer any of that.

But when I left the Torture Room, I was crippled with pain. You see, the Torturer had whacked me with seven words that made me want to scream and cry.

If only I had listened to Dad all those years ago, then I wouldn't be here, crouched on a filthy mattress in the main room of Bangladesh's notorious police headquarters in Dhaka, humming as loudly as possible to try and block out the wails of prisoners being beaten or electrocuted in the Torture Room and clasping my hands tightly together to stop them from shaking uncontrollably. Dad had been right.

'Our people do not become journalists. That is not a proper job. Why did you study law at university if you are not going to become a *vakil*, a solicitor? Look at

Farooqsa'ab's sons. All three boys are qualified now. They have their own practice in Manningham. They are doing so much for our people, helping them with immigration and passports. Each one has bought a first-hand Mesidees with their name on. *Vah bay vah*! My oh my!'

If only I had listened to Dad. Then I too could be driving to my own office in Bradford 8 right now in my shiny new blacked-out Merc with its personalised registration plate: 2AI8A. That's the ultimate status symbol in Bradford – a flash car with your name on it. It lets everyone know that you've made it in your chosen career, be that as a doctor, a businessman, an accountant or a drug dealer.

The 'community' would recognise my unique vehicular tag and they'd wave as I headed past their homes and shops on White Abbey Road, and turn to each other and say: 'There goes Maliksa'ab's daughter. Such a good girl. Always helping her own people.' And other cars would hoot their horns at me, cars called AHM 3D, N4SS4R and HU55E1N, whose young, British-born drivers were just like me, proud to be amongst *apnay lokhi*, our people.

If only I had listened to Dad. Then I would still be part of 'the community'. I'd still be going to weddings, every weekend, where the guests turned up two hours late, stuffed their faces with jeera chicken, Kashmiri pilau and rice pudding and then left. I'd still know all the gossip and tittle-tattle – whose marriage had fallen apart, who had turned down a *rishta*, a proposal. I'd still be desperately reaching for the remote control every time there was kissing on *EastEnders* before Umejee, Mum, could denounce the programme as *basharam*, shameful. I'd still have to eat the ten almonds she gave me every day to give me strength and make my hair shine. I'd still have kind Uncles smiling at me and scary Aunties assessing me to see if I was good future daughter-in-law material.

If only I had listened to Dad, then I would still be what those young lads in their supercharged turbo cars on White Abbey Road say as they greet each other, fist to fist: safe.

But I hadn't listened to Dad. I'd left Bradford in my twenties and moved to London to work as a journalist. And it was while I was filming a Channel 4 programme in Bangladesh about the growing influence of Islam in the country that I, along with my cameraman, Bruno Sorrentino, was arrested by government officials at the border town of Benapole.

We'd entered the country on tourist visas three weeks earlier. We'd had to. A number of articles in international publications about the presence of al-Qaeda members in places like Chittagong and Cox's Bazaar had made the government very nervous about allowing foreign journalists into the country. At first when we were stopped by the authorities we thought it was just a warning – they were going to hold us for a few hours to make us sweat for coming into Bangladesh without the correct permission and then they would let us go. That often happens with foreign journalists. But that evening, as we were driven back to the capital, Dhaka, in a cavalcade of police and army vehicles, it became apparent that this was more serious.

Nobody knew where we were. Our mobile phones had been confiscated. When Bruno and I insisted that we had the right to let somebody in the UK know we were being detained, our protests were ignored.

We spent our first night in a cell. The next morning we were taken to a courthouse. As we were escorted up the steps and into a huge room, photographers and TV crews jostled to get pictures of us. Still I was optimistic as we stood in the dock in front of the judge.

I waited for him to say: 'Okay, okay. We hope we've taught you a lesson. The Bangladeshi government does not approve of what you have done, coming into the country without the proper authorisation, especially at such a sensitive time. We hope you have learnt your lesson and that you will not do this again. You can collect your luggage, which is at the back of the courtroom, and we shall put you on the next flight to London.'

But he didn't.

He said: 'You have entered Bangladesh illegally, and your activities here in the last three weeks have been calculated to bring disrepute to the Bangladeshi people and its government. You have been involved in anti-state propaganda. You are both charged with sedition, which carries a sentence of life imprisonment or the death penalty.'

I laugh.

Nobody else is laughing.

I start to tremble. Then I start to shake. Then a piercing whoosh skates in from behind my head, straight over my eardrums, which puncture. I wince. The whoosh then starts to do a figure of eight over my eyes. Round and round and round. Over and over and over. A stabbing feeling passes from my left to my right to my left to my right eye. Then the tunnel vision kicks in. Do you know those plastic cones that dogs wear to stop them scratching themselves? Well, some invisible person ties one of those around my neck – a black one. And the only things I can see are the ones directly in front of me, objects that are framed on either side by thick black vertical bars, like the skewed rolling end credits of a film.

I can't hear a single thing, apart from a low, slow hum. Like that sound the Aunties in Bradford make when they get together to read the Koran. If only I'd listened to Dad. Then right now I could be sat cross-legged on a carpeted floor in a cosy living room amongst those dear women and Umejee, collecting brownie points from the Angels for reciting my prayers in Arabic, even if it is at an embarrassingly tedious speed.

A young man in a suit mouths something at me.

I can't hear you.

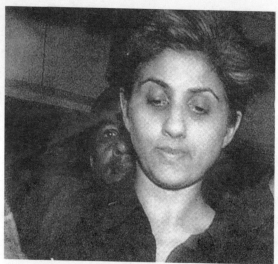

Being escorted into the Dhaka courthouse by police officers.

And the next thing I know is I'm in a large office that has a wooden desk and some chairs and a big cupboard, a kind of dresser, pushed up against the wall in one corner, no windows, and just two tubes of harsh white light. There is a fan above me, but its three blades are drooping from the ceiling like a wilted flower. In another corner of the room is a tiny cell, measuring about seven feet square. There are a dozen men in there. Some are crouched on the floor and some are standing. One man is lying with his back against the wall, I think he's asleep. His head is almost resting on the hole in the ground that I assume is the latrine. It must be. Where else is that stench of watery shit that's making me retch coming from?

The police guards at the desk stare at me.

The male prisoners inside the cell stare at me.

I stare at the person who is sitting on the mattress at the far end of the office. It's Priscilla, the young woman I employed to translate for us for a couple of days towards the end of our filming.

I glare at her. The first thing that comes into my head is that she was the one who informed on us to the authorities, told them that we'd been filming in the country without permission.

Priscilla doesn't look at me. She just looks straight ahead at the wall. At the same spot.

Then I quickly realise. And I want to burst into tears. She too is being detained.

I can't cope with this realisation. That because of me, this girl is in this room. God knows where we are or what will happen to us.

Priscilla doesn't look angry or upset or frightened. She looks nothing. And that's what scares me.

How do I tell her that I'm sorry? So, so sorry?

Do I shout at the officers: 'She hasn't done anything! This has got nothing to do with her! Let her go!'?

Do I collapse on the floor and start to wail, like I've seen the Aunties in Bradford do at all those wakes that Umejee makes me go to? I hate going to those *huthams* — Pakistani women produce such a harrowing sound when they mourn the death of a loved one.

Do I kneel at Priscilla's feet and touch them with my forehead and beg her forgiveness, like I've seen on those rented Pakistani VHS films I've had to sit through with Umejee and Dad? Those overly long over-the-top dramas about a pitiful wife married to a spineless husband living with an evil mother-in-law that could teach *EastEnders* a thing or two about misery and woe.

I don't do anything. I sit on the floor behind Priscilla so she can't see my shame and I can't see her blankness.

The next few days were the worst days of my life.

Even as I sit writing this now, almost six years later, in the magnificent open courtyard of the Victoria and Albert Museum with the temperature at 26 degrees, I feel as though I can't breathe and I'm so cold that the hairs on my arms and neck are standing on end and my stomach is churning so even just glancing at the cakes and pastries that they have on sale in the café here makes me feel like I'm going to throw up and I have to drink cup after cup of black tea to keep me warm and I'm not the slightest bit interested in looking at Bernini's graceful life-size statue of Neptune and Triton or Chihuly's magnificent glass chandelier that hangs in reception or even in buying a postcard or a pencil from the shop.

It wasn't the threat of physical violence. It wasn't the solitude. It wasn't not knowing how long I was going to be in there. It wasn't even the fear of what my detention would be doing to Umejee back home in Bradford.

It was what happened on the first floor of the police headquarters, directly above the Torturer's office, in the Interrogation Room.

* * *

'We are a Muslim.'

It was an announcement Umejee used to make, say, once every couple of months when we were in our teens, or whenever she felt the need. She might declare it to us individually, or in a family setting as we watched TV or ate our evening meal.

And that was fine. Completely unnecessary but fine. We all knew what we were. How could we not?

'We are a Muslim.'

'Yes, Mum. Thanks, Mum. That's great, Mum.'

She'd state it at times when she thought there might have been a bit too much Western intrusion into the house. For example, on a Sunday evening when *Songs of Praise* was on the telly or when there was an ad for sizzling Danish bacon or when I'd taken home a copy of *Vogue* magazine with a semi-naked supermodel on the cover. There was one occasion I remember particularly well when Hanif Kureishi's *My Beautiful Laundrette* was on Channel 4 and it got to the scene where the actress Rita Wolf lifts her top up in front of a room full of Uncles. I think it's the only time I've ever heard Mum scream, rather than firmly proclaim: 'We are a Muslim! We do not do these things! Switch it off! We are a Muslim!'

It was a phrase she would also use in the outside world. In front of strangers who, quite frankly, didn't give a shit.

'What's your name, please?' asked the receptionist at the doctor's surgery.

'Mrs Malik. Malik. Yes. We are a Muslim, please.'

'You look very colourful in your clothes,' observed the old lady at the bus stop. 'Are you from Pakistan?'

'Oh yes. You know, we are a Muslim, please.'

I would smile apologetically at the perplexed third party.

Umejee put so much enthusiasm and pride into one of the few sentences she could speak in English that I didn't have the heart to explain to her that these white people really didn't care what religion she was.

But to her, her faith was everything. It was who she was, not just what she was.

I could only repeatedly correct her on her grammar. Not that she took any notice.

My sister Adeeba, celebrates her Ameen with me, Umejee and Tassadaque, my brother. She had just learnt to recite the Koran in Arabic.

With this explicit and absolute understanding that 'we are a Muslim, please' came the implicit belief that all Muslims have a duty to take care of each other. As the religious saying goes: 'If one part of the body, one limb, feels pain, then the entire body feels that pain.' This Islamic fraternity had a name, which I didn't learn until I was in my early thirties. Until after 9/11 actually. The Ummah, meaning the global Islamic community.

The upshot of the Ummah on a local Bradford scale was

that Umejee and Dad tended to take mainly Muslims as lodgers into our home, and that Dad helped out those Muslims who couldn't speak, read or write English with their various official-form-filling-ins. In return, he could call on favours from 'the community'. That's how I ended up having free driving lessons from a man from Dad's mosque, Mr Rizvi. Or Poor Mr Rizvi as I called him. It took me seven attempts and four years to pass my driving test. That must have really tested his patience – and his faith. Most other non-Muslim instructors would no doubt have given up on me, having screamed themselves hoarse: 'Stop! Zaiba! Bloody hell! Stop! You're going to hit that woman!' But under the rules of the Ummah and Islamic solidarity, Poor Mr Rizvi had no choice but to keep on turning up at our house in his little Nissan Micra and take me out on to the roads of Bradford where, desperately clutching on to his Koranic parchment, he would instruct me through gritted teeth to: 'Stop, sister! No, sister! Stop, sister! Please stop, sister!'

Thank God for the Ummah. Brothers and sisters unite! Without it, I doubt I would ever have learnt to drive. I'm not sure Poor Mr Rizvi saw it that way. In fact, I wouldn't be surprised to hear that since getting into a car with me, he's adopted a white-learners-only policy. Much better for his wallet and his sanity.

I suppose the reason why I never heard the word 'Ummah' until so late on in my life was that it wasn't a term that many people in Bradford used. We tended to use the phrases *'apnay lokhi'*, 'our people', 'the community' to signify that the city's Muslim population should look out for each other. *'Apnay lokhi* who have shops should give good discounts to their own people.' 'It is the role of "the community" that they help us find a decent husband/wife for our daughter/son.'

This was small, inconsequential fry when compared to what the Ummah proper, the global Islamic unity, meant on a worldwide scale. It was the Ummah proper that held protests around the world against the publication of Salman Rushdie's *The Satanic Verses* in 1989; that shouted against the invasion of Iraq in 2003; that supports the Palestinians in the ongoing conflict against Israel; that calls for an end to Russian persecution in Chechnya; that sent millions of pounds in aid to Azad Kashmir in 2005 when the region was hit by a massive earthquake.

'We are a Muslim.'

It was an absolute concept I could draw upon wherever I was in the world. That was the whole point of it, wasn't it?

Even here, faced by a horseshoe of nine Bangladeshi interrogators in the upstairs room of the Detective Branch office on the Mintoo Road in Dhaka where I was being held with Bruno and Priscilla.

Facing life imprisonment or the death penalty for the very serious offence of sedition.

No matter. My religion was going to save me.

'You are a Muslim. I are a Muslim. We are a Muslim.'

We all have a duty to take care of each other.

How could they object to that?

How could they refuse?

How wrong could I be?

The nine men came in all shapes, sizes and ages. Some were round and moustachioed; others were lean and clean-shaven. Some were very dark-skinned, almost black, others were pale. One in particular was young and very good-looking. He had thick hair, a strong jaw line, full lips and long eyelashes. I wanted to say to him: 'You know, you should be a movie star, Handsome; why are you wasting your time serving your country in this dump of a building, Handsome?' But I found it difficult to maintain eye contact with him. He frightened me.

I scoured the panel for a friendly face. Most of the men stared back at me. There was nothing really discernible in those stares – they were just looking at me. Like Bangladeshis do. I'd realised in the three weeks I'd been filming in the country that Bangladeshis love to stare. Much more than Pakistanis. It's not contempt or disbelief or even inquisitiveness. It's just looking. You get used to it.

Then I found it – the third man on my left. It wasn't a friendly face – it was quite stern actually – but there was a balding head, a white beard and a sharp nose. This man looked like Dad. He was the one I was going to direct my answers to.

And then the questions started.

'What is the name of your father?'

'Why do you want to know his name?'

'What is the name of your father?'

'What's he got to do with this?'

'In our country, women are known by the names of their fathers or husbands. Are you married?'

'No.'

'What is the name of your father? Where was he born?'

Right from the outset, I think they thought I was being difficult. I wasn't doing it intentionally. They were asking me personal details about where I was born, how many siblings I had, what Dad did for a living, where Umejee came from in Pakistan.

I couldn't bear to think about family life. I'd shut that out of my mind. It was the only way I could cope. I was in this situation because of my job, because I was a journalist who was making a film for Channel 4, I told myself. I was in this situation because of my job. Why do you ask me about my personal life?

Then the Interrogators stated:

'You are working for the Indian government. We know this. You are a spy who has been sent by them to report bad things and to destabilise our country. How much money did you receive from them?'

'What?! I haven't been sent by anyone. I am a journalist working for Channel 4 in England. Have you heard of Channel 4? It's one of the major broadcasters in the country.'

'We know about Channel 4. This organisation is run by Jews.'

The Handsome One pulled out some papers from a file and read:

'"The British media is owned and run by Jews who are very wealthy. They control the newspapers and the television stations in London." You are a spy, working for the Hindus in the Indian government who are joined with the Jews at Channel 4. Do you know what the Indians have done to the Muslims in Gujarat, even just a few months ago? They murdered them. And do you know what the Jews do to the Muslims in Palestine? You must know that if you are a "journalist" as you say you are. The aim of the Jews and the Hindus is to destabilise and ruin our country. And that is also your aim. That is why you are working for Channel 4 and the Indians.'

'No, that's not at all true. I'm a Muslim too. Why would I ever want to do such a thing? I'm not paid by the Jews or the Hindus. I told you. I'm a journalist, a freelance journalist. I don't work for anybody, I'm self-employed.'

'That is why you have been tempted by the money of the Jews and the Hindus. How much were you paid?'

'No, you're not listening. I only get paid by Channel 4 for the work that I do. I work for many different organisations. And I've never even been to India. In fact, the last time I was at their embassy in London I had to be escorted off the premises because I swore at the woman who refused my application to—'

'You have been engaged in serious anti-state activities. We have evidence of this. You came with the malicious intent of portraying Bangladesh as a fundamentalist country. When you were arrested at the border at Benapole you were entering India.'

'We were just going to do a bit of filming there. I'm telling you, I'm not a spy. That's just rubbish. I am a Muslim. Why won't you believe me?'

'This is an extremely serious situation. Did you know that the punishment for this is life imprisonment or the death sentence? You will never leave this country.'

'Don't be stupid. I'm not—'

Suddenly there was an almighty bang, as if a grenade had been detonated in the room. I jumped so high off my seat I swear my head nearly touched the ceiling.

I must have looked as scared as that London taxi driver a couple of years ago who suddenly stopped his black cab in the middle of Regent Street when a bottle of pop I had in my bag exploded. I've never seen a cabbie move so fast. One second he was at the wheel, the next he was standing on the road outside Hamleys toyshop, shaking and ashen-faced. For some reason I can't explain, I found this hilarious. I couldn't stop laughing, even when he ordered me to get out of his 'friggin' cab'.

I certainly wasn't laughing now.

The Handsome One had brought his fist down hard on the table and was shouting: 'DON'T CALL US STUPID! WE ARE NOT STUPID! WE ARE BANGLADESHI MUSLIMS! IT IS YOU WHO IS STUPID! YOU ARE NOT A MUSLIM! YOU ARE A TRAITOR!'

Oh no! Not again! That same piercing, deafening whoosh that had cut into my head at the courthouse now passed over my eyes and ears for the second time. I couldn't see anything, and the only sound I could hear was that low, slow hum again. Just like the sound the Aunties in Bradford make when they get together to read the Koran.

Please, God. Please, God. Please, God. Put me back in Bradford, reading the Koran with the Aunties.

I was aware of somebody saying something to me, shouting at me.

It's no good; I can't hear you. I can barely see you. It's that tunnel vision again. I can only see what's directly in front of me.

I moved my body round in my chair to look at each of the Interrogators in turn, to see whose lips were moving.

Nine men stared back at me. Not with nothing stares, but with contempt.

For the seven days we were held at the Detective Branch, we all faced lengthy and frequent interrogation. Three or four times a day, for two to three hours at a time. Any time during the day or night.

Where did you go in Bangladesh?

Who did you interview?

How much were you paid to do this?

Do you know how many Muslims are dying around the world every day?

Do you know how many Bangladeshis are starving?

Do you know how the West gives us aid so it can steal our gas?

It was exhausting. All those questions from those nine men under that harsh light in front of that video camera inside that suffocating room.

And of course, I couldn't sleep.

The nights were worse than the days. They went on and on and on. And there was always so much noise at night. New prisoners being locked up in the cell, old prisoners groaning, the female guards giggling, shouting from somewhere in the building, honking from the rickshaws on the main road outside.

Did anybody out there know that we were in here? If I screamed as loudly as I could, would somebody come and rescue us? Why wasn't anybody out there helping us? Why hadn't anyone been to see us? What was going to happen to us? How long were we going to be here? For ever?

I'd noticed that whenever the Interrogators mentioned life imprisonment or the death penalty, they would always pause. I suppose they wanted to see the reaction on my face.

I must have disappointed them. Strange though it may seem, when they said: 'You will never leave Bangladesh' and 'Sedition is punishable by death', they might as well have been saying 'It's a lovely day outside, isn't it? Though they say it's going to rain later.' Right. There was nothing I could offer in response. Their threats were so surreal that they didn't register with me. It was hard enough to believe I was being held in a police cell somewhere in Dhaka, never mind that I might be killed, or even worse, never released.

I'd always had an overly active imagination, but even I couldn't visualise myself being in this shithole for the rest of my life, pacing up and down that room under that tube light. Not being allowed to speak to anyone. Staring at Priscilla. Living inside my head. No thanks. I'd done enough of that already as a child.

And even when I really really forced myself to contemplate what it must be like to be executed – to have a noose put over my head or to stand in front of a firing squad or to have a gas mask placed over my mouth or a needle shoved into my arm (I wasn't sure what form of capital punishment was used in Bangladesh) – I couldn't do it. It was just too bizarre. So most of the time it wasn't actually that hard to cope with the idea that I might never leave Bangladesh. I just didn't think about it.

Instead I forced myself to think about other things, nicer things. Like Umejee, and the way that she used to get me to write letters to Her Majesty the Queen, asking if she could go and work for her at Buckingham Palace. 'I am a very clean lady,' I wrote as Mum dictated. 'My own house in Bradford is very clean. You are very decent people. You are like my family. I want to help you. I will do what you need, cook, clean, iron.' Umejee, like so many other Pakistani women, held the royal family in great esteem. To her, this institution, headed by a matriarch and based on duty, respect, loyalty and *izzat*, honour, epitomised everything a family should be. 'You are like a Pakistani family. I will work for you for free.' Needless to say, we never heard back from Her Majesty. (Though in the years to come, Mum would have the pleasure of meeting the Queen and her offspring on a number of occasions – when she was invited to a summer garden party at the Palace, when she was amongst the 350 guests at Her Majesty's eightieth birthday lunch and when my sister, Adeeba, received an MBE for her work with ethnic minorities.)

Mum's adoration of the Queen certainly didn't extend to Mrs Thatcher. 'Why can't they kick her out? She is no good for this country. You can see from her face that she is a hard woman,' was Umejee's assessment as she watched the miners' strike and the poll tax riots and the long queues at job centres on the news. 'If I could speak English, I would go to London myself and tell her to get out.'

I thought about the way that, because she can't speak English, Umejee calls the Queen 'my mom', pronounces England 'Ingerlernd' and Channel 4 'China 4' and has renamed the singer Tom Jones 'Thumb Jone' and how, when she watches some wrongdoing on the news, she rhetorically asks why people do things that are 'deadly against law'.

The way that she always gives homeless people in Bradford a quid or two, even when I point out to her that they may well spend that money on un-Islamic things such as booze or drugs. 'It doesn't matter,' she says. 'Whatever makes their wretched lives a bit easier.'

The way that she sometimes tells me: 'Zaibee, you can achieve whatever you want in your life.'

The way that I love her very much.

Psychologists often say that for people held in captivity, one of the most difficult aspects is losing all control over what you say, do and even think. With every session the Interrogators were pounding me, like a hammer driving a nail into a plank of wood, making me believe that everything that was happening, the detention, the interrogation, the torture, was all punishment.

For sedition; for anti-state activities; for anti-Islamic activities.

I had to fight back, regain some control.

So I stopped eating. Pretty much from day one of my detention. It wasn't that hard. I had no appetite anyway. And lots of nervous energy. I refused their rice, their vegetables, their fish, their Pringles, their sweets. I only took one banana every day.

This worried the Interrogators. They didn't want anything serious to happen to me whilst I was in their custody. They could break international law and prevent me from having legal or consular access. They could hold Priscilla even though she had done nothing wrong. They could interrogate me for hours and hours at any time of the day. They could accuse me of whatever they pleased. But they couldn't allow me to be physically harmed.

'If you don't take food, we will force a saline drip into your arm,' warned the Torturer.

Still I didn't eat. I'd fasted throughout the month of Ramadan as a child so I knew I could do this. I too could be bloody-minded. Like the IRA hunger-striker Bobby Sands, whose name was graffitied on the wall at the bottom of our road in Bradford 7 for years: REST IN PEACE BOBBY SANDS 1954–1981. (It has always been a mystery to me as to who would have daubed such a tribute in our neighbourhood; we lived in a Pakistani area where there was more concern about what President Zia was up to back home than the welfare of the H-Block inmates. I can only conclude that maybe some Muslim on our street saw Bobby Sands as someone to be exalted, a religious man, with his long wavy hair and beard and knackered blanket shrouding his bare emaciated body; a man who was fasting on much harsher terms than we did during Ramadan and who talked about God.)

Though I had no intention of starving myself to death. I just wanted to become ill so I could be hospitalised and then could let somebody outside of this building know where we were and what was happening. As far as we were aware, nobody knew, though I learnt later that every day whilst we were being detained at Mintoo Road, officers from the British High Commission were at the gate trying to get in to see us. But they were never allowed entry.

As well as stopping eating, I started shouting at the guards who sat at the desk in the corner of the room.

'You fucking cunts! What are you staring at? What have you got to laugh about? Do you think this is funny, hey? Being held in this shithole by your bloody government? Why don't you go and do something useful instead of staring and laughing at me?'

They must have thought I was a madwoman. All quiet and still one minute and then like a howling banshee the next. I couldn't stop myself. I needed to get angry at someone, and there was no way that was going to be the Interrogators, so it had to be the guards. They had no idea what I was going on about or why I was suddenly spitting at them, so they just kept on staring at me, slightly bemused, which riled me even more.

'Didn't you hear me? I told you to stop staring at me! Are you deaf or just stupid? What part of 'fuck off' don't you understand, hey?'

After every outburst, once I'd calmed down, I felt so guilty about my terrible behaviour towards these officers, these pitiful minions who were just trying to make a living, that I had to lie down on the sodden mattress that I shared with Priscilla, put my head on the pillow and pull the mangy blanket over my head. In the semi-dark I tugged at both my ear lobes with my forefinger and thumb and muttered, '*Thoba*, God forgive me.' Like Umejee had taught me at the age of four when I'd called her sister, my Auntie, a bastard when she'd pierced my ears using a sewing needle.

It wasn't only anger that made me scream and shout so. I was trying to get Priscilla's attention. We couldn't talk to each other, that wasn't allowed, and there were always at least three guards in the room to make sure that we didn't. But Priscilla wouldn't even look at me. She just sat motionless on the mattress and stared at the same spot on the wall. Occasionally she would take off her glasses and wipe them on her shirt, but that was about it. Silence. Even when I was only a few inches away from her, I couldn't hear her breathing. What was going on in her head? I couldn't bear to think about it. I knew from my own time of absolute quiet, my Year of Silence when I was a child, that it wouldn't be anything pleasant.

I had very little contact with Bruno, the cameraman. He was being held at the back of the building. The only time I got to see him was when I passed his cell to go to the toilet. Any attempt to speak to him got me shoved along by the female officers who always accompanied me.

We only managed one brief conversation.

'What are those men asking you in that room upstairs?' I shouted.

'I'll leave you a note in the bathroom, behind the mirror,' he shouted back.

Every time I went to the bathroom, which was as often as every couple of hours – sometimes because of boredom, sometimes because of fear, sometimes just to annoy the officers – I checked behind the cracked mirror above the sink. Nothing. Only a gecko that seemed to permanently reside there. My little friend Jez.

I'm not sure where Bruno thought he could get hold of a pen and paper – everything had been confiscated – or what he intended to write in a note. But just the hope that I could have some contact with someone, even scribbled words, kept me constantly checking every possible hiding place in the bathroom.

Behind the toilet, under the sink, inside the plastic bucket, in between the slats on the shutters, above the rusty shower. Like the time I searched all around our house for the flute or clarinet that the Angels had promised me if I stayed up and prayed from dusk to dawn during the Night of Power.

I found nothing then. And I found nothing now.

If ever I needed a distraction it was now. Something to stop me thinking and thinking and thinking about what the Interrogators kept accusing me of:

Hindu spy.

Jewish conspirator.

Muslim traitor.

'No, you are not a true Muslim.'

Was that why I was here, in this Hell?

Not because, as I'd tried to convince myself, I worked as a journalist, and sometimes journalists find themselves detained by foreign governments. But because I was being punished. For not being a proper Muslim.

'If you were a real Muslim, you would not have done what you did. A vicious report about our country, about the Muslims here. We know where you travelled in our country and who you spoke to. We have arrested those people who have assisted you. We shall deal with them.

You see that we have detained Priscilla. There will be more.'

'Please, I implore you, let Priscilla go. She hasn't done anything wrong. She only did what I asked her to do.'

'Do not tell us how to treat our own people. That is nothing to do with you. It is no concern of yours. We shall do with them what we choose. You cannot bring your Western ideas to us. We have our own ways. We work to help our people. You, you have nobody to help you. Where is your Channel 4? Where is your Indian government? They are not here to help you.'

'Please. Can I telephone the British Embassy and tell them where I am?'

'You have no rights here. We decide what happens to you. You have done wrong and you must pay the price. You will not leave Bangladesh.'

Best not to think about that. About the life imprisonment and the death sentence.

Just as I was thinking about Umejee again, and how I used to sometimes try and teach her English from one of my low-rent magazines, such as *Heat*, where the typeface is large and the language simple – 'Kate wins *Big Brother*' – Priscilla walked into the main room and sat on the mattress. She looked drained. I assumed she'd been in with the Interrogators.

She stared at the wall as she always did. But this time I could see that her whole body was shaking. She'd never done that before.

I had to ask her. 'Are you okay?' I whispered.

She didn't whisper back. She screamed. 'They're electrocuting me! They're giving me shocks to force me to turn witness against you!'

Three female officers scurried over. They lifted Priscilla off the floor and placed her at the other end of the room.

When the guards came back to me, I shouted at them: 'Toilet! I need to go to the toilet! Now!'

I walked past Bruno's room, and as I did so, I yelled at him:

'They're electrocuting Priscilla! They're really hurting her! We've got to stop them!'

I was so scared and angry, I too started to shake uncontrollably.

'Please, please, please, sir. I beg you. Don't hurt Priscilla. She hasn't done anything wrong. She only worked with us for a short time. None of this is her fault. She's just a translator.'

Priscilla, who looked like Vera from the Scooby Doo cartoons. With her big round glasses and her cute face. How could she look more innocent?

'Stop electrocuting her. Hurt me if you want to, but please leave her alone. I beg you. I beg you all. I beg your forgiveness.'

One of the Interrogators had come out of the bathroom into the office that they all used. No matter that he had probably just pissed all over his brown slip-ons, I found myself kneeling at his feet with my forehead touching his shoes. And if he had seen those same rented Pakistani VHS films I'd watched with Umejee and Dad, he would have known that what he had to do was gently place his hand on my head and say something like:

'My *bheti*, my daughter, there's really no need for this. Everything will be just fine. We won't lay another finger on Priscilla.'

Instead, he took one step back, away from my furrowed

brow and my grabbing hands, and said: 'There is no forgiveness.'

No matter that it was the month of Ramadan, the holy month of fasting. A time that Dad had always taught me was about forgiveness.

I'm so sorry, Priscilla.

It didn't get any better. On the fourth day of our detention, Saleem Samad, the Bangladeshi journalist who had worked with us as our fixer, was brought to Mintoo Road and put into that tiny shitty cell with the other male prisoners just a few feet away from the corner of the office where Priscilla and I were being held.

It turned out that after he'd heard about our detention, he'd gone on the run from the authorities, but they'd found him by bugging his wife's phone. In the week or so since I'd last seen him, he'd aged about a decade. He looked like a very frightened old man. I suppose he knew what was coming.

He gestured to me from his cell that the Torturer had beaten him with a stick across his legs and on his back and held a gun to his head and threatened to shoot him. That his only food was stale rice and his only water was that from the toilet's cistern. In the crammed chamber he shared with about fifteen other men and boys, frail Saleem assumed the position. He crouched on the floor and stared at the wall.

And that was the worst part of the worst part of my life. Seeing the tortured faces of Priscilla and Saleem. Knowing that I was responsible for their imprisonment and their pain.

It was my fault.

'We have made more arrests. We will find every person that helped you. There is no doubt about that. A lot of people will suffer for your actions.'

I was back in the Interrogation Room. It was three

thirty a.m. That disturbing time of the night when even under normal conditions nothing makes any sense. Never mind now, when I am sitting in front of eight inhumane men in the middle of a room lit only by two tubes of white light, with a video camera filming me, my quivering hands, my trembling body, my darkened eyes, my mournful mouth.

My fear.

'You see that after all these days still nobody has come to help you. Maybe they have forgotten about you now that you have been caught. Even your family – where are they? Why are they not here? You think that you are cleverer than us. But I tell you this – you will be punished for what you have done. You will never leave this country. You will be put into prison for life. You will never go home again. You will rot in Hell.'

Maybe it was the lack of food.

Maybe it was the lack of sleep.

Maybe it was seeing Priscilla shaking.

Maybe it was seeing the cuts and bruises on Saleem's body.

Maybe it was being told I was going to have to live in a tiny shitty cell for ever.

Maybe it was being told I was never going to see my family again.

I couldn't stop myself.

'Who do you think you are that you can accuse me of not being a true Muslim, of being a traitor? Do you think that you are proper Muslims? When you treat people worse than dogs, when you electrocute them and break their bones, when you starve them? Where is the humanity in that? What way is that to treat your fellow

Muslims? I know that Muslims are dying all over the world every day. But is this the way you seek your revenge, by torturing your own people? Even now, during Ramadan, which is all about forgiveness, you continue with your horrific deeds. You are hypocrites. You talk about Islam but you do not practise it. It is you who are committing the sins.

'You cannot tell me that I will rot in Hell. You cannot pass judgement on me. Only God will do that on the Day of Resurrection when I stand in front of Him. God knows me.

'You, you know nothing about me.'

You know nothing about me, about what I do or what I have done. You know nothing about my faith, what I believe in, what I feel or what I think. You know nothing about my family, about Umejee and Dad, how they brought me up, what they have taught me. You know nothing about what it was like growing up in Bradford amongst 'our community' of Aunties and Uncles and amongst *goray*, white people. You know nothing about my life now, the person that I have become.

You know nothing about who I am.

They were full of rage, those men. The Interrogators and the Torturer. That's what I remember most about them. That's what scared me the most. How their faces and bodies were always rigid with fury. I could feel it, something boiling inside them. Like they could kill somebody.

I never once saw them smile or laugh.

When did you stop smiling and laughing?

Were you that angry?

Is that why you did what you did?

Is that why you killed all those people on that day?

1

The Found City (1977)

I was born in 1969 at a red-brick hospital in Leeds that has since been converted into a psychiatric unit. The very first words I heard were the ones uttered by my father: '*La illaha ill Allah, Muhammad ur rasul Allah*' – 'I bear witness that there is no God but Allah and that Muhammad is the Messenger of Allah', the Shahadah, the declaration of faith, whispered three times into my right ear. A couple of days after my birth, my mother took me home to our tiny over-crowded terraced house. I was her third child, born with British citizenship, Pakistani values and a Muslim soul.

'Oh that's a pretty name. But what does it mean?' That's what people say to me when they can't pronounce my name. I reply: 'It's Zay-bar. It rhymes with "neighbour" or "labour". It means "Beautiful One".' Or 'Intelligent One'. Or 'Enlightened One'. I make up any old rubbish, depending on the mood I'm in. In fact it means 'Adorned One'.

I was named after a famous Pakistani actress called Zeba, a superstar who like modern-day icons had no need of a surname. Zeba played the heroine in scores of black and white films from the mid 1960s – most of them tragic love stories with controversial and complicated plots, such as

Armaan, about a young girl who has a child outside of wedlock, a jilted lover who becomes an alcoholic, a mother who commits suicide and a sexual attacker who is murdered. It makes me smile when I wonder if it was in a moment of weakness that my reverential father called me after a screen goddess who appeared in such ungodly films.

My family name, Malik, is Arabic and means 'Master'. In the Koran, Malik is the Angel who guards Hell, assisted by nineteen guardians. 'And when the sinners in the Punishment of Hell cry: "Oh Malik! Would that thy Lord put an end to us!" He will say: "Nay, but here ye shall abide for aye because you abhorred the truth when the truth was brought to you."'

As it turned out, my parents named me well. It's almost as though they anticipated the tension I would endure throughout my life, the tension between the profane and the pious.

I knew I was Muslim long before I knew I was British. And I knew I was Pakistani long before I knew I was English.

It's hardly surprising.

There was the blatant declaration Umejee occasionally made me repeat from the age of about four:

> We are Pakistani,
> Pakistani children are good children.
> We are Muslim,
> Muslim children are good children.

Then there was the Islamic baptism ceremony, the Haqeeqa, that my siblings and I had at the Bradford YMCA, where an old holy man with a long grey beard and a white crocheted cap stood in front of an audience of about fifty Aunties and Uncles and prayed to Allah that we, the four Malik children, would grow up to be good, obedient Muslims.

There was the way Umejee always referred to Pakistan and never England as home.

The way we spoke Punjabi in the house.

The way our food smelt and tasted so different to English people's, and how we used our hands, not knives and forks, to eat. Even the places we bought our food were different – we didn't shop at the supermarket, but at the halal butcher and the grocery stalls that sold lambs' hooves, fresh coriander, bird's eye chillies, ginger and mangoes.

The way we covered our bodies with sparkly *shalwar kameezes* and saris.

The time that Umejee made us leave a children's birthday party when some of the adults started knocking back 'viskey and Coca-Cola'.

The way that Dad treated all white people with the utmost respect and deference. 'Mr Councillor sir', 'Mr Police Officer sir', 'Mr Plumber sir'.

The Aunties, a network of women all about my mother's age or older, who, like Umejee, didn't work and spoke very little English. We always had to show the utmost respect to these women, for a start referring to them all as 'Auntie' even though they weren't (thankfully) blood relatives and ensuring an endless supply of sweet tea and coconut biscuits whenever they turned up at our house, always unannounced and always for bloody ages, so we'd miss *Sale of the Century* and *3-2-1*.

Apart from bringing up their children, the Aunties had

one other function – to maintain Pakistani traditions to the best of their ability and to shame anybody who dared to deviate from them. So they would talk endlessly about Pakistani concepts such as the *halaht*, the situation, with family back home; the *himaht*, strength, they needed to cope with their ailing health – diabetes, arthritis, depression; the *fikr*, concerns, they had about their adolescent daughters and the *rishta*, marriage proposal, they were looking for for a teenage son; the *izzat*, honour, lacking in the British-born generation; and the *perishani*, sorrow, they had to endure as parents of this British-born generation.

The Aunties were masters at letting you know that they disapproved of non-Pakistani habits. It was very subtle – sometimes it was just a look, a hard stare, and sometimes it was just a sentence: 'I see that your daughter is wearing trousers and not *shalwar kameez* at home, Begum.' Like the poles of a tent, the network of Aunties supported and reinforced each other in upholding what they regarded as the moral and social protective cover for their children – the Pakistani Muslim way.

And then there was Bradford. Like hundreds of other Pakistanis, Dad had come to Bradford in the mid 1960s because there was plenty of work in the city's textile mills, particularly on the night shifts. At first, he and the Uncles arrived here on their own from places like Sialkot, Kashmir, Rawalpindi and Mirpur; they worked all the hours they could, alternating shifts at the factories with shifts in shared houses (numbers varied massively from six tenants in a two-up-two-down to an implausible forty) and sending money back to their villages and towns. Life was hard but at least there was freedom – no parents to tell these young men what to do, no Aunties, no wives, no imams. Nobody to tell them not to go into clubs or listen to rock 'n' roll or fall in love with girls in floral miniskirts who drank halves of ale and went by the name of Sybil or Barbara. That was what some of the men did – I can't tell you how many or who, that's a secret the Uncles will no doubt take with them to the grave – but there was certainly a fair number of them who fell in love with Ingerlernd and its ways and its women. I can just see it now: shouting sweet nothings over the deafening sound of the textile looms – 'Oh, you are so beautiful lady, like the film actress Nargis.' 'You what?!' – sharing fish and chips on a damp bench overlooking a bleak, blackened and smoggy Manningham, then bringing her back to your flat, where thirty brown-skinned men with coconut oil in their hair were taking turns to sleep in makeshift beds.

These 'love matches' may have been romantic, but they were also short-lived. As Enoch Powell spurted his 'rivers of blood' speech and the immigration laws were tightened, the young economic migrants had to act fast – they had to get their families over from the subcontinent before the proposed voucher scheme made it much more difficult. So over came the parents, the Aunties, the wives and the imams. And over came Umejee, an eighteen-year-old bride from Lahore who left behind eight siblings and a beloved mother, and Pajee, Dad's elder brother. All of them about to begin a very different life.

As hundreds of migrants became thousands of settlers, hostility grew. The National Front held regular rallies in Bradford, and the Yorkshire Campaign against Immigration (which won around 20 per cent of the votes in some wards in the 1970 general election) distributed leaflets around schools warning white parents that if their kids sat next to Asian pupils they would certainly contract smallpox.

Umejee and Dad shortly after their wedding.

Despite such opposition, by the mid 1970s it was pretty obvious to all – the politicians, the racists, the Bradfordians and the Pakistanis – that we were Here to Stay, and that Here to Stay didn't necessarily mean Here to Integrate. For the thirty thousand or so of us in the city, there was a process of 'settlement by tiptoe' – we took on some aspects of British life by working in its factories and sending our kids to its schools, but preserved Pakistani life through language, religion and culture. We set up our own communities in places like Manningham, Little Horton and Great Horton, where I grew up; we established our own mosques and madrasas; we ran our own businesses – goldsmiths, curry houses, fabric shops; we even set up our own entertainment in the form of Asian record shops and cinemas.

In the early 1970s, the Reverend P.M. Hawkins, the bishop's chaplain for community relations, wrote a pamphlet entitled 'Pakistanis in Bradford' that was designed to explain to the white population the religion, customs and traditions of this newly arrived community:

The Pakistani will not have a very good picture of English people, because the ones he most often sees are feckless, amoral and poverty-stricken in every way. He is not very anxious to become 'like us' until he sees that there are people who live decent hard-working lives within English society. Such people are usually known to him as 'Royal Family'.

I'm not sure that such a brutally frank assessment did much to promote positive Anglo-Pak community relations at the time, but given the fact that Umejee and no doubt other Aunties had tried and failed to become part of the royal family, the most revered institution in the whole of the country, by offering their services as cooks, cleaners, etc., the only other option available to them in this 'feckless, amoral' society was to stick to their own.

Bradford, the city that was once called Worstedopolis, on account of its production of fine worsted wool, the best in the world, was now Bradistan. A home from home for the Pakistanis.

That was why I could never forget that I was Pakistani when I was growing up – because I lived in Bradistan.

But more importantly than that, the main reason why I knew who I was from a very young age – a Pakistani, yes, but a Muslim first and foremost – was because of Dad. You see, Dad was very religious. Which meant that I was too.

You may have heard it stated, particularly over the last few years, that Islam is much more than a religion, it's a way of life, and that everything a Muslim does from the moment he wakes up to the time that he goes to sleep is dictated by God and the Koran. You may also have heard about the five pillars of Islam; the Shahadah, the declaration of faith; Salat, prayer five times a day; Zakat, donating money to the poor; Ramadan, fasting for a month from sunrise to sunset; and Hajj, pilgrimage to Mecca.

Now I have no scientific research to base this upon, but I reckon that the majority of Muslims living in the UK do not fastidiously observe all five tenets. I certainly don't. But Dad did, all his adult life.

So, for example, every morning he would wake up at the crack of dawn to recite his Fajr, even when he'd just worked a ten-hour shift at the mill. From underneath my blanket, I would hear him utter God's name, '*Bismillah Irahma niraheem*', as he headed downstairs to carry out his ablutions in the kitchen sink – hawking mucus from his nose and throat, gargling three times, drenching his face, neck, feet and arms in water, washing out his ears, all the time flooding the adjoining gas cooker, Umejee's spice jars and the lino, so that poor Mum would have to spend ages drying out the kitchen with a mop and cloth before we could have our sugary eggy-bread breakfast.

Throughout the rest of the day, no matter where Dad was or what he was doing, he would always stop to say his prayers. God came first. Even if it meant having his head perilously close to the wool machines he operated at the factory, and their two-foot-long needles that moved so fast you couldn't see them. Or having to park up on the motorway and pray on the hard shoulder: 'Get out your mats and pray to the west.'

My father spent more time at the mosque than he did at home. His regular place of worship was down the road from our house in an old Victorian building that had once been a church, but if the call to prayer came when he was out and about elsewhere in the city, he would often nip into one of the other 'God's Homes', as he called them.

Not that he had lots of choice. Back in the late 1970s, there were just seven mosques catering for Bradford's forty thousand Muslims. Most of these were converted terraced houses, like the one on Southfield Square that's still in use today. And when I say converted, what I really mean is stripped, so that the furniture you would expect to see in a normal residential abode – sofa, bed, table, etc. – had all been removed, but other than that there were few other changes. There was no proper provision for carrying out ablutions, not enough space for dozens of prostrated men, especially on a Friday, no emergency fire exits; such an arrangement was far from suitable.

I remember a story in the news recently about one of these converted houses, in Birmingham, collapsing under the weight of the congregation at a funeral. I wouldn't be surprised to learn that such accidents were once regular occurrences in Bradford.

In the absence of any organised Islamic body, it was left up to Dad and the many Uncles who made up 'the community' to work to improve the provision of religious sites for the growing and by now permanent population of Muslims in Bradford. They had a difficult task.

For a start, they had to battle against the authorities. If you look at the Subject Archive at the Central Library in Bradford, there's a folder entitled 'Mosques', which details some of these disputes. A mosque in the residential Lapage Street was closed down after the Department of the Environment found that: 'The mosque activities involve chanting and during the month of Ramadan, very long hours of use.' Another was shut after it was found to have dangerous wiring, and another was ordered to be closed by the corporation because it didn't have planning permission. When a penalty of forty pounds had to be paid by the mosque committee, one representative stated that: 'It's not a crime to be religious but yet our members are brought to court and fined.' There was a lot of ill feeling. One congregation even stated that it would use physical force to get into their mosque if it was locked up.

Secondly, they had to battle against each other. Throughout the 1960s, Bradford's Muslims had looked after one another, helping other members of 'the community' to get jobs, learn English, find somewhere to live; any differences that there might have been from back home disappeared once it was realised that the priority was survival in this foreign and sometimes unwelcoming land. But as 'the community' became more settled in Ingerlernd, it also became more fragmented, with divisions based on nationality – Pakistani, Bangladeshi, Indian; geography – Mirpuri, Gujarati, Pathan, Punjabi; and denomination – Sunnis, Shias, Deobandis, Barelwis. So deep-rooted were the differences between these factions that they couldn't even agree on the most fundamental things, such as should we class ourselves as Muslims or as Moslems or Mohammedans or Mosalmans, never mind reaching consensus on where to build the next place of worship. Again, if you look at the archive in Bradford's library, you'll see newspaper headlines such as 'Bitter row at mosque' and 'Rival Muslim groups plan city mosques'. So much for the Ummah. So much for 'the community'. So much for 'God's home'. Left to the Muslims in Bradford, God would be permanently homeless.

Like the father who nips down to the shed at the bottom of the garden every evening, I never really knew what Dad did at the mosque. Of course he prayed, but he also went there to chit-chat with his friends. I can only imagine that they talked about the usual stuff – religion, politics, cricket and paperwork. As one of the few men of his age who could read and write English, Dad was always being asked to check official forms for the Uncles – immigration and social security forms, sick notes, marriage certificates, that sort of thing. He was paid in kind for this community service – the odd curry made with lashings of ghee that oscillated in your belly for days, or a juicy bit of gossip. Very occasionally he would come back and share this tittle-tattle with Umejee: 'They say that the imam at the X mosque in Bradford 9 has had to go back to Pakistan because immigration say there's a problem with his documents.' 'They say that the robbery at X jeweller's in Bradford 7 was done by the family's relatives because they were owed some money.' 'They say that the wedding of Xsa'ab's son isn't going to happen now because the family in Pakistan is not happy about the match.' Dad knew pretty much everything that was going on amongst *apnay lokhi*, but most of the time he kept it to himself or only discussed it with other men. That was the rule. The mosque was a place where the Uncles could relax and talk openly without the Aunties snooping. It was hallowed ground for more than the obvious reason. No wonder they were always in there.

Me, I did what I could to get *out* of there.

I really didn't enjoy going to the mosque or the madrasa. I much preferred to read the Koran and say my *namaz* at home. For a start, our kitchen was warmer and it smelt nicer. In the days before tinned pulses, foiled curry pastes and vacuum-packed rotis, Umejee spent hours cooking, making masala from scratch – ghee, onions, garlic, ginger, chilli, coriander, cumin and turmeric for our aloo gobi – boiling chickpeas in the pressure cooker for our keema chana and patting out chapattis on to the smoking *thava*. The spicy aroma of Mum's cooking comforted me. The smell of holy buildings made me retch.

Adeeba, me and Tassadaque being taught to read the Koran by Dad.

The mosque stank of sweaty women and their sandals; the madrasa stank of sweaty teenagers and their pumps. Nobody could afford heating in those places, so the odour froze in the air. Imagine the stench in a Bedouin tent in the middle of the night after twenty nomads have trekked thirty miles across the Sahara in the glaring heat and then devoured a feast of lamb mansaf and gone to sleep. It smelt like that. And it was bloody uncomfortable to sit on the stone floor for so long.

The women at the mosque spent most of their time nattering away at each other. Chitter-chatter. Chitter-chatter. They never stopped – even as the imam started his sermon in the adjoining hall, which was then relayed into our room on some dodgy speakers that kept cutting out so that he sounded like a Pakistani Norman Collier, the northern comedian whose routine was based around a faulty microphone. Have some respect, ladies. You're supposed to be here to pray and reflect, not gossip. At least make an effort to fill in the gaps in the imam's holy lecture.

The madrasa was quite the opposite, very strict. The teacher carried a long wooden stick that he thrashed down on the desk too close to your fingers if you made a mistake. He didn't know how to talk at normal volume, only how to shout, so he was constantly wiping the spittle away from his beard, which was precisely one fist long, as some say it is meant to be (I don't know why). He was a very scary man.

Neither he nor the imam spoke English, so I really struggled to understand what they were going on about. Pretty much all the holy men in Bradford came from back home, from villages and small towns. Their method of Islamic education was to teach the Koran in Arabic by rote and to give their sermons in Urdu or Punjabi, no matter that you had no idea what it all meant. They didn't provide many prayer areas for women, nor did they get involved in pastoral care. It was far from ideal, but I have to say that at least these imams and teachers never talked about jihad or *kuffirs*, non-believers, or martyrdom. It wasn't part of their vocabulary; it wasn't part of our vocabulary. We never mentioned words like that. And we never discussed or challenged or doubted who we were. There was no need. We just got on with it.

I knew that:

If you are a good Muslim, God will hear your prayers.

If you are a good Muslim, you will go to Heaven.

If you are a bad Muslim, you will go to Hell.

It sounded like a fair deal to me. If I kept my side of the bargain, God would keep His, and everything would be just fine.

I would have no need to fear the end of the world, when 'the sun is folded up, when the stars fall, when the mountains vanish, when the oceans boil over with a swell, when the souls are sorted out, when the World on High is unveiled, when the Blazing Fire is kindled to fierce heat, and when the Garden is brought near' (Surah 81:1–13).

I would have no need to fear the Day of Resurrection, when the Angel Raphael sounds his trumpet, one blast to move the earth and crush its mountains to powder, the second to bring all the dead back to life like scattered moths.

I would have no need to fear the Day of Judgement, when the book of my bad deeds is weighed against the book of my good deeds.

I would have no need to fear that as I crossed the dark, narrow bridge over the fires of Hell, it would cut into my feet and I would fall into the flames below, where my skin would burn and would keep alight the fire of the condemned. Where I would be forced to eat the fruit of the *zaqqum* tree, with its flowers made of Satan's heads, which would make my insides burn like molten brass. Where, whenever I tried to escape, I would be pulled back into the searing flames with iron hooks.

Instead, I would look forward to skipping joyfully over the flat, broad bridge that leads into the Garden of Paradise, where I would be met by the Prophet Muhammad at a beautiful pond. Where I would be dressed in fine silk and rich brocade. Where I could feast on the flesh of fowls and fruit and milk and honey. Where I could recline on jewelled couches and be waited on by immortal youths in a climate that is neither too hot nor too cold.

That was my purpose and my goal in life – infinity in Paradise.

And that was why I always looked forward to Ramadan – the month of fasting, when I could learn obedience, patience and discipline and ask for forgiveness. This was a time when I could make God happy and Dad proud.

In theory, I was exempt from fasting on account of my age. You're supposed to start when you reach adolescence, and I wasn't yet even eight years old. But that didn't stop me. And in theory, Dad was exempt from fasting on medical grounds. He was a diabetic, which meant that he was supposed to eat regularly throughout the day. But that never stopped him; even when his blood sugar levels dropped dangerously low and the doctor advised him to eat.

God came first.

During Ramadan, I relished the challenge of waking up in the middle of the night every night for a month to eat toast and jam and a big bowl of cornflakes before I started my fast, trying to stomach watching Dad eat ghosht kerala, lamb with bitter gourd, at four a.m.

And it was a challenge not to eat or drink anything all day. Occasionally I forgot and swallowed the odd midget gem or slurped a glass of dandelion and burdock. But there was no malice. I didn't have the guts to cheat and lie. I knew that my two Angels, my honourable recorders, were monitoring my every move. The sweet smiley one on my right shoulder listing all my good deeds and the earnest, glaring one on my left shoulder making notes of all my sins.

They'd been there all my life, from the second I'd been born, and would stay with me until the moment I died. I knew that on the Day of Judgement my two lists would be weighed. If there was a positive balance I would go to Heaven, and if I was in the red, I would indeed burn in Hell.

I was aware of my Angels most during the Holy Month, and I would sometimes speak to them.

'I'm really sorry, but I just swallowed a bit of water when I was brushing my teeth. Is that allowed? . . . No, it was an accident and there wasn't much . . . Great. I'll be more careful next time.'

I was tempted to give the Angels names but I figured that might result in a point against me, there on my left shoulder. They were servants of God, not my chums.

Of course I was hungry and thirsty and tired throughout the day. And it didn't help that I was often the only one in my class fasting even though there were other Muslim kids there. Maybe their parents thought it was too difficult for a child to abstain for so long. But Dad and I didn't. I got blessings from God – thirty points recorded by the Angel on my right shoulder, one for each day of the holy month – and treats from Dad at dusk when we broke our fast. Cashew nuts, pistachios, dates, strawberry Cornettos, pineappleade and as many packets of Seabrook crisps as I could eat from the cash-and-carry boxes he'd bought.

Alhamdulilla. Praise be to God.

* * *

The fifth and last pillar of Islam states that every Muslim who is physically and financially able must go to Mecca on the Hajj at least once in their lifetime. Dad went every year, without fail; so often in fact that even in a city such as Bradford, where there are a lot of Hajjis (the title given to those who've completed the pilgrimage), Dad was known to all his friends as Hajjisa'ab.

I've never been to Mecca, but I've seen it on TV on Pakistani satellite stations. It's breathtaking. Over two million people go each year. They circle the Kaba, the House of God, built by Abraham and his son, Ishmael, whilst calling out: 'Doubly at Your service, oh God.' How loud must that be? Two million people uttering the same phrase. Loud enough that God can hear it in Heaven. This forty-foot-wide and fifty-foot-high cube, draped in a black and gold cloth, is the centre of the earth, the point that every Muslim around the world kneels towards when he prays.

In the photos I've seen of Dad at Hajj, he's wearing two plain white cotton sheets, one wrapped around his waist and the other hanging over his left shoulder. His hair has all been shaved off and he's wearing open-toed sandals. This is the uniform of sanctification worn by all men at Mecca because all pilgrims, whether rich or poor, stand as equals before God.

And all men and women have to perform the same duties – go round the Kaba seven times and touch the sacred Black Stone. This stone came down from Heaven and was originally white, but has been darkened over time by the sins of humanity. Pilgrims have to undertake seven 'runnings' between the hills of Safa and Marwa, and then walk the fifteen miles from Mecca to Mount Arafat, where

God forgave Adam and Eve. Once there, they have to stand in the intense heat for hours to repent their sins, and then throw stones at the pillars at Mina to show that they reject Satan's temptation.

Every year Dad would tell us about the miraculous things he'd seen and experienced. People getting up out of their wheelchairs for the first time in years, the elderly and infirm finding strength, the terminally ill finding peace, the hungry being fed.

Sometimes he couldn't even describe what he'd witnessed. 'How can I tell you? There are no words I can use. You can feel God everywhere. *Vah bay vah*, it's so beautiful, so calm.'

Not always, though. Dad would neglect to mention the stampede where a thousand people were killed when a bridge collapsed, or the fatalities around the stoning of the Devil when scores were crushed to death, or the fire in the tented city where he was sleeping where hundreds were burnt to death. We heard all this on the news and were worried sick. Was Dad okay? There was no way of contacting him. It was only weeks later, when he finally returned to Bradford, that we knew he had survived.

He would always shrug off our concern: 'Those people are very lucky. What a beautiful thing, to die on Hajj. Then you are guaranteed a place in Paradise. That is God's will.'

I never found out why Dad was more religious than the Uncles or, indeed, any of his siblings. Quite simply because I never asked. It never seemed right to query: 'Dad, how come you say your *namaz* five times a day and read the Koran, and Pajee doesn't?' And it never seemed right to ask Dad's elder brother, Pajee, who lived with us: 'Why in all these years that you've been here have I never seen you pray?' It would probably make him feel very uncomfortable.

I don't know if Dad had always been like that or whether some particular event had made him so devout: the death of his parents, perhaps, or the birth of his children. He never talked about his life; all I know about his past is that he was one of eight children, three of whom died in infancy; he grew up in Sialkot, a region of Pakistan known for its manufacture of sportswear; he taught himself to read and write English under the light of an oil lamp; he worked for the Pakistani civil service as an administrative officer; he was a diabetic from quite an early age; he never met Umejee before they got married; when he came to the UK, he used some of his earnings from the night shift to pay a dentist to have three gold teeth put in; and when he wasn't wearing overalls at the factory, he liked to dress in very natty suits and ride around on his scooter.

When I look now at those black and white photos of Dad from the late 1960s, I see a man standing at the foot of the Blackpool Tower in dark sunglasses, kneeling next to white women at the mill, crouching besides a rose bed in his shirt sleeves, eating candyfloss at a fair. And it feels like I'm looking at somebody else, not Dad. My dad wore a skullcap a lot of the time, carried rosary beads, often sat on a prayer mat and had a dark blue tattoo etched into the skin of his right arm that read 'Allah'.

Maybe things changed for Dad when the imams came over to the UK at the start of the 1970s. I've heard quite a few Uncles suggest that that was when those young male workers first got religion, whether they wanted to or not. The job of the holy men was to make sure that the settlers never forgot that they were Muslims, even if they were thousands of miles from home.

My gut feeling, though, is that Dad never needed reminding of who he was: a Muslim first, whether he was in Sialkot or Bradford.

I remember exactly when it dawned on me how important Dad's faith was to him, more than it was to most of the other Uncles. Some family friends were visiting us from the Midlands, three brothers and their wives. The men sat in our posh living room at the front of the house and the women congregated in the lounge. When I got bored of listening to the Aunties and Umejee going on about Pakistan and relatives and weddings and all the usual stuff, I went and stood outside the men's door. Earwigging. I liked to earwig.

'Business is very good. We are looking to set up a new shop soon. We moved house as well, did we tell you that? Into a semi in a nice part of the town where the *goray*, the white people, live. So we are keeping busy. Same normal things, you know, we work and the wives spend. Ha ha ha! How are *halaht* with you, Hajjisa'ab?'

'*Teek tak, teek tak.* Okay, okay.'

That was about as far as it went with the social niceties before Dad somehow managed to skilfully manoeuvre the conversation from 'Children doing well at school, missus okay' to:

'One day, the Prophet, when he was forty years old, was meditating in the Cave of Hira. He went there a lot, on his own, to think. Then the Angel Gabriel appeared and demanded him to read. "But I do not know how to read," he replied. Gabriel squeezed him very very hard. So hard that the Prophet was very scared and he thought he was going to die, but still he kept saying, "I'm trying to tell you that I cannot read." Then, just like that, by some miracle, the first words of the Koran came to the Prophet and he started saying them. The *surah* just came out from his lips. The first one was Surah 96: "Read! In the name of thy Lord and Cherisher who created, created man out of a clot of congealed blood."

'Then he remembered what he had learnt and he repeated it to others and they remembered it also and then they wrote it down. This is how our *muzab*, our faith, came to be found in the Koran. *Vah bay vah.* How beautiful that is.'

I can't recall how he did it, how he turned that corner from mundane chit-chat to divine revelation, but he was still at it an hour later when I had to take in a tray of tea and *matai*, Asian sweets, and cream horns.

'. . . and when they heard that the Prophet had died, they could not believe it. "How can this be?" they asked. "He is our Prophet." But the Koran teaches us that Muhammad was an *insaa'an*, a man like other men. He had said his final sermon in the middle of the desert: "This day I have perfected your religion for you, completed my favour upon you, and have chosen for you Islam as your religion." *Vah bay vah.'*

Dad could quote at length from the Koran, not as much as the *hafiz*, those revered individuals who could recite the entire book by heart, but substantial chunks, and he knew everything about the life of the Prophet Muhammad, including dates.

'In 570, the Prophet was born in Mecca. He was an orphan, brought up by his grandfather, Abd al-Mutalib . . . In 619, the Prophet's wife Khadijah passed away. This caused a great sorrow to the Prophet as she was a good wife and was the very first person to become a Muslim . . . In 624, at the Battle of Badr, Angels were sent to help the Muslims fight against the Meccans . . .'

'Ah, *chai*. Very nice. Thank you, *bheti*,' remarked one of the Uncles as I placed the tray on our posh onyx table. I swear all three of the visitors rushed towards the teapot and sweets. Something to distract them from Dad's holy soliloquy. Poor Uncles. They just wanted to relax and natter. Poor Dad. He just wanted to . . . I'm not sure, really. He wasn't trying to impress or brag or bore. It was just his way. He was always telling stories from the Koran to his kids, his wife, his friends, the builder, Mr John sir (who was white), his GP, Dr Douglas sir (who was also white), most probably even the imam at his mosque. It made him happy.

I can't vouch for those others, but I loved to sit at the kitchen table with Dad and listen to him as he told us about the amazing miracles the Prophet Muhammad had performed: he split the moon in two, he fed an entire army with just a few scraps, he spoke to trees and rocks, he made water flow from his hands, he blew dust into the eyes of some bad men so they couldn't see him. The Prophet also had the most amazing dreams where he could see into the future. I loved to hear the fantastic stories of Angels and the desert and the sun and the stars and fire and thunder and earthquakes.

Wow! It's like magic, but real magic!

It didn't matter that Dad never read fairy tales to us. I didn't need them, silly made-up fables to help me sleep; this stuff was real, it had actually happened and it was important. It taught me how to live my life. Be a good Muslim.

Dad had his own favourite bits that he would tell us time and time again, such as the miracle of the Night Journey, Al-Isra.

'The Angel Gabriel visited the Prophet one night and put him on a *buraq*, this is a donkey with wings on its legs. They flew all the way to Jerusalem, it is very far away. When he got there, at the . . . what do they call it . . . we call it the Masjid al-Aqsa but the Jews call it Temple Mount, he went up into the sky. The Angel Gabriel took the Prophet through the seven levels of Heaven. In our religion, we call this the Mi'raj. When he got to each one, he saw a different person – Adam, then Jesus and John, then Joseph, then Idris, then Aaron, Moses's brother, then Moses himself, then Abraham.

'Gabriel took the Prophet into Paradise and he spoke to God. Can you believe it, he saw God when he was alive! That is the most miracle! God explained that all Muslims have to pray fifty times a day. Fifty! So the Prophet tells Moses this and Moses says: "That is too much for humans. You have to go back and ask God to reduce it." So the

Prophet goes back, and now God says you must pray ten times a day. The Prophet tells Moses and again Moses says: "No, it's still too much. Go back and ask to lower it more." Again the Prophet goes back. He is very ashamed to ask God. It's not good for him. God says he must pray five times.

'Thanks be to God it is five times! If it was fifty times Salat, we would have no time to eat or sleep! We would be praying all day and night! Ha ha ha! So the Prophet Muhammad returned to Mecca that night on the *buraq*. Only those who were Muslims believed he had been on such a wonderful journey. *Vah bay vah.*'

You didn't get Dad's enthusiasm or his raconteur skills at the mosque or the madrasa. I really didn't enjoy going to the mosque or the madrasa. I could learn the rules I needed to know about being a good Muslim at home. From Dad and Umejee and the Koran.

Such as: 'God has forbidden to you flesh from animals found dead, blood, pork, and any food offered to idols' (Surah 2:173), which translated into no pig or non-halal meat.

Everyone knew this rule and nobody flouted it. So when, one lunchtime at school, we, the Muslim pupils, spotted Usman with a slab of non-halal beef on his plate soaked in onion gravy, we realised we had to act. I'm not exactly sure who the informant was – it wasn't me – but by the time Usman got home, his parents *and* 'the community' knew what he'd had for his lunch and they made sure he never ate it again. I can imagine there were a few slaps and some tears in their house that night. Poor Usman, he was only five years old. How was he supposed to know at that age? The harsh answer is: 'Because he was.'

Some of the rules weren't codified; you just picked them up as you went along. Such as, you must always eat food with your right hand. When I asked Umejee why we had to do that, she answered: 'Because in old times when there wasn't much clean water people kept their right hands to eat and used their left hands for dirty work.'

'But we've got clean water now.'

'Yes, I know, but we have to carry on the tradition.'

And so we did.

'You must never kill spiders. Once when the Prophet Muhammad was travelling to Medina, he was being chased by some men who were trying to kill him. He hid in the Cave of Thawr and a spider spun a web across the entrance to fool the men into thinking the Prophet couldn't be in there. The spider saved the Prophet's life and now we cannot kill these creatures.'

And so we didn't.

'Mum, why does the lady upstairs show her legs and cover her hair?'

We had taken Muslim lodgers into our house: a young Iranian couple who were studying at the nearby university. I'd noticed that they had much paler skin than us and that the food they cooked smelt very different to ours; it was a lot less spicy. I'd also observed that the wife always wore a three-quarter-length skirt and opaque tights and always covered her hair with a scarf. I couldn't understand it; how could she, as a Muslim, get away with showing her legs? My sister and I were never allowed to show our legs.

'They're Shia,' Mum explained. 'People in Iran are Shia and they are different to us. The women wear skirts and cover their heads. We are Sunni. We always cover our legs but we don't always wear a duppata over our hair.' (Of course, there were more fundamental differences between Sunnis and Shias that I didn't understand at that age; also this was a time before the Islamic Revolution in Iran, when the dress code for women wasn't as severe as it became under the Ayatollah Khomeini.)

And so I remembered the rule: 'I walk on the Sunni side of the street and I don't have Shia luck.'

I was very good at obeying the rules. In fact I became quite fanatical about it. So much so that I developed Islamic Obsessive Compulsive Disorder. Whenever I saw a shoe upturned, I had to rush to put it right on the basis that it's an insult to God to show Him a dirty sole. Whenever I saw anyone's feet pointing west in the living room, I would tell them to move them on the basis that it was an insult to God to direct your feet towards His house in Mecca. Whenever I had to recite prayers thirty-three times, I would say them forty times on the basis that I might have made a mistake whilst counting on the segments of my fingers. Whenever I had to say my *namaz*, I did my ablutions twice on the basis that it was better to be overly clean than disrespectfully dirty.

I was a star pupil when it came to observing the rituals of my faith. That was what mattered, wasn't it?

If you are a good Muslim, God will hear your prayers.

If you are a good Muslim, you will go to Heaven.

If you are a bad Muslim, you will go to Hell.

I was a good Muslim because I did all the things that I was told to and I never did those things I was told not to. I always made sure that my hair was covered when I said my *namaz* and I thanked God for my food after every meal and I never touched the Koran with unwashed hands or walked in front of Dad when he was saying his prayers.

Though a lot of the time I didn't understand why. Why some things were *halal*, allowed, and others were *haram*, forbidden.

Like giving your spouse a massage in the privacy of your own home. You see, it came to light amongst the Aunties that one of their friends had a room in her house that she regularly used to knead and press her middle-aged husband. It was as innocent as that. However, from the reaction of the Aunties, I could only assume that such an act was sinful. 'How disgusting!' 'What appalling behaviour!' 'What a thing to teach your children!' 'Don't they have any shame? *Basharam!*'

Everyone got to know about the massaging Aunty and Uncle, just like they got to know about Usman and his beef. But the consequences for the former were more severe than a smack and a telling-off. People stopped inviting the Aunty and Uncle to parties and weddings. They stopped talking to them. They pointed at their house as they went past: 'the House of Sin'. And so did I. Each time I went to school or came home on the bus, I tried to peer through their lace curtains to see if there were any signs of Evil. I'd never seen Evil before in real life but I was certain I'd know it when I saw it. Smoke, maybe, or flames. And horns and hooves. Just because I never witnessed these omens, it didn't mean anything. After all, as I'd been told at the madrasa, sinners are experts at deception, for they have been taught by the Master of Evil, Satan himself.

So there were many sources for the rules that I learnt as a child. Most were from the Koran and Umejee and Dad; some were found in customs and traditions; and some were laid down by the Aunties, *apnay lokhi*, our people, 'the community'.

Of course, I didn't know it back then, but these last two sources had no divine authority. The laws they set had no religious foundation or rationale. They had nothing to do with the Koran and everything to do with culture. But sometimes the two got confused. What was a man-made decree would sometimes be misinterpreted or even knowingly mis-sold as the word of God.

There is nothing in the Koran about it being *haram* for a wife to massage her husband; in fact, on the contrary, the Holy Book encourages intimacy between spouses. 'The community' just made up its own regulations and expected everyone to follow them.

So I knew that if I asked Umejee if I could play in the yard at the back of our house she would say: 'What will *apnay lokhi* say if they see you? They will talk about you. Girls are not supposed to play outside. Anyway, you know it's not safe at the moment.' And I would do as I was told. Not only because that was the rule – boys can play in the streets but not girls – but because it made sense.

Because at that time there was a killer on the loose. The Yorkshire Ripper. He'd murdered four women in Leeds and Bradford in the last two years. They'd all been prostitutes, but a few months ago the body of a sixteen-year-old had been found. She was a shop assistant. Jayne MacDonald. She'd been hit over the head with a hammer and stabbed in the chest and back. If the Ripper had started killing 'normal' girls, then he might come after me and my sister and Umejee.

I was petrified. Every time Umejee went to the shops or the chemist or into town, I sat at the bay window in the living room, waiting for her to return. 'I'll be okay. Nothing will happen to me. God will protect me,' she would say when I begged her not to go. She wasn't interested in getting one of those personal alarms that were being handed out. Neither were a lot of other women, who argued that these little gadgets provided no protection whatsoever from a vicious attack. They armed themselves with knives instead. No man was to be trusted.

They'd been showing it on the news – body after body covered with a sheet or under a makeshift tent. I knew what was under that covering – I'd seen the horrific pictures of Jack the Ripper's victims in the crime books Dad had bought us from the book club. Women who'd been bludgeoned so badly that they didn't look like human beings any more. Like the other photos, in the books about the paranormal, of people who had spontaneously combusted, where there was just a charred heap. Those pictures gave me nightmares. I didn't want to end up like that.

So I didn't mind the rule that forbade me from playing outside.

Good rule, Umejee. Good rule, Aunties.

I stayed in and watched television with Dad. Dad loved to watch the telly. He never missed the BBC evening news. It kept him up to date with the turbulent events back home – the imposition of martial law and the arrest and eventual execution of Prime Minister Zulfikar Ali Bhutto. He was also an avid fan of light entertainment and comedy – Morecambe and Wise, Mike Yarwood, Shirley Bassey, *Mind Your Language*, *It Ain't Half Hot, Mum*. He would chuckle away on the sofa and occasionally you would hear an 'Oh dearie! Ha! Ha! Ha! Oh dearie!' from him. And I would giggle too. How funny!

But then sometimes Dad would order: 'Turn it over, quickly!' And my siblings and I would run at breakneck speed towards the set in the corner of the living room and change channels as quickly as we could. You see, there was another rule. We weren't allowed to watch any form of nudity on the telly.

So we always had to skip the opening titles of *Starsky and Hutch* because there was that gratuitous shot of a bikini-clad girl in what looked like a strip joint where the two detectives are ogling her. The rest of the programme was okay – it was just the first two or three minutes we had to avoid. *Dallas* was a no-no, not just because of naked flesh but due to general committing of sin, adultery, murder, treachery, that kind of thing. And no bra adverts. These were always tricky at a time when we had no remote control for the TV. We all knew that as soon as we heard the words: 'Whether you're . . . or whether you're . . .' we had to jump off the sofa and rush towards that disobedient box. There was no guarantee that we would get there in time – for example if we were busy eating – but it left everybody feeling mighty embarrassed and awkward if we'd got down to the words: 'Triumph has the bra for the way you are.' Too late. We'd seen it all. All that bare flesh.

There are only two instances I can recall when the naked flesh rule was not obeyed. Once was when Dad bought all four of us kids tickets to go and watch Lynda Carter aka Wonder Woman perform at the Alhambra Theatre in Bradford. He knew from the popular TV series that there was very little to the superhero's outfit – a studded tiara and a US flag cape over some blue star-spangled hot pants and a red corset. It seemed even skimpier in real life as she sang and danced on that stage in her knee-high boots. I was grateful for my vanilla ice cream in the interval, something to cool down my hot blushes.

The second time was when ITV broadcast the controversial film *Death of a Princess* in 1980. This was a drama documentary about the true story of the public execution of a Saudi princess and her adulterous lover, which didn't show the Saudis in a particularly flattering light, especially regarding their treatment of women. Despite protests from the Ummah, the global Muslim community, led by the government of Saudi Arabia, who demanded that the film be banned on the basis that it was 'an unprincipled attack on the religion of Islam', it was eventually screened on television. When Dad suggested to Umejee that we be allowed to watch it, to see for ourselves how Muslims had been portrayed, Mum put her foot down. 'No, it is a shameful thing. They cannot see it.'

It was much safer to watch the Asian VHS films that Dad rented from the grocer's shop or borrowed from the Uncles. We might be bored stiff and the plot might be completely implausible and the songs might go on for hours at a time and we might not be able to understand what anyone was saying, but at least we could relax, no need to act as though we had ants in our pants. There was never any nudity or kissing in these movies, romances such as *Kabhi Kabhie* and *Andaz*. That wasn't allowed. There might be a cuddle or a brushing of cheeks or a metaphorical gushing fountain but nothing more than that. Plenty of violence, though, that was okay – in films like *Sholay* and *Don*. My favourite was *Pakeezah*, which means 'Pure of Heart', a beautiful classic tragedy about a woman called Nargis who dances for a living. Or so I thought at the time. Now I know that it's actually about a woman called Nargis who works in a brothel as a courtesan and who is forbidden to marry the man she loves. No matter how hard she tries to give up her immoral life, she can't. In real life, the actress who played the main role, Meena Kumari, also had a tragic existence. She split up from her husband, the director of the film, in a very bitter divorce, and one month after *Pakeezah* was completed, she died in a nursing home at the age of forty, a penniless alcoholic. Of course neither Dad nor Umejee told us that.

Before they were shut down in the early 1980s, Bradford had a couple of Asian cinemas, the Sangeet and the Liberty. In the evening they presented the latest harmless Bollywood blockbuster, but during the day, the projector beamed a much more shocking celluloid. Films where you saw what the world was like before the Prophet Muhammad arrived. Men and women cavorting in the desert, writhing, dancing, feasting, drinking, laughing uncontrollably, wearing very little, lying down before idols.

Then there were films like *The Message*, which showed you how Islam brought salvation to these sinners.

On that big screen, I saw the things that Dad had taught us from the Koran at the kitchen table. That God sent the Prophet Muhammad as a mercy to mankind; that three hundred and sixty idols were smashed at Mecca and then it was declared a holy place; that before he died, the Prophet delivered the Final Revelation of the Koran: 'This day I have perfected your religion for you and completed my favour to you and chosen for you Islam as your religion.' There's a particular scene in the film that I remember in some detail. A middle-aged woman, the mother of a believer, is lying on the ground in the desert, screaming.

Two men are pulling on a lever system, which is attached to two ropes tied to her arms. Every time they pull on the handle, her arms are pulled further and further out of their sockets. She screams, 'There is only one God and Muhammad is his Messenger!' The two men then drive a wooden stake through her heart, and the next shot you see is of lots of vultures circling in the sky.

The film starred Anthony Quinn, who also appeared as a Muslim in other holy films. Dad was a big fan of Anthony Quinn. '*Vah bay vah*, he is a good man, showing the life of the Prophet Muhammad and teaching people about our religion.' Dad used to say (incorrectly) that the impact on Anthony Quinn of making *The Message* was such that he converted to Islam. Like Muhammad Ali. Dad was a big fan of Muhammad Ali too. All Muslims were.

But the thing that Dad loved most, more than watching Muhammad Ali fight or Anthony Quinn act, more than his rented VHS films, his British comedies and his trips to the cinema, was his music. He had a massive record collection that consisted mainly of Indian and Pakistani ballads sung by stars such as Noor Jehan, Lata Mangeshkar, Kishore Kumar and Mukesh.

Some evenings he would sit for hours in the posh living room on the plush gold-upholstered sofa and just listen to album after album after album, carefully replacing each vinyl disc back into its protective clear polythene sleeve once he'd done with it. Beautiful melodies with beautiful lyrics.

Using the colours of flowers as ink and my heart as
    a pen,
I wrote to you every day,

I can't even say in how many ways you torture me
   in every instant,
I dream of you and I keep awake thinking of you,
I am all tangled up in thoughts about you, like a
   thread in a garland.

Sometimes he would sing along; he didn't have a great voice, but that didn't matter. You could tell he was somewhere else. I have no idea where. Sometimes he would call Mum in from the kitchen: 'Begumsa'ab, come and listen to this. Such grace, such poetry. *Vah bay vah.*'

'I can't, I'm too busy.'

'Oh, you're always busy.'

And then back into his dream. Back to his secret place.

I wonder if that's where I get my love of music from. From Dad. Like him, I listen to music on my own. Like him, I go to a secret place. Stretched out on a piano at Ronnie Scott's wearing a long red dress and singing Crystal Gayle's 'Don't It Make My Brown Eyes Blue' to an enthralled audience.

I always loved to sing.

It was Dad who bought us our first four albums. A Barbra Streisand compilation and three Abba records. He'd seen the supergroup on Eurovision and took an instant shine to them.

I wasn't as keen on 'Waterloo' as he was; 'Nina Pretty Ballerina' was my favourite. I sat cross-legged on the floor, in between the two speakers of our Sony hi-fi system, and sang along: 'Nina, pretty ballerina, now she is the queen of the dancing floor, this is the moment she's waited for, just like Cinderella, just like Cinderella.'

I tapped my feet and nodded my head to the music and

I imagined what moves Nina might make as the Queen of the Dancing Floor. A pirouette and then a demi-plié going into a grand jeté. Sometimes I imagined that I *was* Nina, dressed in a tutu and a tiara, floating around some huge stage to rapturous applause and shouts of 'Bravo! Bravo!' It was the only place I could dance – inside my head. You see, that was another rule: no dancing. I'd discovered that when Dad had once seen me jigging away in the posh living room to Barbra Streisand and Donna Summer singing 'Enough is Enough' as he was setting off to do his night shift at the mill.

He came back into the house and told me: 'It's not allowed for Muslims to dance.'

And so I stopped. That was the rule and I obeyed it like all the other rules I'd learnt. That was just the way it was.

I could listen and sing along to Abba as long as I didn't dance. I could watch Robert Powell in *Jesus of Nazareth* as long as I knew that he was not the son of God. I could eat fish and chips as long as they weren't deep fried in dripping. I could wear a skirt to school as long as I wore trousers underneath it. I could run around the school play-ground but not in our back yard. I could watch that great British institution the Queen on the telly as she celebrated her Silver Jubilee, but not that other national treasure, Barbara Windsor, in *Carry on Camping* as she did her chest exercises so forcefully that her bra pinged off. And I could read Brer Rabbit and the *Mandy* annual as long as I remembered that the Koran was the Holiest Book.

Fair enough. I could do that. No problem.

Were you taught the same rules as me when you were growing up? Were you told that you weren't allowed to dance or watch any kissing on the telly? Or that it was a sin to whistle or open an umbrella inside the house because it attracted Satan, or that you could only drink holy water when you were standing up? Or that when you went into a bathroom you had to enter with your left foot first, and when you came out, you had to use your right foot first? Of course, some of these rules weren't rules at all – they were just customs or old wives' tales passed down through generations of Aunties. They were never meant to be observed.

Unlike the fundamental laws set down in the Koran:

Let there be no compulsion in religion. (Surah 2:256)

To you be your religion, and to me, mine. (Surah 109:6)

Those who believe in the Koran, and those who follow the Jewish scriptures, and the Christians and the Sabians – any who believe in God and the Last Day and work righteousness, shall have their reward with their Lord; on them shall be no fear, nor shall they grieve. (Surah 2:62)

O ye who believe! Stand out firmly for God and let not the hatred of others to you make you swerve to wrong and depart from justice. Be just; that is next to Piety. (Surah 5:8)

Whoever kills one human being shall be regarded as having killed all mankind. (Surah 5:32)

These rules are written in black and white. They're very clear. They're not superstitions or stories made up by the Aunties. These are Divine Laws.

So why did you go against them?

Why did you do what you did?

2

Goat Eid (1981)

'Where are your shoes?' Umejee asked.

'Somebody took them at the mosque,' replied Ahsan, my younger brother.

'What? Today? Don't those *bandar*, idiots, have any shame? Don't they know today is Eid?'

Ahsan was the last one to walk through the front door, preceded by Dad, my older brother and Pajee with his walking stick. All four were dressed in *shalwar kameez* that had been pure white when they left. On their return, only Pajee's shirt was still pristine. That was because he had been allowed to sit on a chair at the mosque for Eid prayers. The others had patches of dirt on the fronts of their kameezes where they had been kneeling on the floor. I could see that the bottoms of my brother's towelling socks were almost black. Never mind doing ablutions *before* prayers; it was just as crucial to have a good scrub *after* visiting the mosque.

You couldn't tell if there was a shoe thief operating at the mosque or whether a young lad, in his eagerness to get out of there, had absent-mindedly picked up any old pair of black lace-ups. God help that pilfering boy if he existed. Stealing on Eid, one of the holiest days of the year – a celebration of the time when Abraham sacrificed his son to God – was a pretty stupid thing to do. Stealing in God's House, well, that was just madness. I imagined that for that you got your hands *and* your feet chopped off on Judgement Day; that pretty much guaranteed that you'd never have the ability or the need to nick footwear ever again.

Everyone had risen particularly early that morning. By 7.30, I could hear Dad shouting at my brothers: '*Jaldi! Jaldi!* Or else we won't get a space!' I never realised, until much later on in life when I saw it on the TV, just how packed the mosques were on this day, and how everybody wore white *shalwar kameez*, so that, with their black crowns, they looked like a hall of melting snowmen as they prayed in unison, gradually disappearing down from the standing position to the bowing position to the kneeling position to the prostrated position.

Once the men had left the house, I got out of bed. I stood at the bottom of the attic stairs, listening intently for any sound to suggest that the upstairs lodgers might be awake. Nothing. Even their macaw was silent. They were never early risers but I couldn't be sure. I started to ascend very slowly, all the while keeping my body side-on so that I could descend at haste, if need be. I concentrated my hearing as much as was humanly possible on the silence from upstairs rather than the clatter from the kitchen two flights down. My journey to the bathroom was this tedious every morning and every night.

The Shia couple from Iran who had lived with us for the best part of two years had finished their studies and returned home. No doubt the wife had had to burn or give away her pretty skirts and tights and invest in a hijab now that the Ayatollah had deemed her country the Islamic

Republic. I'd watched it on the news a couple of years earlier, how the Shah had fled with his beautiful wife and how this man dressed in black and with a long beard who looked very religious had taken over, and I still didn't get it – why Muslims were fighting each other. The Koran mentioned Muslims fighting against idolaters, like when Abu Bakr won victories in Hira and Syria, but wasn't it wrong for them to hurt each other? Well that was what I'd always been taught.

Since the departure of the Iranian lodgers, Dad had taken a young student couple into the attic. They weren't Shia or Sunni; they were French, and quite unaware of how to conduct themselves in an Islamic household. He walked around with just a pair of shorts on, and she wore miniskirts and vest tops. She had packets of Tampax openly on display on top of the bathroom cabinet. They held hands and cuddled in public. They played music first thing in the morning when all thoughts should have been focused on God. I squirmed with embarrassment for them, and shame.

I was scared of seeing them, particularly him, in any state of undress as they made the short trip across their landing to the bathroom we shared with them. If we weren't supposed to watch any nudity on the television, I concluded, we certainly weren't supposed to see it in real life. So I crawled up the stairs, very slowly.

The sixth step from the top was the place I had to crouch for a while, to have a final look and listen. One more step up and I would be visible to them. What would I do if I saw them and they weren't fully clothed? Should I run into the bathroom with my head down? There were no guarantees I would get there before they did. It would just be easier for all concerned if I ran back down the stairs to my bedroom and made it look as though I'd already used the bathroom. Save me and them the humiliation.

Except, of course, they didn't care. It was only me who did.

Sometimes I went days without brushing my teeth or washing my face. I knew God wasn't happy with that, He demanded cleanliness, but what could I do? What should I do? Which was the worse sin – being dirty myself or looking at dirty people? I had no idea; Dad had never advised upon that particular dilemma.

I put on my bright orange *lengha*, a long-sleeved shirt dancing with beaded sequins, and a full-length skirt in the same colour. With my chubbiness, I looked like an over-ripe satsuma. Umejee had taken out a pair of *kusay* for me to wear on my feet. Instruments of podiatric torture. My size six feet were unusually large for my age, and my mother had bought these shoes in a Lahore market where size six meant nothing, she'd just guessed that they might fit. They didn't. And what made it worse was that they were made of thin wood and they coiled up at the toes, like Ali Baba shoes. It would have been less painful for me to run a marathon over burning coals. I slid, rather than walked, with all the speed of a geisha but none of the demureness, either tripping up on my skirt or getting caught on furniture.

I begged Umejee to at least let me discard the *kusay*.

'Please, Mum, I can't walk in them, and look, they're making my feet bleed.'

'You only have to put them on today. And they look so pretty,' was her response. 'You will get *swahab* for wearing them.'

Swahab was a word that Umejee often used. It's the opposite of a sin, but it doesn't quite mean a virtue. I don't know what the equivalent is in English. It's like a deed you do to please God, that the sweet smiley Angel on your right shoulder notes down. It's more like a brownie point, I suppose. So on Eid my *swahab* came from having bloody toes and ankles and Umejee's came from laying on a huge meat feast – which was easier said than done. Despite repeated assurances from the halal butcher that her order of minced lamb, diced lamb and chicken breast had been taken down days in advance, when Dad got there, all that was left were a couple of mangy chicken thighs. But this was where my father excelled.

Since losing his job at the textile mill, along with thousands of others, when the whole manufacturing industry had collapsed, Dad had become much more involved in 'the community'. His ability to read, write and speak English not only provided an important service to those Pakistanis with little or no grasp of the language, but was also a great bartering tool. At such a critical time – facing a meat famine on the morning of Eid – he could always call on some favour, either from someone in the queue or from the butcher himself – someone he'd helped fill out a social security form or interpreted for in a driving test. 'Oh yes, Maliksa'ab, we are now getting the money from the gov'ment every week. *Shukriyah*, thank you. How can I repay you?' 'Many blessings to you, Hajjisa'ab. Now I am driving a taxi daytime and night-time. Tell me, what can I do for you, please?' Dad would often walk out of the butcher's with enough chicken breasts to feed the whole of Bradford. Thanks be to God for 'the community'.

* * *

71

Eid was dull. It wasn't like Christmas. There was nothing on the telly, no special *Top of the Pops*, no Queen's speech, it didn't snow, there were no trees or decorations or presents. Apart from the clothes and food, it was just like any other day.

All the excitement was contained in the night before. I say 'excitement'; what I really mean is 'anguish'.

Because Islam operates around the lunar calendar, we had no way of knowing the specific date that Eid would fall upon until the very last moment. We had a vague idea – we knew that it would be towards the end of November, either the 26th, 27th or 28th. On the night of the 25th, we had to wait until we had word from the grandly named Supreme Judiciary Council of Saudi Arabia as to whether there'd been a sighting of the new moon there and therefore whether the following day would be Eid or not.

The kingdom of Saudi Arabia is like the heart of Islam on earth, since that's where the holy cities of Mecca and Medina are and where the Prophet Muhammad was born and died. Muslims around the world obey its commands. The Supreme Council had set up a Moon Sighting Committee, whose members had the job of doing just that, spotting the new moon.

It sounds fairly straightforward. Not so. Some Bradford and other British mosques had charged the committee with incompetence and backwardness.

'They never get it right,' they complained. 'They use old old men to gaze into the night sky. How can we trust the eyes of such *budday*, who couldn't even see a light shining in their faces, never mind the thin crescent of the moon?'

Others resented being told what to do by the Saudis.

'We should use the sighting of the moon here in England. Why should the Arab royal family tell us when we have our Eid? They are not our leaders.'

Every year it was exactly the same. In the evening Dad would go to the mosque, waiting for any news. In a chain of phone calls that ran from someone in Saudi Arabia to someone in a mosque in London to someone at the Council of Mosques in Bradford to Dad's mosque, often all within the impressive time of about thirty minutes, we would learn whether tomorrow was Eid. Dad would come back home – there was no point phoning, the exchange system in Bradford had gone into meltdown – and laugh as he recalled the pandemonium he'd just witnessed.

'The moon has been seen in Mecca but all the imams are giving different advice. The Bangladeshis say they don't trust this so they are not going to celebrate tomorrow. The Indians are doing Eid in two days' time. The Kashmiris are doing it in three days. The families from Lahore and Karachi are all having Eid tomorrow. It's a joke. This is one of the holiest days in our religion. We should all celebrate it on the same day.'

So much for the Ummah, a united global Islam. There was no Ummah even in Bradford, let alone throughout the entire world.

This not knowing when Eid was didn't really help at school.

A couple of months earlier I'd started at the grammar school. It was so different from my middle school in many ways – the building was older and much bigger, there was a well-stocked library, the corridors and classrooms were much quieter, there were more rules. But the thing that struck me most was that I was the only Muslim pupil in my year. At my old school, I had been one of many, so when it came to religious festivals such as Eid, it was assumed that the Islamic pupils would just take the day off. But at the grammar school the teachers were very strict on things like absence, so Dad had to write a letter to the head.

Dear Headmistress,

I am writing to you regarding my daughter, Zaiba Malik.

As a Muslim it is requested upon her to celebrate Eid, a very holy day in our religion.

I am kindly requesting that you oblige and allow her to stay at home on this date which I shall let you know in the future.

Yours faithfully,

Mr M.S. Malik.

Dad's letters, which he printed out on his Remington typewriter, were often full of spelling mistakes or big blobs of Tippex. I had to make sure this particular correspondence to the head of my new school was perfect. I needed to make a good impression.

Right from the start, I was very aware of myself at the grammar school, how different I was to the other girls. They were white, I was brown; they were English, I was Pakistani; they were Christian, I was Muslim. I instinctively knew it was up to me to compensate for these differences. The onus was on me, as the minority, to position myself within the majority. It made some practical sense. I was, after all, the odd one out.

'What's Eid?' some of the girls in my class asked me.

'It's like Christmas.' I tried to inject as much enthusiasm as possible, to make my Holy Day as much fun as theirs. 'We get new clothes (true), we give each other presents (not true), we have really nice food (true) and we go to each other's houses (not true).'

'But why do you have it?' they asked. 'We have Christmas because that was when Jesus was born.'

'Yes, I know that. Well, we have two Eids every year. Eid al-Fitr for the end of Ramadan, the month of fasting, and Eid al-Adha where the Prophet Abraham sacrificed his son.'

I told them the story from the Koran just as Dad had told it to me.

'Abraham had a dream where God asked him to sacrifice his only son, who was called Ishmael. He knew that he had no choice, he had to do it, so he took his son to a stone where he laid him down. The Devil appeared and tried to tempt Abraham not to kill his son but he carried on. Then just as Abraham drew a sword to Ishmael's neck, a ram appeared. His son was saved and Abraham had passed the test that God had set him; he knew that love of God is more important than anything else in the world, even your own children.'

Dad had told me this story, his favourite from the Holy Book, scores of times. And I loved it too. Much more than the girls, it seemed.

My audience of about eight had dwindled down to just two. One of these was Harriet, who I'd classed as a semi-outsider by way of her height (at least a foot taller than the average measure) and her ridiculously bright orange hair and freckles.

'You have two Christmases?' she asked.

I played on this.

'Yeah, it's fantastic. You get presents twice a year, you get to eat lots of nice food, you wear pretty clothes with glitter on and you don't have to come to school. And there are all these amazing stories you learn about. It's great, being a Muslim.'

No matter how much I went for the hard sell on my faith, the girls weren't buying into it.

'But that's silly. How can you not know what day your Christmas is? Jesus was born on the twenty-fifth of December, so that's Christmas Day. You can't just change it.'

'You have to go by the moon. It's when you can see the new moon in Arabia and that's when you know for sure.' I didn't realise it then, but to the girls in my class, I must have sounded like one of the werewolf hunters from the Hammer House horror double bills that were on the telly every Saturday night. A bit scary and a bit mad.

The Malik family in the posh living room.

Soon after our breakfast of vermicelli noodles and hot milk, it was time for lunch. We all sat quietly around the kitchen table and waited for Umejee and the tandoori roast chicken that had been marinating in yoghurt and spices overnight. Pajee broke the silence.

'The *masjid* was very busy this morning,' he said. 'There were some men there that I haven't seen in over ten years, men that came to Ingerlernd at the same time as me and your dad. Where does the time go, hey?'

I couldn't imagine Pajee at the mosque. He hardly ever went. He spent most of his days sleeping or watching television or playing solitaire or smoking Benson and Hedges or coughing or chatting to the Uncles who came round to the house. Mind you, he wasn't that talkative. He never really had been, but was even less so now that his health had deteriorated. He'd started to use a wheelchair and I think that made him really unhappy, the loss of his independence. On a few occasions, without telling anyone he was going out, he'd hauled himself and the chair down the steps at the front of the house and gone off into town. He was very thin and weak and we were worried sick that something awful might happen to him. My brother Tassadaque went after him and always found him a street or two away, limp and completely breathless.

Poor Pajee.

I don't know what his life had been like before he came to England – as I mentioned, nobody talked about that kind of thing – but he seemed to have been ill and painfully gaunt for most of the time he'd been here. In fact he'd always looked uncannily like the keyboard player from Sparks, with his sucked-in cheeks, little Hitler tash and NHS specs. I don't think we ever got to the bottom of what was making him poorly; he was never admitted into hospital. Sometimes the pain was so excruciating he would cry out from his bed: 'Majee! Majee! Mother! Mother! Come and get me!' My grandmother had died when I was about five years old.

I couldn't bear to hear Pajee in such agony. I used to either put my hands over my ears or go to the top of the house where I couldn't hear him. I don't know how my elder brother mustered up the courage to go into his bedroom when he was wailing like that. I found it hard enough to go and see him every morning when he was quiet.

It was my job to take him his mug of tea before I headed to school, and from the very second that I put the two teaspoons of sugar into his drink and started stirring, I started praying: '*Bismilla irahkma niraheem*. Please, please, God, let Pajee be alive. Please, please, God, let Pajee be alive.' Right up to the moment when I nervously said: '*Aslam-o-alakum*, Pajee, Here's your *chai*.'

No reaction. Pajee was lying in his bed with the blanket pulled right over him. I moved forward and very gently prodded him with one finger. I could feel bone.

'Pajee?'

I glanced at his bedside table, at the same objects that had been on there for years – two packets of cigarettes, a lighter, an ashtray, dentures in a glass, a pack of playing cards, a tube of ointment and a bottle of red cough medicine.

'Pajee?'

Cough.

Thank you, God, so so much. Thank you.

Cough, cough.

'*Aslam-o-alakum, bheti. Teek tak?*'

'Yes, Pajee, I'm fine. There's your tea. I have to go to school now.'

'*Teek tak.*'

Dear Pajee.

Sometimes I just wanted to give him a really big tight hug. But I didn't know if that was allowed. Besides, I'd probably break every bone in his body if I squeezed him.

So I settled for just looking at him, making sure he was okay.

Like I was looking at him now, sat at the kitchen table in his smart navy blue jacket, tucking into his Eid meat feast.

Apart from the sound of munching, the occasional request for more nan or more water and the odd put-down by Umejee – 'Are you eating that or are you operating on it?' directed at me as I picked at my chicken leg – we ate in silence. We always did. Mealtimes at our house were so different from the ones I'd seen on the TV, on *Butterflies* and *To the Manor Born* and *Last of the Summer Wine*. I'd never dined at an English person's house and I was fascinated by what I saw on the telly. How they discussed important subjects at mealtimes. The way they stopped masticating when they spoke. How the food was laid out in various floral vessels on the table, which was covered in a red gingham cloth. How colourful the food looked, oranges, reds and greens. Ours was pretty much always some shade of brown. But it was the sound that intrigued me the most. Earthenware lids being replaced on tureens, crystal stoppers being plugged into decanters, a carving knife sawing through a joint of beef, and that clear metallic clink-clink of knives and forks as they chopped up the compartmentalised meat and veg on china plates. I would always be so distracted by those sounds that I lost interest in what people were saying. At our house everything was cooked in the same pot and then Umejee ladled it into our plates at the cooker. There was no selection of dishes to pick and choose from, just curry and chapattis. We didn't need cutlery, we ate with our hands. Apart from Sunday lunchtimes, when I made fish fingers and chips. But even then I could never replicate the sound I'd heard on the telly – that clink-clink, that sound of Englishness.

'All of you. Come in here!' Dad shouted from the living room. We quickly congregated from our various bedrooms, where we were struggling to find something to do.

I had resorted to a bit of dancing. I'm sorry, I know I said that I never danced after being caught by Dad

. . .'Guilty feet have got no rhythm' . . . and really I hardly ever did. But I was so bored at home and I couldn't miss this opportunity of being Nina Pretty Ballerina and spinning around in my sparkling *lengha*. I did it in my bedroom where nobody else could see. But of course I knew that my Angels were watching.

'I'll just do a few more turns and then I'll stop, I promise, and I won't do it again,' I informed them.

Turn, turn in front of the dressing table mirror. Turn, turn so fast that my long, heavy skirt swivelled around my waist and exposed my squat legs. Like a chubby whirling dervish.

It was a good job that Dad hadn't seen what I'd just been up to, otherwise I doubt that he would have given me that tenner and that pat on the head in the living room. I put the crumpled note and the five pounds that Pajee had given me in the security box I shared with my sister, Adeeba, a purple stainless-steel container that only we had the keys to. I kept a meticulous record of all my income and expenditure, right down to the coins I spent on half-pence chews. As I sat going through my now much healthier balance sheet, I heard a commotion downstairs, male voices at the front of the house.

Most of Dad's friends knew to use the back entrance, so I thought maybe someone had an urgent immigration form they needed Dad to read, or maybe an Uncle was giving out boxes of *matai*, multicoloured Asian sweets made of gram flour, sugar and ghee, to celebrate the occasion of their child becoming a *hafiz* – that is, learning to recite the entire Koran by heart. (Astounding though it may seem, we regularly heard news of a kid aged only twelve or thirteen years old who had memorised all one hundred and fourteen *surahs* of the Holy Book, that's around eighty thousand words. The reward for such an extraordinary feat was automatic admission into Heaven for the *hafiz* and a crown of gold more brilliant than the sun for the parents. No wonder the fathers of the *hafiz* had huge grins on their faces when they came round to our house.)

I peered down from the top of the stairs, but I couldn't see anything. It was always very dark in our hallway. You see, the building next door to our house on the right wasn't a residential property; it was an electrical engineering showroom. The window in our hallway looked into the office of this showroom. And hanging on the office wall directly slap bang in front of our view was a calendar. Not one of those inoffensive, unimaginative promotional calendars that bears the company logo all over pictures of its latest products – cookers, heaters, microwaves, that kind of thing – and not one of those cutesy calendars that has a fluffy kitten snuggling up to a sedated puppy. No. Every Christmas, year in, year out, the workers at the showroom clubbed together to buy their boss a gift that they too could enjoy. A calendar showing twelve naked buxom women, blondes, brunettes and redheads, performing such vital tasks as changing a flat tyre or washing a dirty car.

Umejee didn't appreciate the gift one bit.

'*Basharam ahdmee*, shameful men!' and she ordered that the blinds on that particular window remain permanently drawn.

As I couldn't see who was at the front door and didn't recognise the voice, I headed down the stairs.

'Oh, Hajjisa'ab, please, I need your help. We've lost our goat. Have you seen our goat?' The words were said with some urgency but then were followed quickly by a childish chuckle.

Dad made that sound of utter disbelief he often made – 'Henh?' – and raised his eyebrows.

'It was there this morning in our back garden when we went to the mosque, making a bloody noise. Baa, baa, baa.'

I strained to look past Dad to see who this *bandar*, this village idiot, was that kept a goat in a house in the middle of Bradford. We're not in Pakistan any more, you know. It was Mr Aziz. Mr Aziz lived somewhere at the top of our road, at the rough end. With so many back-to-back houses up there, and Pakistani families in constant flux, coming in and out of the country, it was hard to pinpoint his or any of those other residents' exact addresses. I think a lot of them were related and swapped houses as it suited them. We lived at the better end of the road, where there were no back-to-backs, just tall Victorian terraced properties with attics and cellars.

I liked Mr Aziz. He had a fat black moustache broken up by almost parallel lines of white hair that added a comical element to an already jovial face. And he had those dimples in his cheeks that made him look like a naughty schoolboy, even though he was probably around fifty years old. His pale green kameez was splattered with milk stains from his vermicelli noodle breakfast and ghee stains from his unidentifiable lunch.

'We ate our chicken, and Faisal from the butcher's on Great Horton Road came round to do the job on the goat but the bloody thing had gone,' he continued. 'In the last week we had fed it bloody everything to fatten it up – nans, chapattis, parathas. But it was still hungry and it ate the bloody rope we tied it with!' (Pakistani men – including Dad – liked the word 'bloody'. 'Bloody bastard!' 'Bloody idiot!' Those times when Dad became really angry or excited, it was impossible to keep a straight face. His 'bloody hell' would come out as 'bloody health!' 'Oh, you bloody health!')

Mr Aziz was intending to get his brownie points with God, his *swahab*, by slaughtering a goat to celebrate the Prophet Abraham's sacrifice of his son. The plan was then to distribute a third of the meat to the poor, a third to family and friends and a third amongst his own household.

'Maybe God told him to escape, to save himself,' suggested Dad. They both chortled. 'Ha ha!'

Dad offered to help Mr Aziz search for the missing goat. After all, it was Eid al-Adha, the Feast of Sacrifice, also known as Goat Eid. And besides, in between Eid meals there was little else to do. We had no relatives we could visit or who could come to see us. Eid was dull. I wished that we could pull crackers, play parlour games, sing carols around a log fire. Umejee had promised that there would be *ronak* on Eid, a liveliness, a revelry, but it never manifested. These days you can see young boys on the Edgware Road in London or on the curry mile in Manchester causing mayhem by driving up and down in their souped-up cars, blaring their horns, circling under council-erected lights that flash: 'Eid Mubarak', Eid Blessings. They're noisy and showy. Back then, Eid was almost silent. 'Silent Eid. Silent Eid.'

For an instant, I was grateful to Mr Aziz and the goat for the welcome distraction. But then I thought about poor Goatee, with its wise eyes and its pale grey pelt, having its slender throat cut open by a determined butcher, a bearded man wearing an inappropriate white *shalwar kameez*, no apron and a skullcap. He repeats the words: '*Allah wakbar, Allah wakbar.*' God is great, God is great.

Goatee tries to object by kicking with its back legs and a reverse head butt, trying to impale the slaughterer with its horns. But God is not on the animal's side. As it dies, its skin turns black.

I started my own search for the missing animal in the back yard. I knew it wasn't the right thing to do, but I wanted to save it. I looked behind and in the dustbins. I called gently: 'Goatee. Goatee.' How do you attract the attention of a lost goat? By whistling? By holding out clumps of grass? By clicking your tongue?

Then I twigged. Of course! I knew where Goatee was! At that spooky farm place behind the house. I peered over the wall that ran across the bottom of our yard and those of all our neighbours to the left. The drop on the other side was a good forty feet. Still I leaned over as far as I could. I scanned the massive overgrown field, searching for any movement, grass being nibbled or trees being butted. My eyes started to ache. There was nothing. But that didn't surprise me. I bet those nasty secret people had taken Goatee, the ones that worked inside the brick building in the middle of the field and hardly ever came out. The ones that arrived early in the morning before anyone was awake and left late at night when everyone was fast asleep. Oh, but I had seen them, two or three times. And I'm telling you, they were not normal people. They were dressed in short white wellington boots, white overalls, yellow gloves and black masks. Like scary astronauts. They might have tried to hide it, but I knew what they did in there. They carried out experiments on animals. They killed them. I was sure of it. That was why there was a huge fence right round the compound; that was why there were alarms and buzzers everywhere; that was why when our tennis balls flew over into their field and we screamed until we were blue in the face: 'Can we have our ball back, please?' they never replied; that was why there was a rancid smell of dead rodents in the summer; that was why I sometimes had nightmares about being chased by monkeys and giant rats through long grass.

Please don't hurt Goatee. I don't really care about the monkeys and the rats, but please don't hurt Goatee.

It was pointless shouting out to them: 'Can we have our goat back, please?' They hadn't responded to repeated requests for the return of about a hundred balls; they were unlikely to do so now that they had something in their possession that they actually wanted.

Maybe Goatee could escape by eating his way through the wire cage they'd no doubt put him in, and then the brick wall and the perimeter fence.

I headed back into the house and into the posh living room at the front. I stood at the bay window. I often stayed there for hours, staring at people and things outside. The triptych glass gave me a fairly clear 180-degree view of the road and our neighbours. I watched Mr Aziz knock on each of their doors. He wasn't a shy man, which was lucky.

'*Meera bakra gum geeyeh*,' he informed the Pakistani families.

'Oh dearie, Azizsa'ab. We haven't seen anything.'

We'd heard tales of goats and sheep and chickens being kept in gardens in other streets in Bradford, but never our own. I wanted to see how people would react, particularly the whities.

Mrs Peters was our direct neighbour. She was of that age where she had morphed into the Queen Mother. 'My Mom Mom,' as Umejee called the Queen Mother. The

Queen was simply 'my Mom'. It was a resemblance that paid dividends for Mrs Peters – she was the only resident on the road that everybody respected. And just like the Queen Mother, she felt she had to keep something back, to preserve herself, her culture, her way of life, her threatened institution-of-one, and so she always appeared aloof to her brown subjects. Particularly those she couldn't understand. Mr Aziz's English was nowhere near fully formed. He spoke in words, not sentences, and relied heavily on his fat smiles and dimply cheeks to get his message across.

'Please. You see goat?' He grinned at Mrs Peters.

'Coat? What coat?' She pulled a face. Like she was in urgent need of a posy of sweet-smelling flowers to mask the smell coming from Mr Aziz's food-stained shirt.

'No coat. You know. *Bukra.* Goat! Goat!'

From where I was watching, it seemed as though an invisible wall had been erected between the two. Their facial expressions didn't correlate at all. Mrs Peters was scowling. Mr Aziz was laughing. Did not understanding each other's mother tongue extend to not reading each other's face and body language?

Mrs Peters shut her door in the rotund Punjabi's face. He didn't take offence, he didn't know how to. He just waddled next door to the Todds'. This I wanted to see. Mrs Todd was an abrasive woman who thought nothing of letting her Yorkshire terrier, Sid, wrap his gnashers around our ankles. The more we ran away from the wretched thing, the faster it chased us. This would make Mrs Todd laugh. Horrible cow. She knew that we were petrified of dogs, as most Asian kids are.

I heard her first: 'What you doing with a bloomin' goat in your back yard? Do the council know?'

'Not council goat. My goat. My Chrismus.'

'What do you mean, Christmas? It's bloody November.'

I cringed with embarrassment for Mr Aziz. He might not have been aware of Mrs Todd's tone, but I was. Though there was something to be said for such imperviousness; it granted Mr Aziz immunity from most social mores. I often wondered if he was really just taking the piss.

'No, I haven't seen no goat. But I tell you what, if I do, my Sid'll have a good go at it, no doubt.'

'Thank you, dear. Yes, thank you.'

There weren't many whities on our road, but the ones there were disliked by the Pakistanis, the Indians and the Bangladeshis. You see, at one point back in the 1960s, our road had been prosperous – large, solid terraced houses occupied by the white well-to-do. The Asians had come in gradually, and they now formed the majority. They lived by their own rules. They either subdivided their houses to rent out to the students at the nearby university, or they overfilled them with their own brethren. Hardly anyone spoke English. Men with bright orange hennaed hair and grey beards walked around with their shalwars halfway up their calves, while women with white scarves wrapped tightly around their heads and about as much facial hair as their husbands trailed ten steps behind them. People parked wherever they wanted. It was like being in Pakistan. And an escaped goat didn't really help matters.

Wouldn't it be wonderful if we, the Asians and the whities, could put our differences behind us and come together for just one day or even one afternoon? Maybe Eid wasn't the most suitable day to pursue racial harmony, but a few months back there had been the perfect opportunity – when Diana had got married to Charles. We could have had a street party, got to know people on the road properly, made friends with them, realised that we all loved the royal family and the new princess in particular. Loads of other people had done it all over the country; why couldn't we? It could have been a chance for Dad to try apple crumble and Mrs Peters to taste samosas. We could have listened to a bit of Adam and the Ants and a bit of Khabi Khabie. Mrs Todd could have told us a Les Dawson joke and I'm sure Mr Aziz could have entertained us with a funny yarn from back home that would have had everyone in stitches.

Sadly, nobody from either the Asian side or the whities' side had suggested it, and it was something I just fantasised about. Community cohesion. *Come together, oh oh oh oh, come together.*

Mr Aziz disappeared into the passages that ran between some of the smaller houses at the top end of the street. He wasn't used to the exercise – sweat patches had appeared on his kameez, making it go a darker green. He knocked on the door of another set of Maliks who lived about ten houses up from us.

Good idea, Mr Aziz. If anybody's going to find Goatee, surely it's got to be Shahid Malik. After all, that was his job – to make things appear. Shahid Malik was a magician. Not a common-or-garden-pull-a-rabbit-out-of-a-hat magician. He was much more than that. He was an escapologist who escaped from water tanks and sealed boxes like Harry Houdini; he was a daredevil who motorbiked through hoops of burning hay like Evel Knievel; and he was an illusionist who made women, cars and tigers vanish in a puff of smoke like David Copperfield. He'd been on the telly many times, on programmes such as *Wogan* and

Live from the Palladium, and he was the holder of various world records, including the 'Highest Escape in the World' when he got out of a straitjacket whilst dangling from a helicopter at an astounding 1,800 feet. Dad had once taken us to see one of Shahid's shows. I watched in utter amazement as he wriggled and squirmed out of a steel chain that was tightly wrapped around his entire body as he hung from a burning rope. As the flames drew nearer and nearer towards his writhing frame and the audience gasped with horror and excitement, I wondered if Shahid, like every other Asian son or daughter in Bradford, had to put up with his parents saying to him: 'Look, *bheta*, all this magic business is fine for a short time, but when are you going to become an accountant or a *vakil*, a solicitor?'

We were very proud of Shahid in Bradford, of what he had achieved. He was our very own Bollywood superstar, with his full head of hair and dense moustache, his black leather suits and sports car. He was the only reason I had to be proud of being a Pakistani from Bradford.

'Oh, Shahid Malik's my cousin,' I used to lie to the girls at school. I could – by virtue of a shared surname. I had to – to impress them. 'And I go round to his house for dinner once a week, and when I'm there he makes my food float above the table and then he makes it disappear! It's amazing!'

I had complete faith in Shahid. He had the magical power to bring Goatee back to Mr Aziz. I strained to see what was happening at the Malik house. Brick walls obscured my view. I wanted to see Shahid utter the words: 'Hocus pocus, abracadabra,' turn round three times, click his fingers, then WHAM! – in a puff of smoke Goatee would appear, baaing contentedly, having spent the last few hours God knows where, probably in that mystical black hole where rabbits and leggy blonde assistants go as they wait to be recalled to their respective magic hats and boxes. My heart sank as I watched Mr Aziz move down the steps to the adjoining house. There'd been no reply at the Maliks. Shahid was probably tied up somewhere.

By now it was after four p.m., and getting dark. If Mr Aziz wanted to have his Eid dinner, he really needed to get his skates on. He was spending too long chatting to his neighbours, accepting sympathy in the form of cups of tea, glasses of Coke and meat samosas. He was only halfway down the even numbers.

This was the side of the road where the Wicked Witch lived.

The Wicked Witch lived with her elderly mother, who was infirm and only stepped out of the house on the hottest days of the year. Even then she would be dressed in a nightie, dressing gown and woolly hat. She would sit on a dining chair at the front of the house, and when she wasn't sleeping she would wave at anyone who went past. Umejee loved old people. She still does. She always chats to them at the bus stop or when she walks past their homes. 'Hello, darling. You fine, darling?' she asks.

Umejee would sometimes try and get one of us to go and give the old woman a plate of biscuits or some Asian sweets. But we wouldn't dare, because of the Wicked Witch. The first time I saw the Wicked Witch, I thought she was Pakistani. She had dark brown glossy hair and olive skin. I thought she was very pretty. I'd named her Meryam. But then I saw her on her way to work once, marching past our house in her white uniform with tan tights on. I should have sussed from her exposed legs that she wasn't a Muslim. Turned out she was a racist.

'Get out of my way, you bloody Pakis!' she screamed at a trio of children who were doing nothing in particular on the pavement. They were no more than six or seven years old, and you could see that they were petrified of her. From that instant she became very ugly. Her nose extended like Pinocchio's. Her coiffed hair became straggly and dry. And her face lost its roundness and became sharper. She stopped being Meryam and started being the Wicked Witch.

Every morning the Wicked Witch headed past our house, her heels alerting everyone to her movement. She had excellent posture; she walked like Miss Jean Brodie, a snooty nose-in-the-air-pile-of-books-on-the-head walk.

I never saw her at work, but I guessed she had a job at one of the make-up counters in one of the department stores in town. Her face uniform consisted of eyelashes lacquered in multiple layers of black mascara, three shades of blusher, and bright red lipstick. When she returned home, I could spot her a hundred metres away because of those lips – as flawless as they were when she left home eight hours earlier.

In a way, I felt sorry for the Wicked Witch. I guessed she was lonely, looking after her old mother. And if she hated Pakis, she couldn't have chosen to live in a worse street. It must have driven her mad how many of us there were there. There was no getting away from us. We were everywhere. Bradistan.

Poor old Mr Aziz. He was about to get it in the neck and he had no idea. Whilst he'd been busy drinking *chai* in someone's living room, I'd watched the Wicked Witch teeter home. She was wearing a black fake fur coat clenched in at the waist with a black plastic belt, and very high patent stilettos. Under the street lamps she looked like one of the women from the Human League. Or a successful prostitute. She always dressed like this, always walked around on her own. Even after the mutilated body of a woman was found at the bottom of our road two years earlier, near some bins, underneath an old carpet weighed down with stones. Barbara Leach, a twenty-year-old student at the university; the eleventh victim of the Yorkshire Ripper. She had been hit with a hammer and stabbed with a screwdriver.

It was petrifying to learn that the Ripper had murdered a woman so near to our home; that he had probably passed our house, maybe looked into our back yard. He had been so close.

Even when they caught the Ripper, a lorry driver called Peter Sutcliffe, and put him in prison for the murder of thirteen women, we still felt scared. After five years of semi-naked tortured bodies being found in undergrowth, alleys, fields and dumps, the fear had kind of sunk into our bones and we couldn't just extract and discard it.

It took us a long time before we felt safe enough to walk the streets again. Not so the Wicked Witch. Nothing frightened her. Not the Yorkshire Ripper, and certainly not Mr Aziz.

Poor old Mr Aziz. Knocking on the Wicked Witch's door at the end of the day when she was probably putting her mother on a commode and then trying to scrape all that crap from her own face was probably not a good idea.

'Fuck off! Just fuck off!' she screamed at him, before he'd even opened his mouth. And slam.

Good old Mr Aziz. He threw his hands in the air. And laughed.

'Oh fuck fuck!' He rolled his head from side to side and up and down, all at the same time, in that Pakistani way. 'Indeed yes. Fuck fuck!' he kept repeating.

An X-ray would surely reveal that Mr Aziz's brain was composed of onion bhajis, cemented together with mango lassi. He didn't think as much as the other Pakistanis I knew. Which was a good thing. He just took things as they came. He trundled down the road, still waving his hands in the air.

Finally he knocked on the door of the house directly opposite ours. I was now standing in the middle bay window, trapped between the glass and the oval onyx table. I could stare for England. Apart from school, this road was my life. I still stare, watch people move, listen to them speak, see how they interact with each other. I become so engrossed that my jaw drops and my eyes become fixed. I make no attempt to hide my snooping, my earwigging.

It may have appeared futile for Mr Aziz to knock on that particular door. All the lights were off. But Mr SB never turned his lights on. At least not in those rooms at the front of his house. He lived in perpetual darkness. Ever since his wife and son had left him. He was an alcoholic, or certainly a consistently heavy drinker. I imagine that he drank the same thing as all the men did on those Bolly-wood films I'd seen – Viskey and Coca-Cola. He had very dark skin with even darker circles under his eyes, and when he lost his temper his eyes trembled and he spat every-where. That was Mr SB.

I called him Slime Ball, when in fact he was as thin as a rake. He rarely came out of his house. Only to go to the corner shop to get booze, fags and sliced bread. He never walked in a straight line, always in a higgledy-piggledy manner, and I'd also noticed that the left side of his body hung down lower than the right side. Oh no, Mr SB! You really need to amend your ways, because you're in serious trouble. Look, the sins that are being recorded on your left shoulder are too heavy for you, they're weighing you down. There's only one way you can balance that out – by doing some good deeds. At least start by washing yourself and your clothes.

On a good day Mr SB would wear a soiled shirt and creased trousers on his excursion. On a bad day he would go with a soiled vest and a filthy checked *koti* wrapped around his lower body. On a scale of one to ten of people I knew who looked like they'd come straight off the boat from back home, Mr SB was a nine. Whenever I saw him I felt as though somebody had poured a litre of ghee over me. I felt sticky and sick.

His wife had left him after he had banged her head on the drain outside their house. I'd seen him do it. It was about ten p.m. There was screaming on the street and a young child crying. Everyone on the road ran to their windows to see what the furore was about. Mr SB had his wife's long hair in his hand and he was shoving her head against the metal grate of the drain. She was bleeding and begging for mercy. He was shouting something incoherent. This continued for about five minutes, and just as it looked like she might pass out, an Aunty from further up the road ran out of her house and rescued her. We never saw the wife or kid again.

In their absence, Mr SB's lace curtains went from white to yellow to near black. And he grew thinner and thinner. He had no visitors. Nobody spoke to him.

Except Mr Aziz.

'Have you seen my goat, ya'ar?' he called as he knocked on the window. I stared at the rotting door, waiting to see if it opened. The lace curtain flickered and Mr SB's head popped up unexpectedly from the bottom of the window. It looked as though he'd been asleep right beneath it. He looked more disorientated and dishevelled than normal.

'Were you asleep, ya'ar? It's not even five o'clock!' Mr Aziz exclaimed.

'What do you want? I'm busy.'

'Oh ya'ar. Have you seen my goat?'

Mr SB shook his head and ducked back into his squalor. I could only imagine what it was like in there. Newspaper instead of toilet paper. Viskey bottles that looked full but on closer inspection had two packets of fag ends swimming in Mr SB's piss. Maybe in his most inebriated state he would take a swig from one of the bottles in the hope that the stub ends plus his alcoholic urine would have distilled into something tasting like his usual tipple. But he couldn't stomach it. Lying on his back on the floor, he would just be able to raise his head and spew the nicotined liquid on to himself. That, I concluded, was the reason why he always had brown patches on the chest of his shirt. Sometimes I wondered if he'd killed his wife and son and sat their dead bodies on the sofa. For as long as rigor mortis stiffened her body, he could hit his wife as often and as hard as he wanted.

Goatee was nowhere to be found. I'm sure Mrs Aziz was worried about losing her *swahab*, her opportunity to donate food to the poor on this holy day. I'm sure Mr Aziz was despairing about his missing third of the goat, that part of the animal he had hoped to fill his fat belly with that night. It wasn't difficult to picture Mr Aziz at his dining table, salivating on to the four sheets of kitchen roll tucked into the top of his kameez, biting into a leg of meat so huge it looked like it could only exist in a cartoon. He became a Viking, on his head a helmet with Goatee's horns attached, pleasured grunts forced to come out of his nostrils, having found no exit point through his stuffed mouth. Losing his dinner was what made Mr Aziz unhappy. Not problems with his family back in Pakistan. Or his finances. Or his kids. He could deal with all of those by ignoring them. He couldn't ignore his rumbling gut. He shuffled back home, looking sorry for himself, his hands trying to soothe his corpulent stomach. I'm sure he didn't go hungry that night. Mrs Aziz would have rustled something up for him, chicken biryani or keema roti. But he would have dreamt of goat curry all night.

Mr Aziz never found Goatee. For years people would ask him: 'Mr Aziz, have you got a goat this Eid? Are you going to provide us with a feast?' Then they would laugh. They had no idea what had happened to the animal. I did, though.

If Abraham tried to sacrifice his son and his son became a goat, then if you tried to kill a goat on Eid it would become a man. That was why Goatee had escaped. It was all very well to have miracles happen back in Koranic times – people were used to them then: the splitting in two of the moon, the healing of the sick, the journey through the heavens. But can you imagine the fuss if a goat had meta-morphosed into a man in front of a crowd in BD7 in 1981? No, it would have all been too much. So Goatee had to make its way to the disused plot of land at the top of the road. While munching on some grass, the transformation had occurred, without witness, without gasps.

Human Goatee now works as a bus driver and has three kids of his own. He has never told anyone his secret.

3

The Night of Power (1982)

Those sixty minutes between three and four a.m. must be about the loneliest time there is for normal people in normal conditions (I'm excluding prisoners, addicts, the homeless, depressives and senior politicians, who I imagine feel lonely most of the time).

I've never been a sound sleeper, five hours is a good night for me, and I can function quite well on less, but what does me in is seeing that one red electric bar on my cheap Goodmans digital alarm clock disappear from 02:58 to form 02:59. The next hour is spent doing what I can to distract myself from glancing at the clock again until I can feel pretty confident it's reached at least 04:01. So I'll listen to the World Service, read a book, do a Sudoku puzzle or try to fathom the rules of American ice hockey from the TV. But of course I never get it right. I peek too early and I see that the flashing red light is reading 03.21, and I shudder. Not even halfway through yet – still thirty-nine minutes to go!

Three to four a.m. is a dangerous time to be awake. It's the surreal hour when nothing functions as it should; it's when everything gives the illusion of being serene but is actually quite disturbed. I know that things are happening all around me, I just can't see them. Divine decisions are being made about what will happen to who when the sun rises – who will suffer and who will flourish. Decisions about every single human being on earth.

But that's not what frightens me, the thought that my time might be up. I hate that three to four a.m. hour because it's a neither-here-nor-there time – it's neither the end of one day nor the start of another; it's neither night nor morning. It's a confused time that adds to my confused state. You see, I am a neither-here-nor-there person. A British Muslim.

And though I can now finally cope to some extent with the fairly constant flux in my head, I can't deal with being surrounded by muddle. I need things to be just so, to be in their place and to be certain. And when they're not, like at three in the morning when even the space around me isn't at all sure what it is, I feel very unsettled.

Three to four a.m. is the time when my legs ache with a dull pain and I have to kick off my duvet because I can't bear its weight and then seconds later I have to pull it tightly back around me so that only the top half of my head pokes out because, in my state of quivering alertness, I become convinced that I can feel something stroking my foot, some invisible being, some spirit. It's trying to be gentle and it doesn't mean any harm, but it freaks me out. The spirit senses my fear and stops. It hangs around for a while and then leaves. I don't see anything, there's no apparition, no white mist or vaporous form. It's just a feeling. A hazy, indistinct feeling.

I don't know if we're supposed to believe in ghosts. Some Muslims are really into their superstitions and black magic. There's one Aunty, a friend of Mum's, who recently changed her surname because she thought hers was bringing her bad luck, and another who went to see a mystic to lift a curse she said had been put on some members of her family who were suffering from severe depression. A few times I've heard Aunties talk about having their palms read or buying potions to ward off evil. In extreme circumstances a 'holy man' may perform an exorcism if they think that *jinn*, ghostly beings, inhabit your soul and are forcing you to commit wicked deeds like renouncing your faith or having no respect for your parents. You won't be surprised to learn that you can watch these exorcisms on the Internet, though I must warn you that they say that those who watch such banishments of evil on YouTube may find that they too become possessed. Take heed.

Jinn was a word we heard a lot when we were growing up, though not so much now. When we were naughty, Umejee used to say: 'The *jinn* must be visiting you today. Ask Allah for forgiveness.'

So we would pinch and tug at our ear lobes with our thumbs and forefingers for a few seconds, as we'd been taught, until they went bright red and started to really hurt, and we would repeat: '*Thoba. Thoba. Thoba.*' Forgive me. Forgive me. Forgive me. It's a ritual I still perform I would say on average about a couple of times a week, when I've wished another driver who's pulled out in front of me dead or when I've condemned tourists blocking up Oxford Street to burn in Hell. You can always spot a sinful Muslim a mile off – just look for throbbing crimson lugs.

The *jinn* are made of 'smokeless fire' and can fly; they can't be seen by humans and they live in a parallel world to ours where they have free will, which means that they can be either good or bad. One *jinn* called Iblis used his freedom to refuse to bow down to Adam when he was asked to do so by God. His disobedience led him to be thrown out of Paradise and sent to Hell for Eternity, where he was renamed Satan. Satan thus vowed that, in revenge, he would lead all humans astray. He uses his massive army of *jinn* whisperers, *qareens*, to murmur into the chest of every man and woman and urge them to give in to their corrupt desires and to worship deities other than God.

To combat the work of the *jinn*, there is the Light of God, the Angels, who can assume pretty much any form, including that of humans, and can move faster than the speed of light. Some of the senior ones, the Archangels, are given special duties, so, for example, Azrael is the Angel of Death, who separates the soul from the body in the dead. If a person was bad, the soul is wrenched out, but if a person was righteous, it comes away like 'a drop of water dripping from a glass'.

Nobody but God knows how many Angels there are in total, though it's thought that they outnumber humans. And for one night only, every year, when the gates of Heaven are opened, all these Angels descend to earth. This is the Night of Power, the holiest time in the Islamic calendar, which marks the anniversary of the Prophet Muhammad receiving the first verses of the Koran in the Cave of Hira. It's also known as the Night of Decree, the Night of Measures, the Night of Excellence, the Night of Majesty and the Night of Predestination. Call it what you will, the idea is the same – to stay up all night, read the Koran and think about God. Praying throughout this one night is the equivalent of praying for a thousand months, which works out at precisely eighty years and four months, a lifetime. And on this one night, God forgives all your past sins and answers all your prayers. It's worth losing a night's sleep for.

So once a year, on the twenty-seventh day of Ramadan, me, Dad, Adeeba and Tassadaque would sit at the kitchen table from dusk until dawn, praying and reading the Holy Book. (Ahsan was exempted from this vigil on account of his age.)

Now that I think about it, I wonder if that tingly ethereal feeling I get now in the hour between three and four a.m. when I'm wide awake, of some other presence in the room, some supernatural being, has something to do with the sensation I used to get as a child when I stayed up during the Night of Power and when, for one miraculous night only, I could hear and feel the flutter of Angels' wings and even see them, thousands of them, hovering above us in our kitchen.

The Night of Power always started off with great enthusiasm and excitement. This was our Night Before Christmas, a truly magical time when amazing gifts would be bequeathed to the faithful, delivered not by a ruddy-cheeked portly man oozing out of a red suit reeking of sherry with bits of mince pie nestling in his beard, but by the most beautiful, pure and gracious winged beings, whose astounding presence made even the Prophet Muhammad faint.

As the sun set, Dad placed several copies of the Koran in the centre of the kitchen table, along with a jug of water and four glasses. Veneration is thirsty work. We sat in the same positions as at mealtimes, Adeeba to my right, Tassadaque to my left and Dad at the top end. We all had our heads covered and socks on our feet. Dad had his grey and green striped blanket wrapped around him, which made him look like a Talibani. We knew from past experience that it would get very chilly in the middle of the night.

Then, without so much as the firing of a starter gun or a 'They're off!' we quietly started our marathon holy session.

I didn't really have a plan as to how I was going to last the night. I wasn't a big tea or coffee drinker and it wasn't the done thing to nip out into the back yard for a bit of fresh air. It was just a case of starting at the beginning of the Koran and seeing how far I could get. Dad stuck to his silk-wrapped copy, whilst the rest of us read from a version that had a larger typeface. All the better for tired eyes. As the youngest, I was also the slowest, but I was determined to do the best I could. I wasn't too concerned about having all my past sins erased; apart from the occasional rudeness to Umejee and Dad or the odd lie to my teachers about why my homework was late, I reckoned I was leading a fairly uncontaminated life. But I did need God to answer my prayers – well, one particular prayer. There was something specific I wanted from Him, something really important.

And that was a clarinet. Or a flute. Either one – it didn't matter. It could be a shiny brand-new one, like those I'd seen displayed in the window of Woods music shop, priced around £150, or a second-hand one for a bit less – I wasn't bothered.

I just needed a clarinet or a flute so that I could be a bit more like the other girls at school. I could fit in. Make some friends and not stand out any more. The only Muslim in my year, the only Pakistani. No matter that I didn't know how to play the clarinet or the flute, or even how to read music. That wasn't important. What mattered was that from now on things were going to change. I would join the orchestra, the girls would see that I wasn't so different from them and they would become my friends. Simple. All I needed was an instrument; the rest I could do myself. And as Dad didn't have the money, the Angels would bestow one upon me. That was what the Night of Power was all about. Rewarding good Muslims.

'Dear Angel Gabriel, I know that you can hear me right now on this holy night. I have been a decent person and I do my very best to obey God and the Prophet Muhammad. Though I know sometimes I make mistakes and I'm very sorry about this. Please please can you look after everybody in our family in Bradford, especially Pajee who is not very well. Can you please take care of our family in Pakistan and give them food and money. Please will you look after all the poor and the poorly and the hungry people in the world. Please will you stop all the fighting and the wars in the world. Please will you look after Princess Diana's baby William and make sure he grows up a healthy boy. Please please I will do whatever you ask of me in the year ahead but please please I beg you can I please please have a flute. If it is not possible to have a flute, could I please please have a clarinet. Umejee says that playing a clarinet will make my cheeks very big so I would like a flute but really I'm not bothered. A flute *or* a clarinet will do. Please, this is very important to me. I am asking for many things to help other people but I am only asking for one small thing for myself.'

As I beseeched the Archangel, I raised my cupped palms so that they covered my mouth. I didn't want anybody to see what I was praying for. It was private, between me and Angel Gabriel; don't they say you should never tell others what you wish for because then it won't come true?

Actually, if truth be told, I was ashamed; I felt guilty

that I was only half-heartedly asking for the things I was supposed to want – peace, an end to famine, good health – and that my real motivation for staying up all night was to get a silly wind instrument. I tried to decipher the whisperings of Dad and my siblings; it would make me feel so much better if I knew that they were asking for a new car or a hi-fi or an electric guitar, but no luck. I couldn't even make out if they were requesting in English or Punjabi, let alone what was on their wish list. Nevertheless, I continued. I had to.

As I saw it, the choice I had was either to be selfish tonight and face the wrath of God on the Day of Judgement, which was many many years away, too far in the future to worry about now, or to be altruistic tonight and have no friends for the entire duration of my schooldays. For me, there was no choice.

The fear of being alone and lonely was the natural stimulant I needed to keep me awake. Even when the combination of the tube lighting overhead, the gentle hum of four people reciting, the sight of Dad gently swaying to and fro in his cosy blanket, and basic fatigue conspired to lull me into a deep slumber. I forced myself to stay awake by pinching my cheeks and holding my eyelids apart.

Concentrate. I must concentrate. I can do this. I have to do this. If I fall asleep, the Angels will never give me what I want. What I need.

'It's only one night. It's only one night,' I kept repeating to myself. 'After tonight, you won't have to sit in class on your own or go to lunch on your own or spend breaktimes on your own.' Whenever I felt my eyes shutting or my breathing slowing down, I put down my Koran and put my hands together and rocked quite forcibly backwards and forwards.

'Dear Angel Gabriel, please please please . . .'

I managed to complete the first chapter of the Koran and was now on the second. Good. Satan's attempts to distract me from my mission by making my eyes heavy with fatigue had failed. But he wasn't easily dissuaded; his remit was to never give up. He breathed icy air into the kitchen, hoping that our lips would freeze together and our hands would become numb, rendering us unable to read the Holy Book or turn its pages.

My whole body shuddered, as though somebody had walked over my grave, or as though the Devil had tried to enter my soul.

Dad, who had shown no signs of flagging all night and was charging through his Koran at great speed, glanced up at me. He didn't say anything, he was just checking to see if I was still awake. Yes, Dad, I'm wide awake, cold but awake. Satan won't get the better of me. I could see that my siblings were hitting the wall, and so I recited the

Koran with more vigour than I had done all night to try
and compensate for their weariness. And that was when I
became aware of the warmth and the calm.

> On the Night of Power the Angels and the Spirit
> descend by their Lord's permission, with all His
> decrees. That night is peace, till the break of dawn.
> (Surah 97:4–5)

Of course at three a.m. our kitchen, our house, our
entire road was quiet, but this was another type of quiet
that I'd never heard before. I knew from going to the
madrasa that when you pray you should enter a state of
mind where you're not aware of your surroundings because
your entire focus is on God. That's why Islamic teachers
encourage their students to gently sway as they read
because it puts them into a trance where they can block
out the world around them.

I couldn't hear the ticking clock above the mantelpiece
and I couldn't hear anybody reciting Arabic. It was as
though I'd gone deaf. But I didn't panic. For a couple of
minutes, everything was deadly silent and still, and then
I heard a flapping sound behind me. It was very low and
very slow but very definite. Like the sound of a single
sail on a tranquil sea. And I could feel a light flutter on
the back of my neck. Normally when we let our budgerigars out of their cage and let them fly around the living
room, I would run out screaming. I hated having something flying around my head, but this was different. I
didn't panic.

'Dear Angel Gabriel, I know that you are very close to
me right now on this holy night. Please please please . . .'

It didn't occur to me to tell my family that the Angels were right there, in our kitchen. As far as I was concerned, there was nothing strange or bizarre about seraphs floating around our sink and cooker and fridge-freezer; this was what was supposed to happen, this was what the Night of Power was all about. Each person around that table would sense the Angels in their own time.

Just as now when I'm awake in the middle of the night and I feel something stroking my foot and I know it's not evil but I don't want to see it, back then in the kitchen I didn't have the guts to look behind me. I didn't want to see the Angels close up. But I did look out of the window. The black night was no longer black but a pale grey. Thousands upon thousands of pairs of sheer white wings were circling the sky. Each pair was about the height and width of an average man; there was no form, no body or head or halo or feathers as you expect there to be with Angels, just two tethered wings made of some material resembling tracing paper. Occasionally a pair would swoop down on a house that had its lights on, fly straight through a door or window and then reappear a few seconds later.

I could hear a strange noise from outside – it wasn't a monotone but rather made up of two distinct and intense sounds. There was that low, slow flapping I'd just heard behind me in the kitchen but on a much louder scale, this time more like a massive flotilla of sails on a calm sea, which came from the infinite host of Angels flying in the night, and then below that there was a drone so deep it was more like a vibration than a sound.

And there, way up in the slate-grey sky, hovering horizontally above all mankind, was the Angel Gabriel. Even though it says in the Koran that the Archangel is so big that the distance between his ear lobe and his shoulder is more than the distance a bird can fly in seven hundred years, I could see his entire shape. His main body was like that of a butterfly's but without the antennae. He had hundreds of wings, which were feathered and so blindingly white that they made the entire earth gleam and me squint. He had no face but an aura of extreme solemnity. After all, he was here to do the work of God. And though this was a joyous night for those who believed, I knew that the Archangel was also able to pull entire cities out of the ground, using just the edge of one of his wings, if God so commanded. No wonder Dad always talked about the Angel Gabriel with such respect.

I had witnessed a truly beautiful thing. How fortunate we were, those who stayed awake during the Night of Power. Those Muslims in Bradford 7, in Yorkshire, in England and all around the world. The Ummah. This was what we saw and heard and felt and knew whilst others slept.

Once I'd experienced such a miracle, I had no problem staying awake until dawn. I managed to get through almost three chapters of the Koran and I prayed for a flute/clarinet so many times that my throat was sore and my mouth was parched. I was knackered. But that was okay, it was a small price to pay for such a big change. No more Zaiba the Loner. From now on it was going to be Zaiba the Accepted, maybe even Zaiba the Popular.

I resisted the temptation to search for my instrument until I returned from school. No doubt the Angels would be very busy throughout the day delivering ceasefires and harvests and vaccines. Best to give them a bit of time.

That morning, I put on my uniform and got the bus to school. The year before I'd passed the eleven-plus and been given an assisted place because of Dad's low income. I had started at Bradford Girls' Grammar with much hope for my future. I was going to become a doctor. As Dad said: 'Education is the most important thing in Ingerlernd' and as Mum said: 'I am very happy that you are going to a girls' school. I won't have to worry about you.'

As it turned out, none of the above statements proved to be true. I never became a surgeon; fitting in was more important than grades; and Mum spent a lot of time fretting about me.

You see, I was trying to straddle, balance, juggle, whatever, my life at home with my life at school. And at the same time I was at that age when I was trying to work out who I was besides a Pakistani Muslim schoolgirl. Someone who enjoyed drawing, singing, reading, sewing, collecting stamps and, probably most of all, fantasising. It wasn't easy. I struggled.

Let me explain in more detail. I'll describe to you the day after the Night of Power, starting from 'That morning, I put on my uniform and got the bus to school.'

In fact there were two buses, the 576 and then the 680.

The stop for the 576 was a few metres down the road from our house. Its final destination was Halifax, miles away on the outer edge of Bradford, but I had to stay on it only for a few minutes as it trundled up the lower half of Great Horton Road – past dingy terraced houses with shiny shalwar kameezes hanging out to dry, fruit and veg shops with all the labels handwritten in Urdu, corner shops selling the *Jang* newspaper, travel agents advertising cheap flights to Pakistan, solicitors providing immigration advice, taxis blaring out Punjabi classical music. Our own little world. Bradistan.

At the junction with Cross Lane I got off the 576 and walked over to the 680 bus stop on Arctic Parade, from where you get one of the best 'former mill town' views over Bradford. Crooked rows of blackened houses smoking away, decrepit factories that have been forced to give up the habit, and the magic faraway countryside, the amphitheatre of hills that promises so much.

The 680 was an altogether different ride to the 576. Its passengers were white and the areas it travelled through – Clayton, Thornton and Allerton – were white too. The houses here were larger, had pretty uncemented gardens at the front and clean net curtains, and underwear flapping unashamedly on the washing line for all to see.

I knew what was behind those curtains – I'd seen it once when I'd been invited to Amanda Parker's home for tea. The pink, cream and green floral sofa, the pewter tankards on the mantelpiece, the porcelain dogs on the dresser, the real dog on the windowsill, the brass plates etched with shire horses hanging on the walls, the framed tapestry that read 'Home Sweet Home' over the door, the wooden cross with Jesus on top of the telly and the burning coals in the fireplace. How fascinating. I took it all in; so this is how English people decorate their houses, this is how they live. Umejee was right all along – white people are very different to us. I had suspected that all along, but now that I'd seen it for myself, I knew it was true.

Upstairs on the very back seat of the 680 bus were sixth-formers from the grammar school, like figures from a Tamara de Lempicka painting – sophisticated, no-nonsense, dangerous women with their lubricious red lips, sleek defined curls, flamboyant dresses and feminine arrogance. They chain-smoked and carried art folders and albums such as Bob Marley's *Exodus*. Wow! I was desperate to stare at them, but they were all behind me and there were only so many times I could pretend to glance out of the back window as though I was looking for something. I wanted to learn from them, be like them, be part of their world. Me, with my greasy hair scraped back and tied in a plait with a blue rubber band, my yellow shirt with its white patches on the chest and back where my anti-acne cream had bleached the cotton, my baggy men's sweater to hide my developing form, my ugly clumpy brown and beige shoes, my tent skirt and my trousers.

Those bloody trousers. They were the bane of my life. Dad wouldn't let me wear just a skirt to school – 'It's not allow,' he would resolutely and regularly state. So as hundreds of girls went straight through the school door every morning, no fuss, I lurked near a large oak tree at the top of the hill. When the coast seemed to be clear, I struggled to take my flared trousers off over my clumpy shoes – not that easy to do when underfoot is all damp and slippery – and put them in my bag. I hated having to perform this covert exercise every morning; having to hang around until I was as sure as I could be that the school bell was just about to chime and that most of the pupils would already be inside the building so nobody would spot me undressing. But no matter how discreet I tried to be, my classmates knew about the addition to my uniform.

'Why do you wear trousers when you come to school?' Some girls asked out of curiosity, others with malice.

'I'm a Muslim and it's not allowed for me to show my body,' I explained.

'But you've got tights on; nobody can see your legs.'

'It's our religion that you have to cover yourself up properly.'

'Why aren't you allowed to show them?'

'So men don't stare at me. When I come to school or leave or when I'm at home I never show my legs. It's okay for me to wear tights inside school because there aren't any men here.'

'Yes there are. There's Mr Hargreaves and the science assistant and the gardener. Why don't you have to put your trousers on when you see them?'

'Oh, I don't know.'

'But if you're wearing tights then nobody can see your legs. Your skin's covered up.'

No reply.

'Why is it okay for you to show your arms, then?'

No reply.

'We go out with bare legs in the summer and nobody stares at us.'

No reply.

'Why is it so different for you?'

No reply.

They couldn't get it and I couldn't explain. Because I'd never had to. I'd just done it all my life, put trousers on underneath my skirt, put a shalwar on underneath my kameez, put a *lengha* on underneath my top. No questions asked. That was the way we did things. Obey God and don't ask questions. How could I tell them that showing your legs was what white people did, not me, not us, the Pakistanis, the Muslims? Shame, shame. If I told them that, they'd never talk to me again, and I was already struggling for friends.

How I wish Umejee had been a fan of Noel Coward; then she might have acted upon his sage advice:

Don't send your daughter to school in trousers,
   Mrs Malik,
You may be keen to secure her place in Paradise,
But I can assure you that it's not very nice to have
   girls leer with contempt in their eyes,
They can be oh so cruel, there's really no need to
   give them extra fuel,
So, Mrs Malik, throw those darn pants in the bin,
You won't be committing a sin,
Merely enabling your daughter to fit in.

No such luck. Mum only liked Engelbert Humperdinck and Freddie Mercury.

Inside school, things didn't really improve. We had assembly every morning, a religious ceremony with two prayers and two hymns and notices. Dad had written to the headmistress asking that I be exempted from attending this gathering as well as religious education lessons, and so at nine a.m., as hundreds of girls filed into the main hall, I worked my way against this giggling traffic up a flight of stairs and into the library. Some mornings I would just sit and read for half an hour as I was supposed to, but actually for the most part, I might as well have been in that prayer hall with all those Christians. Because if I heard them singing a hymn that I loved, I would have to sing along. And I loved a lot of hymns: 'I Vow to Thee My Country', 'Holy, Holy, Holy', 'We Plough the Fields and Scatter'.

There were good acoustics in the library on account of

the wooden panels and high ceiling. There was nothing to stop me; Dad wasn't around and every pupil and teacher was downstairs in the congregation. I belted out: 'The Lord's my shepherd, I'll not want, He makes me down to lie, in pastures green, He leadeth me, the quiet waters by.'

I couldn't justify singing about or to Jesus. I knew Dad wouldn't like it and I knew that the Angel on my right shoulder was frowning and shaking its head whilst the Angel on my left shoulder was making a note of my offence. But what could I do? I loved to sing. Hymns, Abba, Barbra Streisand, Dexy's Midnight Runners, Tears for Fears, songs from *Oliver!*, the Pretenders. Anything. (Apart from 'Onward Christian Soldiers' – the lyrics of that particular hymn made me feel uncomfortable. Were they marching as to war against us, the Muslims?)

I had to have some fun.

Life was difficult enough.

I don't know what it was like at your school, but at ours, factions were created pretty much from week one. These were based on various things: whether you were arty or sporty or academic or musical, where you lived, your social status. Like attracts like. It's a simple fact of life. And once those tribes are established, they're very difficult to penetrate.

I had no like to attract. No other Muslim or Pakistani.

From the very start, I was the girl who wore trousers to school, didn't go to assembly or RE, never invited people round to her house, never went to any parties; the girl whose sister had to come to parents' evening because her mum and dad didn't speak very good English, who got picked up from school in a clapped-out old Datsun, who had two Christmases a year but didn't get any presents and who, for a few weeks every year, didn't have to go up to the dining room because she wasn't allowed to eat or drink or something weird like that.

What did I have in common with girls who either wore lambswool V-neck sweaters and tied polka-dot silk scarves around their necks and made fairy cakes for the summer fete, or cut six inches off the bottoms of their denim skirts and three inches off the bottoms of their T-shirts and drank cider and black on the back seat of their boyfriends' cars, whose mothers got their hair washed and set at some swanky salon in Ilkey, whose fathers drove a new company car every year, whose gardens had apple trees and a golden retriever and whose living rooms had a drinks cabinet rattling with bottles of gin and vodka? Almost nothing.

I did my best to stress things from my life that the girls might find interesting: living on the same street as the world-famous magician and escapologist Shahid Malik; knowing all the words to The Jam's 'A Town Called Malice'; staying up really late on Saturday night to watch the Hammer House of Horror double bill and not covering up my eyes once. I even told the odd lie: 'I sneaked out of my bedroom last night when everybody was asleep and I went to Leeds on the bus to see the Police in concert. I got back at three this morning.' No matter that the band were touring in America.

My efforts to impress the girls – whether true or not – amounted to nothing. You see, there was so much about my life I couldn't tell them. That the only holiday anybody in our house had was Dad when he did his annual pilgrimage to Mecca. That I had an elderly Uncle who lived with us and who was in a wheelchair. That Umejee was part of a committee run by the Aunties where she put a bit of money aside every month so that she could pay for her children's weddings once she'd found suitable partners for them. That in addition to doing my homework in the evenings and at weekends, I had to read the Koran in Arabic and in English. That Dad had been a textile worker until he'd been made redundant. That men with baggy white trousers and little caps and women with baggy white trousers and headscarves were pretty much the only visitors to our house. That the only time I went out at the weekend was with Dad to WHSmith to buy books or with Mum to a wake or a wedding. That they should fear what would happen to them on the Day of Judgement with all this bare flesh and talk of boys. That last night, when I'd stayed up all night for the Night of Power and asked for a flute, I'd seen the Archangel Gabriel.

I did what I could to get along at school. I studied hard, read, sang, listened to music, painted, chatted to the girls a bit. But not very much. I had very little to say to them. Which is why there's so little dialogue in this chapter. In fact you may notice that there's not very much dialogue at all throughout this book. I was a quiet child who lived inside my head. In my school reports, the teachers often commented that 'She works thoughtfully' and 'She is a thoughtful member of the form contributing quietly' and 'She always works with quiet interest.'

I did what I could to get along. I imagined, fantasised that I was other people – important people – in other places.

A city gent who one morning decides to leave the rat race for good by boarding a train with only his briefcase and travelling to a quiet village miles away, where, after first being treated as an outsider, he is then hailed a hero when he rescues a farmer from a fire.

An Olympic swimmer who has undergone life-saving surgery and spent months in hospital and who, against all odds, swims for her country against some stiff competition and wins the gold medal and is greeted home by the Prime Minister as a heroine.

A 747 pilot who has just come out of the shower and who is being helped to get ready for his press conference by three glamorous air hostesses who bring him, in turn, his pressed uniform, his cup of coffee and his cigarettes and who congratulate him for his heroism in flying his plane single-handedly across the Atlantic from London to New York after his co-pilot had a heart attack.

There were many more fantasies but those were some of my favourites. I'd imagine for hours during morning assembly, lessons, at breaktime, at bedtime. Sometimes I even imagined when I was reading the Koran when I should have been concentrating on God. '*Thoba, thoba.*' Forgive me, forgive me. I couldn't help myself. Maybe that was why God didn't listen.

Normally I was never in any rush to get back home after school. It would only be curry and homework and Koran. But this was the day after the Night of Power. I didn't even wait for the school to empty before putting my trousers back on. You can all stare. Tomorrow things are going to be different. Everything's going to change once I get my flute or clarinet. I'm going to be popular. Just you wait and see.

I jumped off the 576. In the distance I could see the Wicked Witch walking up the road, heading home after a day's work. There wasn't anybody else around. Maybe they were all too busy with whatever they had asked God for. Shahid Malik, the escapologist, with his new strait-jacket; Mr Yusuf, the shopkeeper, with his new cash till; Mr Aziz with his new goat *and* a new meek wife for his son – after all, that was a fundamental wish of most of the Uncles and indeed Aunties, an obedient daughter-in-law who just got on with the cooking, cleaning and child-rearing without any fuss or bother. Lucky man. God'll fix it for you. And you and you and you. I wondered what the Wicked Witch would ask for if she was a believer – for her mother to pass away? For all the Asians in the street to move out?

'*Aslam-o-alakum*, Umejee.' Mum was in the kitchen, cooking lamb bhindi. 'I'm just going to get changed.'

I had to do this properly – not tell a single soul that I'd asked for something as wasteful as a flute or clarinet and not make it look like I was desperate to find my gift. Slowly does it. I took off my school uniform and put on my Asian clothes – I even covered my head with my *dupatta* to please God. And then I started the hunt.

There, behind the radio on the fireplace in the kitchen, was a letter addressed to me. Ha! The instructions: GO TO THE CUPBOARD IN THE FRONT ROOM WHERE THE KORANS ARE KEPT AND THERE YOU WILL FIND A BRAND NEW SILVER FLUTE. ARCHANGEL GABRIEL.

I took a deep breath and opened the envelope. No card, no map, no directions. Just the latest set of commemorative stamps sent by the stamp club of which I'd been a member for a few years.

Oh well – on with the hunt. Up in my bedroom I lifted my pillow. No, nothing under there. Nothing in the pillow-case. Nothing under the bed either, apart from my purple safe, and there was no way, miracle or not, that you could fit a wind instrument in there. I searched the cupboards, the drawers of the dressing table, the bathroom cabinet, behind the toilet, the sofas in the posh living room, behind Dad's records, in the oven, the fridge, behind the televisions, underneath the dining table.

It's got to be here somewhere. It says specifically in the Koran that for those who pray throughout the Night of Power, their wishes will be met. I'd kept my side of the bargain and I had no doubt that the Angel Gabriel had kept his. It was just a case of finding the damn thing. It might be in a swish black case, lined with red silk, like I'd seen at school, or maybe there was no box, just a bare instrument. It could be anywhere. There was no need to assume that it would be in the most obvious place. I kept searching. Nothing.

It might still take a few hours for it to turn up. There must be other people with more urgent requests – a new kidney, a job, a son. So I waited a while and then retraced my steps. I even checked inside the budgie cage. Still nothing.

I sat on my bed. My head felt light. What was all that about? Was I the only Muslim in the whole world not to get what I had asked for? Was God angry with me for asking for an extravagant and unnecessary item? Or had I done something else wrong? What? I had prayed, not just last night but many many times before. I fasted. I read the Koran. I didn't show my legs and only females saw me in my leotard and swimming costume. I didn't pray to Jesus. I only occasionally sang songs about him. I never read the Bible. I only ever ate halal meat. I didn't talk about boys like the girls at school. I didn't shave the hair on my head and dye it bright red like Stephanie Gibson did. I didn't wear lipstick and mascara and eyeliner to school like Julia Armitage did. I didn't curse the teachers like Vanessa Doyle did. I didn't go to nightclubs. I didn't complain about my two lives. I didn't have any friends.

What more did I have to do? I'd always been told that if you are a Muslim, a good Muslim, God will listen to you and reward you.

So where was my flute? My prize. My only hope. So I wouldn't be so lonely any more.

'Go to bed now. You must be very tired after last night,' said Mum.

'Yes, Umejee. I am very tired.'

The Night of Power had sapped my strength.

This was the year that you were born, wasn't it? On 15 December, at St Luke's, the hospital at the back of our house. You were the second of four children and your parents nicknamed you Kaka, Little One. You know that your home was only a few streets away from mine. Did I ever see you? I was reading the official report and it says that you always took religion seriously, even from an early age. So you might have stayed up from dusk until dawn during the Night of Power.

Did you get what you prayed for?

What did you pray for? Probably not a flute or a clarinet, like me.

Did you ever see the Angels in your kitchen or up in the sky?

Or was it the evil *jinn* that you saw that night?

Is that why you did what you did?

4

The Year of Silence (1984)

When people ask me that question, as they often do –
'What's it like to be a British Muslim?' – I forage around
for some profound remark, some succinct yet heartfelt
statement. And I never get there, I never find it. I either
go on for ages so that I contradict myself or bore the inter-
viewer, or I just say: 'You know, it's too difficult to explain.'

But a few weeks ago, when I was nosing around the
garden shed that Dad built in the back garden – which
isn't really a shed at all but a large storage room, somewhere for Mum to keep her things, her squares of material, her glasses and jugs, her Thermos flasks, her toasters
and irons – I stumbled upon that profound thing.

It was a VHS tape.

This VHS tape was in an orangey-red cardboard cover
with the initials TDK printed on it in gold. On the spine
of the tape was a yellow label. On that label was typed:
'TOTP + QUEEN (ENGLISH SONGS).

'TOTP' was secret code for us kids for *Top of the Pops*,
which we also called 'Turn Over the Page' in front of
Umejee and Dad to throw them off the scent. Even after
the programme had got rid of its semi-naked dance troupes,
Pan's People and Legs & Co., Thursday evenings were
always tense. Could we get away with watching TOTP in

real time as it was broadcast on the telly, or would our parents utter that damning sentence, 'You're not watching that *sharam thee bakwas*, that shameful rubbish; switch it off,' against which there was no appeal, aside from surreptitiously pressing 'Record' on the video player.

No matter that we were taping over one of Dad's favourite Islamic films. Hence on the yellow label of the TDK cassette I found in the shed, 'TOTP + QUEEN (ENGLISH SONGS)' was written beneath the words 'The Message', which had been crossed out using a green felt-tip pen. But our corrupt English songs weren't immune from expurgation either. Our carefully typed title had also had a black X crossed right through it and had been replaced with the scrawled heading: 'Mehfil-E-Qawwali'. This too had been struck out and in one corner of the label in faint blue ink I could just make out the word 'Superman'. Over that in unequivocal solid black marker pen was the title 'The Hajj 1991'.

And those words remained. Nobody dared to face the wrath of Dad or Allah for taping over the holy pilgrimage.

There were other cassettes too. An entire filing cabinet of old VHSs in the garden shed – 'Ben Hur' next to 'Izzat' on top of 'Xmas TOTP' adjacent to 'Aulea-E-Islam' above 'Diana Wedding' behind 'The Hajj 1994'. And I just want to tell you something freaky: that when I tried those mouldy tapes, which were by now at least twenty years old, in our VHS player a few weeks ago, the only one that actually showed any pictures was 'The Hajj 1991'. Images of hundreds of thousands of Muslims – including, somewhere in there, Dad – walking around the Kaba in Mecca, a white sea floating around a black rock. All the other cassettes – *Back to the Future*, *Only Fools and Horses*, *Sholay* and *Pakeeẓah* – just sizzled in black and white on the screen, emitting that insanity-inducing monotone buzz. Interference. It was like something out of *Poltergeist*. I was convinced that as soon as I put the tape labelled 'Live Aid' into the machine, some demonic spectre was going to come out of the TV set and get me . . . 'They're here.' Just like you said, Dad.

So that small black plastic TDK VHS tape, an inch deep, five inches long and three inches wide, with its confused, scribbled yellow label and all its crossings-out and all the obliterations and restorations, symbolises to me what it's like to be a British Muslim. The conflict, the competition between the two; British v. Muslim.

Anyway, up until my mid teens, I thought I was doing quite well with this conflict, certainly I was doing my best. Mixing and matching.

A bit of English – coleslaw and potato salad, Agatha Christie, The Jam.

A bit of Pakistani – *matai*, sequins, Datsuns.

A lot of Muslim – Koran, Ramadan, prayers, Eid, the Night of Power, ablutions, halal food, modest dress.

I wasn't ecstatically happy, but when are teenagers happy?

Then, in the autumn of 1984, just as I was turning fifteen, I stopped talking. I didn't plan it. I didn't mean to do it. It just happened. And an important thing to understand is that the longer I stopped talking, the harder it was for me to start again. I just couldn't get the words out. They were stuck in my throat. My siblings had always been aware of my tendency to sulk but this was different. Quite, quite different.

After the long six-week summer holiday, I returned to

school to hear stories of what everyone had done in their time off. Travelled around Europe, bought another pony, been swimming for the Yorkshire team, participated in a short-lived but full-on romance.

Julia Reynolds always had plenty of tales about boys on account of her beauty, her slimness and her permatan. She was always much darker-skinned than me because she spent all her school holidays abroad at her parents' villa in Spain. She would often compare the shade of her arm or foot against mine; there was no contest. I'd spent my summer indoors in Bradford 7, and so on the skin colour chart I was Dismal Grey next to her Rich Praline.

This particular time Julia was telling us about how her parents had held parties at their holiday home over the six-week break.

'They invited their friends round for dinner and by the end of the night they were dancing topless on the tables.'

If you're like me, you have a gallery of images from your childhood that will always be there in your memory. And if you're like me, you view these images in a slightly bizarre way. So when I now recall Julia's narrative, I see her sitting on a school desk and her skin colour is almost black – Warm Espresso – and her hair is very glossy and above her head is a big bubble and in that bubble are scenes of depravity. Her mum and dad, also very dark, are cavorting around with their arms in the air. There are other people in the bubble – ladies with leather skin, crinkly cleavages and bleached blonde hair, and pot-bellied balding dads wearing too-tight Speedos. Everybody is intoxicated and so their bodies are quite elastic. They dance with loose limbs. No moral backbone. Julia is watching from the side, but nobody cares that she is witnessing all this wicked behaviour, not even her own parents. Ungodly people. Just like the ones I'd seen in the videos with Dad, films that showed us how the earth was before the Prophet Muhammad arrived. Sinners wrapped around each other, sweating in the heat and dust.

My six-week break wasn't anything like Julia's. I hadn't gone abroad, in fact I'd barely left Bradford 7 all summer, but by the time I returned to school that September, I had made a major discovery. I'd realised that Rudyard Kipling was right: 'East is East and West is West, and never the twain shall meet.'

And that was when I started my Year of Silence.

Maybe once or twice in the summer holiday, one of Umejee's friends would arrange a day trip for us, mothers and daughters. This particular year Aunty Fatima had

planned an outing to Hornsea Pottery and then to nearby
Bridlington. We were all to meet outside a primary school
at eight a.m. to set off in the coach at 8.30. Of course we
didn't leave Bradford until after ten, much to the conster-
nation of Captain Barry, as I had named our bus driver.
The Aunties were fussing around as they always did.

'Take your shawl out of the boot. You'll feel cold on
the motorway.'

'No, I'll be fine.'

'Believe me. This bus will get very cold. *Gorays*, white
people, are too mean to put the heating on, and the driver
will not stop on the motorway for you, so take your *chadar*
now, I tell you.'

'No, I'll be fine. I have brought with me a big Thermos
of *lassi chai* which we can all share.'

'It would be better not to drink it on the bus. It will spill
everywhere, then the *gora* driver will get very angry and
he won't bring us back. Then what will we do?'

'I am not sitting next to Zahida. We have not spoken to
each other for many months. She didn't have the decency
to offer her condolences when my father-in-law passed
away, not even a phone call.'

'But this is a good chance to make up.'

'It is not my duty to do that. If she wants to talk to me,
I am right here. I'm not dead.'

There were as many explanations for setting off late as
there were passengers. Even I had a reason.

'No, Umejee. I'm not going to sit next to her for the
entire journey. Why can't I sit next to you?'

Mum was trying to get me to sit next to one of her
friends' daughters, Uzma, who was just a bit younger than
me. She was always pushing the Aunties' female progeny

on to me, trying to get us to become best buddies, advising that: 'It's good for you to have Pakistani girlfriends. Then you can learn about our *ahdhat*.'

'I already know about our ways, Umejee. What more do I need to learn?'

Apparently quite a bit, according to Nadia, the daughter of one of the richest Pakistani families in Bradford, who came to our house more often than I cared to entertain. Nadia took it upon herself to teach me about 'our culture'.

'In our culture, it's important to marry someone that your family knows well so that you already know what their values and standards are. That way, if there's any problem, the two families can get together to sort it out. So me, I'm going to marry my second cousin from Pakistan when I get to eighteen. I need to finish school first so I've got my education. It's all planned. It has been for years. Our families get on really well, you know, because they're related. We're going to have a *shaadi* here in Bradford and then one in Pakistan. I'm going to have dancers and music and I'm going to wear a maroon *lengha*. Do it traditional. I've been looking at films to see how I can do my make-up. You know that you can get really good make-up artists these days. Mum's been buying my jewellery whenever she goes back home. Then I'm going to live in Pakistan. Better for the kids there, learn about our religion and our culture. Do you want to see a photo of my fiancé?'

If she wasn't going on about her future *shaadi* (which was years away), Nadia was demonstrating the choreography from the latest Bollywood film or the most fashionable way to tie a sari. She had no interest whatsoever in the Top Ten or *Smash Hits*. When I tried to tell her that I'd got an A minus in English or that I'd bought *The Unforgettable Fire* by U2, her eyes would glaze over. She wasn't the slightest bit interested in me and my ways and I wasn't the slightest bit interested in her and her ways. I'm sure she thought I was stuck-up and too Westernised; certainly I found it strange that she was as Pakistani as my parents, even though she had been born in England. How did that happen?

It wasn't unusual for me to hide in the bathroom when I knew Nadia was coming, to get away from her lessons in 'our ways' and her tacit disapproval.

I suppose she was harmless enough though. Unlike Uzma. Uzma was the complete opposite of Nadia. Nadia was a good girl, into her traditions and *shaadis* and *izzat*, honour, and a fluent Urdu speaker, and all the Aunties loved her.

Uzma was modern, and only her own mother loved her. I was petrified of her. She had short cropped hair and she wore jeans – and a tight pair at that, so you could see the shape of her backside. And as everyone on that coach knew, that was the ultimate sign of a naughty girl, a trouble-maker. Denim equals degenerate. Uzma's mother also had modern ways – she was the only Aunty I knew who was a divorcee. A transgression that meant that most of the other Aunties either shunned her completely or talked about her behind her back and I mean literally behind her back. Even as Uzma's mother sat towards the front of the bus, you could hear the whispers.

'*Vah bay vah*! Have you seen what clothes she has let her daughter come out in? She has lost control of her own children. No surprise, without a father. How can they have any respect?'

I'd seen Uzma at a couple of weddings and she was always quite brash – refusing to converse in Punjabi or

Urdu and venturing into the strictly no-go men's section. She didn't give a shit what anyone thought of her. Particularly the Aunties. She never described them as such to me, but I was sure that if I asked her what she thought of her mother's friends she would reply: 'They're just a bunch of interfering old biddies.'

Oh God, what was I going to talk to Uzma about for the next two hours? She'd take one look at me in my mauve nylon *shalwar kameez* with its bright red and yellow embroidered front that attracted everything around it because of static – everything but boys; she'd take one look at me and think: 'What an idiot!'

I knew I should have worn my roll-neck striped sweater and my sister's flared flannel trousers. I might have been hot but at least I would have looked cool.

'If you don't wear *apnay* clothes, our clothes, you won't go with me,' Mum had argued the night before. 'We are not going on a *gora* holiday. The bus will be full of *apnay* women. What will they think if you turn up looking like you are in some Ingerlernd fashion show?'

There was always something. Even a day out to the seaside could never be straightforward, could never be fun.

Well, Uzma barely said a word to me on the bus. She put on her Walkman, danced in her chair, sang loudly and out of tune to George Michael's 'Careless Whisper' and blew the biggest pink bubblegum bubbles I'd ever seen. Occasionally, when I could, I'd take a furtive look at her. I didn't know many 'modern advanced Pakistani girls', as Umejee liked to call them. So that was what they looked like.

By the time we got to Hornsea Pottery, things were starting to relax a bit. We had a quick tour around the factory and then the Aunties purchased various knick-knacks – mugs, ballerinas, doves, that sort of thing – to place on their mantelpieces amidst their Koranic panels and family photographs. Umejee bought a cute shepherdess to add to the rural-themed ceramic collection that stood below her two Haywain paintings in the posh living room.

And then to the seaside, to Bridlington, with its partially deceitful town slogan of 'Beautiful, Bracing Bridlington'. We all headed down to the beach, everyone, that is, apart from Uzma. She disappeared on to the promenade with its flashing lights and hooting games and gangs of boys. Oh no! Our only Western-dressed person, our only symbol of assimilation had deserted us. I was mortified with embarrassment. Bridlington wasn't like the cultured Blackpool we'd visited numerous times with Dad. There the locals were used to Asian women in traditional dress taken out for the day by their husbands from nearby places like Manchester, Blackburn and Burnley. Bridlington, on the east coast, wasn't as cosmopolitan. I could sense it in the sea air. We stood out. We were the enemy.

'Help us, Uzma. You're our only hope.'

Too late. Without Uzma, the pasty white men in their swimming trunks and the pasty white women in their bikinis saw an army of around forty Pakistani women invading their beach, not from a battleship or some other seafaring vessel, but from a rickety old bus driven by the traitor, Captain Barry. These enemy soldiers were dressed not in khakis, but in the most inappropriate uniform of highly visible, brightly coloured sparkling *shalwar kameez*, flapping uncontrollably in the wind, and they were armed not with guns or swords but with something more deadly – the stink of lamb kebabs, vegetable samosas and chicken tikka. The white troops, camouflaged against the sand, went on the defence.

'Fuck off, you Pakis!'

'Yeah, get out of here, you wogs!'

Then, just like that, I heard it.

'Fuck off, you white shit.'

All the Aunties stared at me. It was me. I had said it, without even realising. I waited. No action from the whities and no action from the Aunties. To their credit, the Aunties kept on shuffling on to the beach, undeterred by the hostile environment they were walking straight into. Brave soldiers. They had adopted a strategy of 'smile and ignore' for years, and as far as they were concerned, it worked. Like it still does with Umejee when she goes shopping for fruit and veg at the market and she knows that the sellers are being racist by ignoring her or throwing her change at her but she grins at them and calls them 'dahling' or 'love'. 'Dahling, how much these grape?' 'Yes, love. I need apple, please.' This tactic of turning the other cheek doesn't work for me. On occasion, Mum has had to physically restrain me, like the time a shoe shop owner was very rude to her because of her poor English and I threw the rack of stilettos he had on display at the entrance of his business at him.

'Don't! Don't! He'll call the police! Then what will happen?' she screamed, and dragged me away.

'I don't care! Let the police come! I haven't done anything wrong!'

I have to respond to abuse with abuse.

Like the time I was sat in a National Express bus at Bradford Interchange, waiting to depart, and the two old women in front of me were looking out at the station forecourt.

'Oh, just look at all those Pakis,' one of them remarked. 'They breed like rats, don't they?'

'Oh, I know,' replied the other. 'It's disgusting, isn't it? They're disgusting, aren't they?'

I had to interject.

'It's better being a rat than fucking dead old cows like you two.'

That shut them up.

And the time when a middle-aged man accused me of jumping the queue in a supermarket and told me to 'Fuck off home back to your zoo, you Paki cunt. What are you doing over here anyway, you fucking monkey?' As he was taken away by security, the only way I could think of letting him know how full of rage I was was by spitting in his face.

The only time I didn't dare say or do anything was when I was walking through Nottingham city centre one Saturday afternoon and a bunch of skinheads were coming towards me shouting 'Zieg Heil! Zieg Heil!' Then I just turned round and ran as fast as I could.

These incidents don't happen that often, but I never forget them. They make me shake with anger.

They don't like us but they love our food.

They don't like our colour but they want to be brown.

'Who do these people think they are that they treat us like this? We're not *bandar*, idiots. Why should we take it?' I shout at Umejee, the pacifist.

She replies: 'Why do you want to cause trouble for yourself? Because they are rude to me, it doesn't mean I should be the same to them. I know what they are doing. I'm not blind. You have to be smart about these things. Don't lower yourself to their level. *Sabr kar*. Have strength.' Words of wisdom.

But even as I paddled in the cold Bridlington sea with my shalwar bottoms rolled up to my ankles, I kept a protective eye on the Aunties as they slept, snored and spilled out of their deckchairs, and I prepared my next riposte, in case it was needed.

'Up yours, you white bastard.'

Not very subtle or ladylike, I know, but effective.

On the trip back on the bus, everybody was quiet. Except Uzma, who had now decided she would talk to me.

'I had a great day. Went up to the promenade and met this group of lads, they were a bit older than me. We went on the fruit machines then we had sausage and chips and then we went to the gardens. I had such a laugh. One of them gave me his telephone number.'

Oh God! I knew everyone was listening in. Even the Aunties who couldn't speak English knew what Uzma had been up to. I didn't want to denounce her, but I could feel the pressure from every woman on the bus for me to tell Uzma that she was a disgrace.

I heard one Aunty behind me take in a sharp breath and say: '*Thoba*, forgive her. Like mother, like daughter.'

What to do? I hated these constant T-junction dilemmas at the best of times – should I turn left towards White England or turn right towards Muslim Pakistan? Did I want to appear as some errant disrespectful youth or a dour guardian of morality? But today I was supposed to be on holiday. A day free from conflict. A day away from judgement. No, such a day did not exist. I did the best thing I could. I pretended to fall asleep.

I think the only person who had any fun on our summer holiday was our driver, Captain Barry. I think he really warmed to the Aunties, the way that they tried to converse with him in English: 'You go swimming in sea, sir?' 'You like fish and chip or you like our kebab?' We had a collection for him when we got back to Bradford and the lucky bloke walked away with about ten pounds and all the vegetable samosas and onion bhajis he could eat. Oh, and with Mum's praise: 'You are very good man, very decent man,' which made him blush.

He certainly seemed like a decent man.

But you never know. You see, when I think of Captain Barry now, I'm always reminded of this story I read in the newspaper about a bus driver who ferried elderly and disabled Asians around Bradford. He did it for some years. But then he got the sack. Turned out he was standing to become a councillor for the BNP.

So that was my summer holiday in 1984. Nasty racists on the beach. Meddling Aunties on the bus. I dreamt of a summer holiday where I could get away from Bradford. Just be me. Not the Paki the bigots had seen; not the meek girl the Aunties saw; not the weirdo the girls at school ignored.

'I went to America for a month.'

I was back in my classroom at the grammar school. Groups of girls were comparing holiday notes, and although nobody had invited me to speak, I had prepared this particular cock-and-bull story in some detail – God knows, I'd had the time over the six-week break. So even though the groups showed little or no interest, I had the confidence to recount my holiday adventure.

'I've got relatives there, my mum's family. They left Pakistan a long time ago and they've done really well. They've got a big house in New York and they work in banking. My cousins are really handsome and they showed me around. We went to the Empire State Building and the Statue of Liberty and Central Park and Barneys. I flew there on my own. Oh, it was a great holiday.'

I have to warn you that at this stage of my teenage life I had become Walter Mitty. Out of necessity, rather than desire. It was a survival technique. And like the hole I got into once I stopped speaking and then couldn't start again, once I started telling lies, I couldn't stop.

I wasn't pretending to be some intrepid wartime pilot or brilliant life-saving surgeon or courageous soldier, like Walter Mitty. I was just pretending to be a schoolgirl with a fairly normal life.

'Oh! what a tangled web we weave when first we practise to deceive.'

'How long did it take to get there?' came the first hostile question.

'Oh, not long. Just about four hours.'

'When I went to New York last year, we were on the plane for ages.'

'Well I was asleep most of the time, so maybe it was longer than that,' came my first retraction.

Closely followed by my second: 'Actually I think I got that wrong. I just went away for two weeks.'

And my third: 'My mistake. My Uncle doesn't work in a bank. He's got his own business. He runs a grocery store.'

In the space of one lunch break, all my hopes that this school year was going to be different, that I was going to have friends, confidence and presence, that I was going to belong, just slipped away. I could see it happening right before my eyes. There was that look of vexed disbelief on the girls' faces. Like I was some nutcase.

Liar, liar, Zaiba liar.

Though I never ever admitted to fibbing. I stuck to my guns even when the situation became preposterous: 'No, really, my Uncle *IS* a minister in the Pakistani government.' 'No, really, my family *ARE* millionaires in Pakistan.'

Facing their interrogation was like Walter Mitty being hauled in front of the enemy:

> Walter Mitty lighted a cigarette. It began to rain, rain with sleet in it. He stood up against the wall of the drugstore, smoking . . . He put his shoulders back and his heels together . . . He took one last drag on his cigarette and snapped it away. Then, with that faint, fleeting smile playing about his lips, he faced the firing squad; erect and motionless, proud and disdainful, Walter Mitty the Undefeated, inscrutable to the last.

But my predicament was worse. I wasn't so heroic or victorious. I'd been caught out. I always got caught out, which made me feel like a pathetic failure. I don't think the girls ever believed a word I said. And why would they?

If you put all my fictions/imaginings together, the picture you got of me was of a girl who came from some wealthy flamboyant Asian dynasty, even though my dad dropped me off at the school gates in a rusty Nissan Stanza that he'd recently acquired from one of the Uncles in exchange for some translation work he'd done on an immigration form; who had the most glamorous social life outside of school, even though inside school I was a loner; who turned men's heads, even though I was hirsute and rotund; who had the most amazing à la mode wardrobe, even though I wore woolly tights in the summer and a too-small duffle coat in the winter.

Girls can be very cruel and unforgiving. I was trying my best to be someone they might like, someone not so different from them. But my plan backfired. They didn't like me at all. They either ignored me or talked about me. I could never work out which was worse.

I was reading something just now, one of those web pages that throws out a bizarre question to the whole world and then waits for somebody to post a reply. And the bizarre question that's being asked is: 'Why did Walter Mitty imagine himself facing a firing squad?'

Of course someone has responded; in fact, two people have.

One talks about how even though this is contradictory to Mitty's other reveries, in which he survives and receives much adulation, standing in front of a firing squad is in fact his ultimate daydream, the one where he sacrifices his own life for some greater good. This posting receives three gold stars out of five.

The other person states that this fantasy 'symbolises his exasperation with what has become, for him, an intolerable existence given his alienation and lack of fulfilment'. This response gets four gold stars out of five.

And I know why. For Walter, there was a gaping hole between where he was and where he wanted to be, and he didn't have the tools or the ability to fill that hole. So he coped as best as he could. By dreaming.

I too coped as best as I could. Also by dreaming. And by not speaking. I think in part my Year of Silence was probably down to basic biology – awkward teenage hormones – but in the main, it was a conscious action by me, a protest. Against having to live my two distinct lives.

One at home that was *Bismillah irahma niraheem*, garam masala, *thoba*, *Amar Akbar Anthony*, duppatas, *izzat*. One at school that was *Midsummer Night's Dream*, *amo*, *amas*, *amat*, pineapple upside-down cake, A-line skirts, Duran Duran, pinky-white flesh.

Two lives. Each glaring distrustfully at the other and then turning its back on it. Neither party had proclaimed against the other as such, but there had been a breakdown in communications and I was supposed to be the broker, the negotiator, trying to get a handshake, to arrive at some friendly workable agreement. For the sake of all parties. But after numerous failed attempts, I had run out of options and patience. And the last straw for me was the complete collapse in talks on my return to school after the summer holiday. I know my tactic had been less than honest, all that stuff about going to New York, but I had no choice. I had to do what I could to get white English school life to get on with Pakistani Muslim home life. And when deceit didn't work and I couldn't think of anything else, I gave up.

'If you two lives can't be bothered to make an effort with each other, why the hell should I try?' I thought. 'Just watch, I can be difficult too.'

I ended my role as diplomat and started my own campaign, my Year of Silence.

This was easier to do at school, as most of the pupils ignored me anyway and I was normally so quiet that the teachers didn't really notice my vow of silence. But at home, after the first few weeks, my self-imposed muteness drove my poor family up the wall.

'Why won't you say anything?' Umejee kept asking me. 'What's wrong with you? Why don't you speak?' She was very worried about me.

I just grunted and shrugged my shoulders. What could I say? How could I explain?

After a while, my family did the right thing and didn't expect any response from me, aside from the odd nod or shake of the head. I was so stubborn, I remember that I once slipped on some ice and the school nurse bandaged my hand up, and though Mum asked me many many times what had happened to me, I wouldn't respond.

Things became quite fraught at home. What I was doing was very frustrating for everybody, including me, but the longer I maintained my silence, the harder it was to stop. So I didn't.

Sometimes I would go and sit in Pajee's bedroom in the cellar and watch him play solitaire and smoke B&H fags. We didn't talk and he didn't ask me what was wrong. I liked that. Maybe he knew. We just sat there, in silence, listening to the small noises. Pajee coughing, me coughing, his Zippo lighter snapping shut, him inhaling, Mum's footsteps in the kitchen above and the occasional giggle from next door's children.

Sometimes I would go and sit at the top of the house, on the window ledge in the attic, where it was also very peaceful. Mum and Dad had stopped taking in lodgers, as their daughters were now teenagers and it wasn't appropriate to have male strangers in the house. This was a good thing, as it meant there were two fewer people battling for the bathroom in the morning, and also I now had a wonderful view out of the side window. You could see right over the city centre, way past grey Bradford into the green countryside. I thought about what life was like out there. What did white families do at home? What were they doing right this instant? Probably nice things like horse-riding, barbecues and swimming. No conflict in the countryside.

So in the Year of Silence, I withdrew from my two opposite lives and started to occupy another world. The one inside my head, where I had control, importance, a personality, friends and one life.

I'd always done this. Pretend. Don't most children? At night when I was trying to get to sleep. On the bus heading to school. On a Sunday afternoon when there was only a cowboy film or motor-racing on the TV. At lunchtime when I was sat on my own in the school canteen.

I dreamt that I had been awarded the Nobel Peace Prize for bringing an end to the war between Israel and Palestine; that I was a lauded fashion designer in demand by all the stars; that I was a cricket player in the Pakistani national team who scored a century against England; that I was the wife of the captain of the Pakistani cricket team, Imran Khan.

I was content in my head, where everything was just fine, exciting even. I didn't need real conversation, real dialogue with real people – especially not with Umejee and Dad. It was at this time that I began to wonder how it had happened that Dad, who had come from a poor village in Pakistan, and Umejee, who couldn't read or write English, had as their daughter a girl who read plays by Alan Ayckbourn and books by H.G. Wells and was about to play the part of Manco the Messenger in the school production of Peter Shaffer's *Royal Hunt of the Sun*.

(Fortunately for me, this was mainly a non-speaking role and on the few occasions I had to break my silence on the stage I justified this to myself on the grounds that I was speaking not in English but in Quechua, the language of the Incas.) I know that most teenagers don't feel a great affinity towards their parents and are often embarrassed by them, but at that age the schism between me and them seemed so massive that I couldn't help but wonder whether I'd been adopted. Taken away from my real parents, an English family with dark hair and dark eyes. I don't mean to sound like an ungrateful snobby cow, but that was what it was like for me then. I just couldn't make much sense of how, in just one generation from my parents to me, things were so different between us – our language, our culture, our outlook. So after weeks of rehearsal for the Schaffer play, when the curtain went up three nights in a row, I didn't even think to invite them to see me in it, because:

1. They wouldn't understand the play.
2. They wouldn't understand why I wanted to be in a play.
3. They might get annoyed that I was prostrating myself in front of the Inca sun god Atahuallpa, chanting: 'Sapa Inca, Huaccha Cuyac, Quya, Pachacutic, Viracocha, Inti Cori.'
4. They would get annoyed that I was wearing an orange robe that only came down to my shins and exposed my lower legs in public. No matter that I wore an amazing gold mask with pheasant feathers that hid my identity from the audience so nobody would ever even know it was me.

I can tell you that in the Year of Silence, the worst thing wasn't not talking. It was that terrible terrible feeling of not belonging to Umejee and Dad.

It seems that I wasn't the only one in Bradford struggling to work out who I was, what I was doing and where I was heading.

The 1960s and 1970s had been decades of just getting on with it for the Asians – you put your head down, you make your money, you have a few kids, you go back home. But that had never happened. We now had British passports, were going to British schools, were working in British factories and on British buses. We were British. We were Here to Stay.

So why put up with all the shit? The National Front marches, the racist attacks, the low pay, the poor housing conditions, the immigration controls, the police brutality.

'I pay taxes out my ass but they still harass me.'

Time to take action. Time to organise. No time for passiveness. No time for turning the other cheek. Did you hear that, Umejee? Radical leftie anti-racist groups were formed up and down the country. In Bradford there was the Asian Youth Movement, set up a year after a violent confrontation between Asian lads and the NF in Manningham. The AYM's slogan was 'Here to Stay. Here to Fight.' And there was also the United Black Youth League, an organisation that saw twelve of its members put on trial in 1982 when police discovered their stash of petrol bombs. In court, the Bradford Twelve argued that they were acting in self-defence; that they had to protect their own communities against a proposed skinhead march because nobody else would. 'Self-defence is no offence.' They won their case.

This period in the late 1970s and early 1980s was all about politics. About being black. No matter if you were Muslim, Hindu or Sikh. Brothers and sisters. We were all black. Religion and culture didn't come into it, they were irrelevant. If you look at photos of the Free the Bradford Twelve demos, you'll see men in turbans, men with Afros, women in saris. In defence of the mosque, the temple and the gurdwara.

But then it changed again. Bradford Council set up race relations units and equal opportunities policies that gave its citizens the right to be different, for communities to have their own identity and values. It also funded the new Council of Mosques, a vocal and organised group of men who were there to speak and act on behalf of the city's Muslims. And only the Muslims. And so it became all about Islam. Muslims wanted halal meat served in schools, to withdraw their children from religious assemblies, to allow them to wear more modest uniforms and to have segregated physical education and swimming lessons for girls. These were precisely the things I'd already been doing for years. I didn't get it at the time, but Dad was a pioneer of multiculturalism, meaning the right of every community to 'maintain its own identity, culture, language, religion and customs', as defined in the city's race relations plan.

And so by the mid 1980s, 'the community' that had previously described itself as 'black' or 'Pakistani' or 'Asian' now described itself as 'Muslim'. Religion took precedence over colour and nationality.

And it was at this very time when 'the community' grasped more tightly than ever before on to Islam that my practice of religion fell away.

I didn't read the Koran or fast during Ramadan as often as I used to. I didn't pray for a solid twelve hours throughout the Night of Power. I didn't want to stay at home during Eid. I certainly stopped going to the mosque. And I only occasionally watched those Islamic videos that Dad rented. It was still there, my faith, I could still hear it around me and in my head, but I had placed a gag over it so it now sounded muffled, less clear. It was the only way I could do the other things that I wanted to do.

Like read 'bad' books, trash novels like *The Thornbirds* and *Flowers in the Attic* and *Vogue* magazine. Every month I saved up my spending money so I could pore over every single model in there, staring at each one for hours. I was dumbstruck, fascinated and completely in awe of their astounding beauty, the level of beauty you know you will never ever see in the flesh. Not even Julia Reynolds came close. There were the dimensions of their limbs, long and slender, their flawless complexions, their chic flamboyant clothes, their erotic poses. I knew it was immoral what they were doing – displaying so much flesh, flaunting themselves so – but I couldn't help myself. It was romantic, elegant, civilised and mature. This was the adult life I desired. Stepping out of a New York cab in a cream wool coat, at a dinner party in an off-the-shoulder taffeta gown, walking my Dalmatian in knee-high black leather boots, on a yacht in a Pucci sarong.

But I knew I could never square that with God or Dad or Umejee. Never mind that I had neither the face nor the figure for such aspiration. So I did the next best thing – I copied the pictures of the striking *Vogue* models and put them on my bedroom wall. They were up there for a few weeks before Dad told me to take them down.

'It's against our religion to do a thing like this. You can only worship Allah.' *La illaha ill Allah*. There is no God but Allah. Idolatry is a major evil.

> Allah forgiveth not that partners should be set up with Him; . . . to set up partners with Allah is to devise a sin most heinous indeed. (Surah 4:48)

I knew that from those videos we watched when we were younger, where the clay and wooden totems of three hundred and sixty gods were smashed to smithereens in Mecca when the Prophet Muhammad arrived there. It was pointless telling Dad that the amateur gallery Blu-tacked above my bed wasn't a shrine where I bowed down and prayed to these women; that I just liked to draw. So I shrugged and did as he asked.

At the time, situations like this provided me with justi-fication for my continued silence. It didn't make any sense. Why some things were *halal* and some things were *haram*. Why was it okay to have family photographs on display around the house, but not my pencil portraits? Why weren't we allowed to watch *Top of the Pops* when many of the

Bollywood films also featured semi-naked dancing girls and when one of Dad's favourite films, *Pakeezah*, was all about a courtesan? Why were the *shaadis* in Bradford arranged marriages when the Asian dramas we watched were always about girl and boy falling in love? Why was it okay to play records by the Police and Nusret Fateh Ali Khan and sing along to them but not dance to them? I didn't understand, and to be honest I didn't dare to ask, and so I stayed silent.

It's ironic to think that at the same time I fell into this silence, 'the community' in Bradford was starting to roar. We dealt with our own issues of trying to work out who we were by using opposing strategies. I retreated into myself and it marched forward, demanding to be recognised, to 'maintain its own identity, culture, language, religion and customs', demanding multiculturalism, particularly within the area of education.

Not everybody was a fan of this new concept. Ray Honeyford, the head of a mainly Asian school in Bradford, Drummond Middle, had written a number of articles for various publications including the *Times Educational Supplement* and the obscure right-wing periodical *The Salisbury Review*. He argued against the council's policy of a multicultural, multiracial education, stating that such an approach would be harmful to Asian pupils by preventing their integration into British society, and would disadvantage those white children who constituted the ethnic minority in inner-city schools. He also objected to the lengthy periods of time for which some parents took their kids out of school during term-time so they could go back to Pakistan.

In many ways, Honeyford's argument made sense.

Surely the priority of a British education should be to teach all its pupils how to read and write in English, and surely it was more important for kids to be in classrooms in Bradford than in *khotis* in Pakistan? The problem with what he said was how he said it. For example, he described Pakistan as 'religiously, unimaginably intolerant, barbaric and arbitrary in its dispensation of justice', as 'the heroin capital of the world', where there is 'corruption at every level' and 'which cannot cope with democracy'. He also described one Asian parent as 'a figure straight out of Kipling . . . His English sounds like that of Peter Sellers' Indian doctor on a day off', and he wasn't very tactful when describing a meeting: 'the hysterical political temperament of the Indian subcontinent became evident in an English school hall. There was much shouting and fist waving. A half-educated and volatile Sikh usurped the privileges of the chair by deciding who was to speak.' And he used offensive terms such as 'Asian ghettos' and 'negroes'.

Demonstrations were held at Honeyford's school gates. He was branded a 'Ray-cist' and there were calls for him to be sacked. The national press picked up on what was happening; for the right wing, Honeyford became a cause célèbre, an advocate of free speech and Britishness; for the liberal left he was a liability, a throwback to colonial times. Assimilation versus multiculturalism. This had become a major debate.

These were difficult days for many Bradfordians – the Pakistanis (Why is the focus just on us?), the Indians (Why isn't any of the focus on us?) and the whites (What's going on?). And particularly for Bradford's newly elected mayor, Mohammed Ajeeb, the first ever Asian mayor in the country. It was a big deal for us – this Pakistani man, the son of a poor craftsman, an immigrant, donning the tricorn hat, the ermine robes and the chain of office. Right from his initiation speech he had laid out his dream – to build bridges between the city's diverse populations and religions, for everyone to live in one society.

Everyone, that is, apart from Honeyford. Ajeeb joined in calls for the headmaster, the destroyer of racial harmony, to go. That year, 1985, the two men had only one thing in common: they both had to receive police protection because of death threats.

I once interviewed Ajeeb for a Radio 4 documentary and he showed me some of the hate mail that had been sent to him.

> To the coloured Lord Mayor. We don't want you coloured people over here. Get out, you blacks. You have caused enough trouble and you are not wanted. No coloured Lord Mayors here.

In another letter:

> You are a racist by your interference in Drummond Road School. We have never been in favour of Asians, immigrants, Indians. Why don't you do the honourable way and resign now. Signed Mr Anti-Immigration.

He told me that when he went to a football match to receive a cheque in aid of the families of the fifty-six victims of the Valley Parade fire, his speech was drowned out by the cries of the white fans: 'Honeyford! Honeyford!'

I also went to visit the former headmaster, at his home

in Lancashire. He was in the early stages of Parkinson's disease and looked quite frail. I asked him if he had any regrets about that whole episode.

'No, not really,' he replied. 'I don't think it was particularly extreme or offensive in any way. I regretted the effect it had on my pupils. Most of the pupils and parents were on my side and they were forced to make a fuss, they were manipulated by those with an axe to grind, people in race relations. Multiculturalism is dead. It never worked. And British people are not racist.'

The Honeyford affair was a pivotal point for Bradford. It was really the first time that there was a marked distinction in the city – them and us. Muslims and everybody else. From then on right up until the present day, Bradford has been seen as a city of discord, a city of racial and religious tension, a tinderbox about to ignite. And it has burnt, more than once.

At the time, I watched the protests at Drummond Middle School on the news. Children just a bit younger than me waving placards. Parents shouting 'Honeyford out!' These people seemed so certain of who they were and what they wanted – 'the right to maintain their own identity, culture, language, religion and customs'. They were proud and confident. Me, I couldn't work out who I was or even how I felt – ashamed, embarrassed, unique, blessed? I think this was because the gulf between home and school life was wider for me than it was for the pupils at, say, Drummond Middle or most other schools. There there was safety in numbers. I was the only Muslim and the only Pakistani in my year. I had no allies, no support. The onus was on me to fit in. To integrate. To assimilate. To be like a white girl. But I couldn't do that. Because Dad was a fierce supporter of multiculturalism, even though he didn't realise it, and I was a symbol of multiculturalism, even though I didn't understand it.

The right to be different. The right to be a Muslim girl. Modifying my school uniform, not attending morning assemblies, being granted exemption from religious education lessons, being given permission to take days off for Eid. For me, the right to be different equated to: to not be like everybody else; to not have friends.

Hence the Year of Silence. What else could I do?

After many tortured months, things came to a head one Saturday lunchtime. It was exam season and I was revising in my bedroom. Umejee called me downstairs, to the kitchen.

'What is wrong with you? Why won't you speak to anyone?' She'd asked me that question many many times, but this time I could tell from her tone and the look on her face that she meant business. I knew that shrugging my shoulders or grunting wouldn't suffice. I stood, focusing my gaze on one specific tile on the kitchen lino. Silence.

Umejee tried to encourage me: 'This is no way to live. You can't go on like this, without speaking to anyone. We're all worried about you. Whatever it is, you can tell us.'

Silence.

I was concentrating so hard on the tile that I lost all peripheral vision. But when I lifted my head, I could see Umejee's face. She looked worried.

And then it all came out – first the tears, then the words. Blimey, the words! I had broken my silence. At long bloody last. Even though I'd had the odd conversation at school, these had been in English, and now I could hear my own voice speaking broken Punjabi, more broken than usual. It sounded strange.

'*Meh hush nee.* I'm not happy.'

She listened as I told her about not fitting in, not having any friends, how I wasn't like the other girls.

And then she said: 'We will help you. We will find you some friends. We're here for you. You have your family. That is the most important thing. We care for you. We all love you very much, Zaibee.'

It didn't really resolve anything: it didn't make me more popular or accepted at school, it didn't stop me from telling fibs, it didn't stop me from fantasising, it didn't merge my two lives into one; but that was all I needed to hear.

'We all love you very much, Zaibee.'

My Year of Silence had ended.

Did you ever feel that?

Did you ever look at white people and see them in a way that confused you?

We are different from them, there's no doubt about that. How we think, how we act, what we want.

And did you ever look at your mum and dad and see them in a way that confused you? That's a really uncomfortable feeling. Like you don't belong to them.

It's not easy, growing up here.

Did you find it difficult?

Is that why you did what you did?

5

Pajee's Wake (1988)

I see Dad. He's sitting in the plane, in an aisle seat. The two seats next to him are empty. He mainly looks ahead but occasionally he glances at the vacant chairs and then out of the window. He says no to the watery dhal and warm orange juice that's offered to him by the middle-aged PIA air hostesses. He looks very sad.

He told us on the phone. Or rather he tried to tell Umejee. He rang from his village in Sialkot. At that time the phones in Pakistan weren't always reliable and the news had to be repeated a few times before it could be confirmed.

'Pajee has died.'

By the time we were told, Pajee had already been buried – Islamic law states that if possible, a person should be buried on the same day that they die. There was no autopsy. I'm not even sure if there was a death certificate. I just remember Umejee saying something about gall stones or kidney stones. Pajee was laid to rest in the village where he grew up just outside Sialkot, next to Majee, his mother.

It was nearly fifteen years later that I visited Pajee's grave. I was pleased to see that his was one of the most impressive headstones in the cemetery. It was raised up to hip level, in grey speckled marble. I'm sure his name was etched on there somewhere. The writing wasn't in English but I could recognise numbers marking the year he died. We never knew the date Pajee was born and neither did he. He was part of that generation of Pakistanis who'd had birthday-less lives. It wasn't difficult to point out the dead who had always lived in the nearby village – their graves were denoted by a tiny slab, if at all. Those who had moved to the UK or whose families had sent remittances were buried at the foot of more ornate monuments. Whatever the wealth, they all had one thing in common: they all pointed in the same direction, towards the Holy Kaba at Mecca.

'Hey, *jaldi sarf kar*. Hurry up and clean it.' The grave was covered in leaves and dog shit. The decrepit cemetery warden had been neglecting his duties, safe in the knowledge that most of the families of the dead were now based far away in Bradford. You would have thought that a man old enough to soon be lying in this place would take a bit more care of it. Dad stuffed some rupees into his hand and ordered him to start washing. He scurried back with a jug of water and a balding brush that looked as though it would do a good job of stroking rather than shifting any shit. I removed the foliage and left the excrement to the old man.

Dad took particular offence at the wild dogs that had made the cemetery their home. For Muslims, dogs are dirty animals, never to be kept as pets. He tried to shoo them away, but they looked back at him with unflinching disdain. They'd be spoilt for choice for bones, I guessed.

The burial site is a holy ground where the most fundamental religious things happen. This is where the dead leave the earth and journey to another world. It is also where Angels hover, overseeing and protecting the graves. This place is ultimately what Islam is all about – the After-life, a judgement of our deeds, our sins and our faith. This is where Eternity begins. But somehow it all felt so final.

I don't know how long it takes for a body to decompose, but I could envisage Pajee's skeleton through the marble – arms, legs, a pelvis, a ribcage and a toothless skull. For as long as I could remember, he had always looked like a living skeleton, with very hollow cheeks and no fat on his body, just an uneven layering of skin – taut across his face and arms, wrinkled on his neck and hands. I got a strange sense of comfort knowing he didn't look much different where he lay now.

Dad and I attended to my grandmother's grave. We'd bought a couple of bags full of red and yellow petals at the cemetery entrance for two rupees. Their perfume, concentrated in the bag, dissipated once we started throwing them over the dry soil. It would just be a matter of hours before they were bleached by the midday sun. I wished I could pay the warden to put fresh petals on Pajee's grave every week, or at least to keep it tidy. It could well be another fifteen years before I next visited his resting place. I stood there for as long as I could before Dad insisted on leaving. '*Hudafees*, Pajee,' I whispered under my breath. In my mind's eye I blew him a kiss. And I remembered that Sunday many years before when we prayed for his soul.

For the forty days of mourning, a frayed beige cotton sheet was placed over the television. The family photos that normally gazed out from the top of the set were now laid down, acting as weights to ensure that the screen remained covered. White pieces of cloth were draped over the sofas and layers of material covered the carpet, the table, the cabinet and the hostess trolley. Luckily, we were never short of pieces of material in our house.

Umejee was a hoarder of bits of cloth. Some she had salvaged from the discount buckets at the local Asian stores at fifty pence or a pound per sheet, but the fancier ones were purchased on trips back home. They were compressed into suitcases that lay all over the house – in the attic, in the cellar, on top of every wardrobe and cupboard and underneath every bed. Open any one of these cases and the smell of Pakistani markets would waft out, a pungent sweet/spicy smell like chicken and doughnuts being fried together in a giant *karahi*. Wedged in between these suitcases were bin liners into which squares of fabric not ostentatious enough to be made into *shalwar kameezes* were relegated. They were clean but dull – browns, creams and whites, with no embroidery or beading. They varied in size from a few inches to large enough to cover a room. And that was what we did on the day of the wake – draped all the furniture and carpet in bland material so that the only objects left exposed were the ones that bore God's name – the plaques inscribed with verses from the Koran, the calendar with photographs of Mecca and Medina and the huge wall hanging of the Kaba.

There had been no invitations sent out. This, like most other things in 'the community', was done through word of mouth. There was a network of Aunties who took it upon themselves to telephone each other at such times. It was impossible to know how many or who would come to the house for the wake. But that was just the way. Nobody would be turned away. There was one guarantee, though. That no one would turn up on time. There was nothing disrespectful about this – being late is a Pakistani trait.

The bell first rang at two p.m. Two women I recognised as the wives of Dad's friends came into the kitchen. They were Kashmiris, dressed in white *shalwar kameez* with their heads wrapped in white *dupattas*. What appeared to be stray threads were actually grey hairs spread unevenly over their scalps. Enviably thick plaits dangled down their backs, tied with coloured elastic bands. No make-up and no jewellery. These women were *saadi*, plain, and this was the uniform they'd adopted whether they were at a wedding, a party, a funeral, out shopping or at home. They sometimes allowed themselves a flash of colour in their accessories, such as a ribbon in their hair or a cardigan woven through with gold thread, or silver open-toed sandals. You would often see women like this in and out of shops on White Abbey Road, shops that sold roll upon roll of fabric from India and Pakistan – silks, taffetas, georgettes in every conceivable colour and every imaginable shade. After hours of pondering, they would eventually emerge with plastic bags – often recycled and inadvertently advertising competing businesses – and I would assume that folded in there would be something garish and sparkly. Maybe there was, but you would never see it adorning their frames. They only ever wore *saadi* white. It was like being in a shop selling pick 'n' mix and only ever buying Polo mints.

The two women, both in their late thirties, but looking a decade older, said their sombre *salaams* and sat down on the living room floor. They both picked up a copy of the Koran and started to read.

Over the next couple of hours the doorbell rang with increasing frequency, so that eventually Umejee shouted from the kitchen, where she was cooking sweet rice: 'Leave it open! Nobody's going to break in and steal something. Not on a day like this.'

It wasn't difficult to find something to wedge the door with. In the hallway, dozens of pairs of shoes – sandals, trainers, lace-ups and slip-ons – were piling up as everyone entered the house barefoot.

There was a discernible spectrum of smells in the corridor. Stand near the front door and the stench of sweaty footwear made you want to retch. The women were often more guilty than the men – they didn't have the protection of socks to soak up the odour. There is a line from one of my favourite books, *To Kill a Mockingbird*, where Harper Lee describes the town of Maycomb as a place where 'ladies bathed before noon, after their three o'clock naps, and by nightfall were like soft teacakes with frosting from sweating and sweet talcum'. I wished I had the audacity to put such a suggestion in the Aunties' shoes: 'Try washing and Johnson's Baby Powder.'

Once you headed down the hall, the aroma of curry battled with the stink of footwear. Neither smell won, but they formed an even more sickening union. You had to get to the far end of the corridor near the kitchen before there was any nasal salvation – just the fragrance of tender lamb masala.

Whenever Umejee cooked, she would always fling open all the windows and doors at the back of the house, no matter what the weather, so that a current of air drifted through the kitchen. She hated that sticky substance that some Pakistanis had on their furniture, especially on the kitchen units. It was only visible close up, but you could feel it and smell it. Layer upon layer of ghee that had vaporised from umpteen curries of palaak gosht, aloo chana and masoor dhal and then solidified on to cold surfaces. It was so glutinous you could readily attach bits of paper to it. No need for Post-it notes or fridge magnets in a Pakistani kitchen.

As Mum busied herself with getting the food ready, I pretended to do likewise, chopping radishes and cucumber for the salad.

'Just leave that and go in there,' she instructed me. 'It doesn't look good if nobody from the family is reading.'

'But I'm helping you with the food, Umejee.'

'That's not important. Go in now,' she demanded.

I'd delayed this moment for as long as I could, but now I had no choice. I covered my head with a *dupatta* and went into the living room. It was packed full of women. They sat around a glass table that held four copies of the Koran – each one divided into thirty booklets. The more times it was read, the faster Pajee's soul would lie in peace in his grave. An Aunty was appointed to keep count.

Gingerly I picked my way through the seated bodies, taking care never to raise my feet above the Holy Book. I picked a chapter from the table. 'Not that one, they've been done already,' said an Aunty. 'Take one from there.' She pointed at the smaller pile. I took my copy and lowered myself into one of the few remaining spaces, wedged between the sofa and the mantelpiece. It was probably better for me to stay out of sight. I was embarrassed by how slow my reading of Arabic was. It took the average Aunty half an hour to complete one chapter. After three hours I was still on my first one.

But that wasn't the only reason why I wanted to hide.

Over the last decade or so, I had made little effort to get to know the names of the Aunties or anything about them. There were a few of Mum's friends who regularly came to the house who I had the odd conversation with, but on the whole I tried to avoid them. You see, I didn't understand them. Not just their language; what I mean is that I didn't get them, couldn't relate to them, which made me wary and scared of them. Who were they and what did they do and what were they about and what did they think and feel?

They weren't like Umejee because, well, she was my mother, and I loved her. And they weren't like the mothers of the girls at the grammar school, who drove fancy cars and had dinner parties and wore twinsets and tweed skirts and pearl earrings and went to the beauty salon. Those mothers were always well turned out, smiled a lot and chatted about jolly things – the weather, holidays, horses and baking. Why couldn't the Aunties look and behave like those mothers?

Most of the time they looked hunched and sad, and I knew from my earwigging sessions what they talked about: basically two subjects, their health and scandal.

The first often made me squirm.

'Look at my feet, the doctor says they're swollen because of my sugar problem.'

'The infection has passed to my kidney so sometimes there is blood when I go to the toilet.'

The second often made me angry.

'They say that the last time he went to Pakistan, he got married to a woman there and he hasn't even told his wife here about it. *Vacharee*, poor thing.'

'I was told that their family is getting social security even though they have a business. That's how they can afford a brand new Mesidees.'

'I've heard that her daughter has run away from home. How can she do such a thing to her family?'

You could never put a foot wrong in Bradford, because if you did, the Aunties would know about it. And they would talk about it. Pass it on. Let everybody know. It was paralysing and suffocating, that fear of: 'What will *apnay lokhi* say?' The community?

I'd experienced it a number of times, most recently when I'd applied to universities beyond Leeds and Bradford. 'Why does she have to move away from home? Can't she study her digree here?'

Didn't the Aunties have anything better to do with their time than opine? Anyway, what did they know about growing up in Ingerlernd? How difficult it was.

It was impossible to avoid the Aunties – there were hundreds of them, and they were everywhere: in our living room, at the Asian shops, at the English shops, on the bus, at weddings. It was beyond me to remember all their names, so just as Umejee had devised a method of classifying the Aunties using postal districts – 'Mrs Khan from Bradford 5', 'Mrs Shah from Bradford 7' – I set up my own system. This would allow me to distinguish between those women I could greet with nothing more than a cursory yet polite '*Aslaam-o-alakum, Aunty-jee*' and then ignore, and those I might make more of an effort with. The crude sub-divisions were:

Skin colour. Quite simply, I wanted the Aunties to be as pale-skinned as the mothers at my school and other whities. I thought that if they looked a bit like them, they might act a bit like them, be cultured and civilised. I certainly wasn't alone in pursuing this Aryan ideal. In the Bollywood films I watched with Dad and Umejee, the baddie was always dark-skinned, almost black, in contrast to the heroes and heroines, whose faces and bodies had an incandescent white glow – even after they had been kidnapped, tethered to the back of a horse and dragged through mud, paddy fields, rocky mountains and a lake. And in the real world, fair skin was a condition and selling point of pretty much all the matrimonial ads in the back of the Asian newspapers: 'We are looking for husband for our daughter, Razia, who is 21 years old and has completed her BA Honours. She is slim, very pretty and has wheaten complexion.'

Origins in Pakistan. This was something else that I'd picked up from films and ads and everyday life. That if you came from a rural area back home, you were not quite the village idiot, but certainly regarded as less sophisticated and elegant than the women from the big cities like Islamabad and Lahore. City women knew not to jump the queue at wedding buffets no matter how hungry they were, and not to pile their plates with the equivalent of their own body weight in curry and rice, and not to shovel this food into their mouths whilst all the time spitting and shouting at a waiter for: 'Coke! Coke!'

Ability to speak English. Surrounded by 'the community', Pakistani family, friends, shopkeepers, GPs, bus drivers, etc., the average Aunty in Bradford had almost no need to speak English. Like Umejee, they could get away with a vocabulary limited to a few essential words – hello; goodbye; dahling; How much, please? No, too much, you give me discount. For more complex communications, such as a hospital appointment with a white consultant, they could always rely on their bilingual children to interpret. Not my mother, though. My Punjabi and Urdu were so weak that when the women started talking about anything over and above basic civilities – '*Aslam-o-alakum, bheti. Kessi ho?*' Hello, daughter. How are you? – I would smile, say, 'Just one moment, Aunty. I'll be back in a minute,' then run to the bathroom, where I would sometimes hide for hours.

Whether their children were educated. The way the non-English-speaking Aunties could redeem themselves in my eyes was if they placed an importance on their progeny's schooling. Those who boasted about their kids' academic success and of plans to go to university – even if it was invariably to study law, medicine or accountancy – went up in my esteem, whereas those who had been planning their children's weddings since they were pretty much toddlers – 'Yes, it has been agreed since he was a boy that Ahmed will marry his second cousin from Pakistan. I have been saving up for the bride's jewellery for many years' – I defined as 'backwards'.

As far as I was concerned, if the Aunties could desire the perfect Bradford-born second-generation child – one who spoke fluent Punjabi and Urdu, said their *namaz* five times a day, stayed at home, wanted to get married at the age of eighteen, made regular trips to Pakistan, and knew the names of all the women in Bradford and the nature of their ailments – then I in turn could wish for the perfect Aunty – a pale, urbane, erudite, English-speaking lady with intelligent offspring. Which is why I only ever had one favourite Aunty who I looked forward to seeing. Aunty Farah had a wavy bob, latte-coloured skin, high cheekbones and the added bonus of freckles (a facial feature I had only ever seen on English people). She had worked her way up from being a teacher to a headmistress, sent her kids to good schools, could discuss with me the merits and failings of Thatcherism for my politics assignments and, rather uniquely, knew some of the words to Barry Manilow's 'Bermuda Triangle'.

Of course I was just as guilty of making ill-informed judgements about the women as they were of having preconceived ideas about me. But I didn't see it that way at the time.

I cowered in the corner of our living room and silently read the Koran.

'You have to read out loud so the Angels can see your lips move,' ordered one of the interfering Aunties.

'I know what to do, just let me get on with it,' I mumbled under my breath.

I bowed my head as low as possible to prevent any further criticism, but I couldn't stay in that or any other position for more than a few minutes. It was so uncomfortable sitting on the floor for hours, squeezed in between so many people. Only the very elderly were given exemption to sit on chairs. Occasionally if someone stood up to go to the bathroom they would fall upon their co-readers, unaware that their legs and feet had been pricked by pins and needles.

Apart from the odd cough or the entrance of a late-comer, the only sound in the room was a gentle murmur as the women recited verse after verse from the Holy Book. Low-level drones mixed with higher-pitched hums so that the room reverberated like the string section of an orchestra. In fact, from all you could see of the crouched women, curved backs of varying widths and lengths, their forms also resembled such instruments – violins, cellos and double basses. Within that hypnotic sound, I too became entranced by what I was doing, reciting the lines of Arabic scripture.

I imagined Pajee watching us from the ceiling. I'd never seen him read the Koran. What would he make of all this? All these women praying for him? I was sure he'd be very grateful for anything that helped. You see, it's said that the first forty days in the grave are quite uncomfortable, there's a lot of tossing and turning, and as Pajee didn't have the benefit of much padding on his scrawny frame, all those rocks and stones must have really been hurting him. Our prayers were supposed to relieve that pain.

We read for hours until Umejee suggested we stop. I wasn't even halfway through my second chapter; it would take me at least another hour to complete it.

'Give that to Aunty,' Mum suggested. 'She'll read the rest of it for you. You go and tell the men next door that we're nearly finished.'

I tiptoed past and over the women and knocked on the door of the posh living room. My brother opened it. 'Tell Dad we're nearly done.'

The Aunties' efforts meant that the Koran had been read a total of twelve times in the space of about six hours. Just how much faster Pajee's soul would rest in his grave, I wasn't sure. My school physics lessons had taught me that speed equals distance over time. There was no similar equation for speed of tranquillity for the dead equals number of times Koran read over time taken to read Koran.

The doorbell rang once more. I thought it might be some wily Aunty turning up late enough to avoid reading but in time for food. That always happened at *huthams*. It was actually the imam from Dad's mosque. He'd been to various homes that day for various reasons and now he was here to say the final *duwah*, prayer, for Pajee. I caught a glimpse of him. He was smartly dressed in a crisp starched white *shalwar kameez*, a black waistcoat with gold buttons and a hard tall hat that distinguished him from the other Muslim males in their embroidered skullcaps. Even though he wouldn't see them, the imam's arrival was enough to prompt the Aunties to rearrange their headscarves to make sure that their hair was completely covered.

As he joined the men, the doors of all the rooms were flung open so that the women could hear his prayers. Amongst other things that I didn't entirely understand, we prayed to God to forgive Pajee for any ill deeds he might have committed in his life and to give us, his family, strength. Once the imam had finished, the connecting doors were again closed and the women were left alone. This was the part I dreaded.

All eyes focused upon one Aunty, a short woman, her body as round as her face, and I guessed aged in her late fifties. She moved to the centre of the room. A glass of water and a box of tissues were brought in for her, and she placed them on the table where the Koranic chapters lay. She coughed, looked down and then up towards the ceiling. As she opened her mouth, the first thing I spotted was her yellow teeth, not many of them left but enough to contrast against her dark skin. Then I saw that her lips were stained a deep deep red, not from the application of lipstick but from years of chewing *paan*, betel. From this not very attractive orifice came the most beautiful and haunting sound, like a requiem that bypassed your ears and went straight for your soul. That made every hair on your body stand and then made you shudder. This woman had as much resonance in her solo voice as our entire school had when it sang hymns on speech day.

It didn't matter that I couldn't understand what the words meant. I was totally gripped by this lament that was somehow deafening yet whispered, agitated yet serene. This was the sound of grief.

I'd heard Aunty's voice before, at a previous wake. Even then, aged no more than ten and not even having the faintest idea who had died, I had to choke back the tears. Now, hearing the same elegy, this time for Pajee, my tears stood no chance.

What was I crying for? Well, for my wheelchaired Uncle and the pain he'd suffered most of his elderly life. All those times he'd cried out for his mother. All those times he'd lain in bed, doubled up in agony. Poor Pajee. From as far back as I can remember as a little child, he'd always been an old man, more like a grandfather than an Uncle. I don't think he'd had a great life, either in Bradford or in Pakistan. I don't know why he hadn't; I hardly knew anything about him. He just had that look in his face that told you so. The one where his eyes didn't blink for a while and his thin lips were perfectly horizontal and he just stared at the floor. The one that makes my stomach turn when I think about it now.

Though most of the time when I remember Pajee I don't see his gaunt face – only his bedside table, with his packets of Benson and Hedges, his Zippo lighter, an ashtray fast approaching full, his playing cards, his false teeth, his spectacles, his tube of ointment and his sickly-sweet cherry medicine, which I can almost taste going down the back of my throat.

Pajee wasn't a religious man as such – he didn't pray or read the Koran and he couldn't fast because of his medication. Though he had been on Hajj to Mecca just a few weeks before he died.

But he was a good man. He'd never done anyone any harm. He rarely lost his temper. He was kind. He bought us sweets and books and an Atari home console. He loved us as though we were his own children. I prayed that this would be enough to get him into Heaven, to spend infinity in Paradise where he could 'recline on jewelled couches' and be waited on by 'immortal youths with bowls and ewers and a cup of purest wine that will neither pain the head nor take away reason; with fruits of his own choice and flesh of fowls that he relishes'. The alternative, forever residing in the 'flare of sparks and fire . . . amidst scorching winds and seething water, in the shade of pitch-black smoke, neither cool nor refreshing', was just too grim to consider.

'Please, God, look after Pajee. Don't hurt him any more.'

Pajee on pilgrimage in Mecca just before he passed away.

I was the first to cry, but I knew others would soon follow. Without the Koran or tittle-tattle to distract them, the Aunties were now lost in their own thoughts. Melancholy descended on the room. I could feel it and it made me cry even harder. I knew what these women were thinking about. It was that word Umejee often used – *perishani*, 'the sorrow that we endure'. At a time such as this, at a wake, when all focus is on a life that has been, it's impossible not to contemplate your own existence, your past, present and future. Which was what made the Aunties weep.

You see, what I didn't mention earlier when I was telling you about the Aunties going on about their illnesses was that I couldn't bear to snoop in on their conversations after a while, actually not because I was squeamish or bored, but because I found it too upsetting. It was too distressing to listen to the details of the sickness that they talked about the most. Depression and anxiety. *Perishani*. It seemed that so many Aunties suffered from either depression or anxiety or both. They still do. I was listening to a Radio 4 report yesterday that said that the suicide rate among older Asian women is twice that of white women the same age.

I could hear them sobbing about how poorly they were – sleepless nights, no appetite, no enjoyment of life, heart palpitations, loss of hair, severe headaches, dizziness. About feeling that they had nothing. About how they had no one to confide in. About how they were on medication to help get them out of bed in the morning and then to help get them to sleep at night. Some had been taking tablets for years, the old-style antidepressants that were prescribed in the 1970s, the highly addictive ones that were difficult to come off.

There's a dark line in a song by the Fugees that always reminds me of my mother's friends: 'Tragic depression made her lose all her teeth.' I'd noticed that most of the Aunties sat in our living room were wearing dentures, even the younger ones.

And there's another song, a Punjabi song that the Aunties themselves sing: '*Nah roh eh dil*, don't mourn for this life.' That always gets me.

I started to cry so hard that one of the women patted me on the back and said: '*Sabr kar*. Have strength.'

But you don't understand, Auntie. I feel ashamed of myself. For wishing that you were more like the English women I see at school every day in their beautiful cars and clothes with their poise and sophistication. How could I be so ungrateful? When I know what you have given up for me.

Economic necessity had cost the Aunties their sanity. They had married young in Pakistan, left their extended families and moved to the UK, a new country with a new religion, new culture, new language and new rules.

Of course there were benefits to coming here – regular employment, access to better health care and education and a higher standard of living. That was why they had come.

But there were also significant disadvantages that weren't so tangible; a loss of self, a feeling of isolation, a sense of insecurity, all of which, over time, manifested themselves in a yearning for the old, an incomprehension of the current and a fear of the future.

I know that various measures have been put in place over the last few years in the UK to encourage immigrant communities to integrate – English language classes, the citizenship test, lessons on British culture and customs –

which is all very well, but it's not that easy. Giving up your home and moving elsewhere. Especially when the place you've come from is so different to the place you're going to. You can't just switch off and forget everything you know and feel and think.

I see it with Umejee when she goes back to Pakistan. She's a different person. She relaxes more, laughs more, does more. That's because she's at home. There are probably thousands of people out there who shout: 'Well why doesn't she move back there then?'

Maybe she should.

Or maybe she and the Aunties should have made more of an effort when they first came here – become fluent in English, got a job, lived amongst white people. But to be honest, I'm not sure that would have made Bradford seem any more like home to them.

And now Umejee and the Aunties have children for whom Bradford really is home. Kids with a different language, culture and mentality to them. That makes them feel even more alone. Even more stuck.

Life has been, still is and probably always will be difficult for the Aunties. Most of the time they're just treading water, kept buoyant by medication, resignation or faith. They have little choice but to carry their *borj*, their burden. No wonder so many of them are hunched over.

The women in our living room were grieving for themselves as much as mourning Pajee's death. I never went inside, but I knew there were no tears being shed inside the men's room next door. Life was easier for them. No, not easier, but different. It was unusual for wives to work, but it was compulsory for the men. Work meant mainly manual labour, in factories, in curry houses or on the buses.

The need to support two families, the immediate family in Bradford and the extended family back in Pakistan, meant long hours. More hours spent toiling meant fewer hours thinking about 'stuff'. I have no doubt the men thought about things; they just seemed able to cope better.

I pleaded with God.

'Please, God, look after Pajee. Please, God, look after Umejee and Dad. Please, God, look after the Aunties and the Uncles.'

I heard laughter in the room.

I looked up and saw smiling, animated faces. Some of the Aunties were giggling. For an instant I felt defrauded. I was still in that holy zone. How could the Aunties change from such a wretched, despondent state to one of merriment in an instant? In fact, how dare they? I needed at least a couple of hours to come back down to earth, and here they were comparing notes about their daughters-in-law. 'Mine is very good in the kitchen but she can't clean the bathroom properly.' 'Be grateful – mine can't even make a chapatti that's round! Ha ha ha!'

Never mind. Who was I to judge? I was very grateful to them, to 'the community', for turning up and praying for Pajee. They'd performed a *swahab*, a good deed, which hopefully would allow my Uncle to find peace in his grave that bit faster. Most of them didn't even know Pajee. But that was what the Aunties did, they just turned up at *huthams*, read the Koran, prayed and wept and then chatted and ate. Thank God for the Aunties. Who else could you rely on to do that? I couldn't complain about them now.

Even as they devoured the lamb and chicken curries, eating as though this was their first meal of the day. Even as they sent me back and forth, back and forth to the kitchen for more rotis and more rice. Even as they gossiped about X and how he had left his wife and kids for another woman, and a *gori*, a white woman, at that.

As stomachs filled up, the living room emptied out. Pair by pair the fetid sandals disappeared from the hallway. We were left with piles of dirty dishes, stained cloth coverings and our own thoughts. Adeeba and I tried to hose down the cauldron pots before they were returned to the caterers. I would be back at school the next day. There was no point telling anybody there about my Sunday – they wouldn't or couldn't understand. I hadn't even told anyone of Pajee's existence, never mind his death.

Did you ever go to a *hutham*? Could you hear the women from the room where the men sat? Then you'll know the sound.

That unbearable unhuman sound.

The sound that your mother no doubt made when you did what you did.

Why did you do that to her?

Why did you do what you did?

6

Nightclubbing (1988)

I'd never been over 'the tops' before. Surely the M62 was the fastest and most direct way to drive to Manchester from Bradford? But Melanie had other plans. Her parents lived on a farm just outside the village of Shelf, and this rural terrain was familiar to her. 'The tops', as she referred to it, was the collective noun given to all those single roads running over the various moors, Crosland Moor, Moss Moor and Rishworth Moor, that provided a natural buffer between the once-warring counties of Yorkshire and Lancashire.

The three of us – Melanie, Sara and me – were heading to Manchester University for a three-day A-level politics seminar. This was the first time I'd been away from home alone, unaccompanied by either parent or teacher. I wanted to see what it was like in the adult world, the English world. I was planning to go to university the following year and was terrified of how I would cope. I had only ever known home, family, school, weddings, Aunties, books, dreaming and not much else.

Squeezed in on the back seat of Melanie's aptly coloured black and white Fiat Panda, we left behind the Bradford I knew – Pakistani Bradford, with its overcrowded grey terraced houses, the fused smell of frying onions, chilli, garlic and ginger, the Nissans double-parked on the streets, ornate with beaded seat coverings, gold tissue box holders and miniature Korans dangling from the mirror, obstructing the driver's view – and entered a more verdant, more subtly perfumed, less inhabited, calmer Bradford with its farmhouses and hanging baskets and Jeeps and sheep. White Bradford.

I know most cities have a dual identity – an urban centre juxtaposed with a suburban circumference – but Bradford felt more schizophrenic than most because of its divided demographics. I could almost guarantee that between leaving a specific street in the city, namely Moore Avenue, to arriving just beyond the fringes of Manchester city centre, I would be the only Asian in that corridor. Pakistanis don't do the countryside. And it showed on my face.

As the A roads out of the city centre dwindled into B roads, then country lanes, and as we climbed ever higher up 'the tops', I feared that if I moved even an inch in the back of the Panda, we would all topple over on to the M62 below. As Melanie and Sara chatted away about boys, I sat very still and stared out at the fascinating landscape – vast reservoirs, miles of dry-stone walls, unreachable summits, sheer drops, the farm near the Calderdale turn-off that stands precariously in the middle of the motorway, and then Saddleworth Moor. Even if you weren't aware of its history – the murderous campaign of Brady and Hindley and child graves – a chill would pass over your body and your skin would erupt in goose pimples. Like a reverse oasis, this was a barren and desolate patch in an otherwise lush setting.

(About a decade later, whilst working on an ITV crime documentary, I visited the Black Museum in Scotland Yard.

The museum isn't open to the public, only to police officers. The reason for that is because of the gruesome objects that are on display there – the bath that the serial killer Dennis Nilsen murdered his victims in, and the pot that he used to boil their body parts, photographs of the women mutilated by Jack the Ripper and the noose used to hang Ruth Ellis. The curator was an ex-policeman who had worked on the Moors Murders. He told me that he had listened to the tape that Brady and Hindley recorded of Lesley Ann Downey screaming and begging for her life. 'For ages after, I couldn't sleep,' he told me. 'I couldn't even lay my head down on the pillow. Nobody should ever have to hear a sound like that in their lives.' Now, whenever I drive past Saddleworth Moor, I have to turn up the volume on my radio.)

Signs for Ashton-under-Lyne and Oldham notified us that we were nearing Manchester. By now it was night and the lights of the city sparkled ahead of us. We were still high up in the Pennines and could gaze down on the ordered lines of yellow motorway lights stretching as far as the eye could see, then disappearing into pitch black. And the random flickering of red and white lamps. Nothing else was visible, just lights and the dark. It was mesmerising.

Something whispered to me: 'It's beautiful, isn't it, Zaiba? You know, this is what Heaven looks like.'

Yes, it is beautiful, I replied. And so peaceful. It wasn't quite what I expected Heaven to look like. There were no rivers or fountains, no jewelled couches, no fruit or flesh of fowls. Just thousands of twinkling pinpoints.

We arrived at Manchester University. It was Friday night and the city centre was filling up with smartly dressed people. Men in suits and women with coordinated shoes and bags. Within an hour of arriving at the halls of residence where we were staying, Melanie and Sara had decreed that we were to spend the evening at a nightclub called the Hacienda.

'It's where everyone goes,' they announced.

I'd heard about the infamous Mancunian club. In my record collection, like many others, amongst the singles and albums was only one twelve-inch – 'Blue Monday', by New Order, the best-selling twelve-inch of all time. I knew there was some connection between the band's lead singer, Bernard Sumner, and the Hacienda. Maybe he owned it? Or maybe he played there? And I'd read interviews with Tony Wilson of Factory Records, who ran the club. He didn't look like a man who knew anything about music, but he made things happen. Curiosity and delusion got the better of me. The chance that I might bump into either one of these men and instantly be signed up to Factory (as, of course, I was bound to) was enough for me to flout the ban on nightclubs, one that until now I'd done a pretty good job of obeying.

I watched Sara as she got ready for our night out – I couldn't help myself. She thought nothing of removing her clothes in front of me and standing naked as she decided what to wear. Her limbs were long and toned and her skin was darker than I expected. She put on a pair of jeans, a black belt done up on the final hole so the excess leather draped down one thigh, and finally a mid-blue T-shirt, which she tucked into her trousers. Her hair took much longer to arrange – she put on a bright red beret and couldn't decide at which angle it should sit. Eventually she let it rest at the back of her head so her golden curls fell evenly over her face. The final touch was to spray the fine mist from an atomiser, which left a luminous sheen on her face.

Sara had an asexual cherubic beauty, but there was something else about her. She looked popular, confident and grown-up. I wanted to look like her, but I fell at the first hurdle.

I tried to extend my party prep time by brushing my hair repeatedly and painstakingly applying my Constance Carroll lipstick to my mouth and eyes. So deep was the purple shade that in low light I looked like a poor imitation of a Goth. I reached for Sara's bottle and sprayed my face. I thought this was a way of fixing my make-up so it would stay put all night. But instead my cheap face paint ran. I'd unwittingly finessed my Goth impersonation.

How was I to know what to do to get ready for night-clubbing?

I'd only ever been once before in my life. Four years earlier, when in a desperate attempt to fit in and do what everyone else was doing, I'd persuaded Dad and Umejee to let me go to a 'birthday party'.

'Why do you need to go?' asked Umejee. 'You see these people at school all the time.'

'Our religion does not allow parties,' stated Dad. Not true. We often went to parties – celebrations of weddings, Koranic readings and indeed birthdays.

Finally, after weeks of negotiation and information, they said yes. It was a girls-only affair; it was under the supervision of various parents; I would check that the food I ate was halal. In fact there was no such festivity. I was sneaking off to a disco called The Time, The Place.

This was the Friday-night haunt of the girls at my school, and what happened there in one night often provided enough material to keep them gossiping until Wednesday lunchtime. I couldn't imagine what it looked like or what went on there.

What to wear? Well, I had the sparkly colourful *shalwar kameezes* that I wore to weddings and Mum's friends' parties. I toyed with the idea of adapting one by cutting the top to an English shirt length and getting rid of the extra material on the bottoms so they resembled trousers. I sampled a cheap cotton *shalwar kameez*, one that Umejee wasn't going to miss. If I sewed up the hem on the short-ened shirt it didn't look so bad, but there was so much cloth on the billowing shalwar that any amendments made it look like a pair of the clown trousers that the Thompson Twins wore. It wasn't going to work. I looked ridiculous. I rifled through the wardrobes of every family member. Could I get away with one of Dad's three-piece suits worn in the style of Annie Lennox? Or cut up one of my mum's saris without her knowing and look more flamboyant like Cyndi Lauper? Not really.

I resorted to lying.

'Can you believe it! My parents have gone out and I've lost my house keys so I can't get the brand-new black dress I bought specially for tonight,' I told Melody and Hannah. 'So I'm going to have to wear what I'm wearing now.' We were in the toilets of Sunwin House, the only department store in Bradford, getting ready. The cubicles were full of incontinent old women who sat on the loos for ages before you heard them urinating, and only then for a few seconds. They tutted as they struggled to get to the mirrors that we had monopolised. 'You youngsters, hey. You don't know that you're born.'

Hannah was wearing a short short denim skirt and high-heeled white court shoes. Her top was skimpy and pink. She was the only living person I ever met whose legs were as long and as thin as the pins of a Barbie doll. Melody's attire was a bit more sober. A crisp white shirt worn with three-quarter-length black trousers and a pair of braces. The two girls were dipping into the same pots of make-up – pink blusher, pink lipstick and emerald-green eyeshadow. They hung huge fake gold hoops on to their ear lobes that would have made Umejee proud.

Suddenly they looked about five years older than me. I was dressed in a bright green silk shirt with a Chinese stand-up collar and grey flannel trousers that flared out at the thighs and tapered in at the ankle, making me look exactly like the jester I was trying to avoid resembling. I averted my gaze from the mirror – in it I looked like a fool, but in my head I looked as fashionable as the girls. I multitasked my red lipstick, using it to cover my lips, cheeks and eyes. With my round chubby face and brown pallor, I looked like a bruised Cox's apple.

Melody and Hannah hadn't invited me to the club. I'd asked them days in advance if I could join them. I was desperate to find out what the girls at school got up to at the weekend. They were fairly indifferent, so much so that when I arrived at Sunwin House I was half expecting them not to be there. I don't know what I would have done if they weren't. There was no way I had the courage to go to the club on my own. I didn't even know where it was. And after all the fuss I'd caused at home about wanting to go to 'the party', heading straight back there wasn't an option.

'I think Clare's brother fancies me. I've seen him looking at me on the bus,' boasted Hannah.

'Clare won't like that,' said Melody. 'She bitches about you behind your back, you know.'

'Tough luck. I hope he's there tonight.'

'If David is there, do you think I should talk to him?'

'Yeah. Why not? He's really good-looking. And you know that he's going to France to play for the school rugby team?'

I could contribute nothing to this exchange – the only boys I had any contact with were my two brothers. And I was pretty certain that Hannah and Melody didn't want to hear about them.

The Time, The Place was in the basement of some building in the city centre. If the job of the security guard was to keep an eye on underage drinkers, he wasn't earning his crust. I recognised girls from lower years from school, aged twelve or thirteen, huddled in groups. The factionalism that was evident in the school playground was replicated here. The posh, courteous girls dressed head to toe in pastels from Benetton were in one corner. Then there were the posh, rude girls who I'd heard comparing their first sexual encounters in the locker room. They wore clothes from Miss Selfridge that were more structured, with big belts and pleats. Finally there were the flesh-exposers like Hannah, with their bare legs, midriffs and backs. I couldn't tell you where their garments came from. Probably borrowed from their mothers.

I was expecting something like the school hall – just one large room – but The Time, The Place had a cavernous set-up. Lots of chambers that made it difficult to get your bearings. It was also very dark. The only light came from a bright blue neon sign behind the bar and the scores of cigarettes that were constantly being lit.

Hannah and Melody had disappeared and I was left on my own. What was I supposed to do? I was surrounded by people I knew from school but I didn't have the gumption to interrupt their groups. What would I say to them anyway? Do you like my top, the one that I wear to school all the time? Does your mother really let you out of the house dressed like that?

I found an empty seat on the edge of the dance floor, sat down and stared. At the giggling hordes of girls, having fun. At the clusters of young men. Most of them were handsome. Some were even beautiful. Laughing. Confident. And tall. Maybe money bred height as well as good looks. Gradually males and females began to interact. I watched intensely, stared to see if I could learn. I couldn't hear the words that were being uttered, so instead I analysed the body language, how they stood, where their hands went and how they leaned into each other, pretending that such intimacy was needed above the din of the music. A number of times, when I thought my crash course in socialising was complete, I tried to launch myself off my stool and into the various coteries. No joy. I didn't have the mettle. It was like my body had been frozen by the dry ice that I was immersed in. I couldn't even make the short trip to the bar. And so I stayed there for as long as I could bear, all too aware of the quizzical glances that were being cast in my direction: 'What is she doing here?'

The groups became couples and the talking became whispers and kisses.

'What are you doing here?' I asked myself. 'You don't belong here. You should be at home.'

I tried to distract myself by singing inside my head to the Human League's 'Mirror Man' and Heaven 17's

'Temptation'. I tapped one foot so it looked as though music was the reason why I had come to the nightclub. I tried to look cool, but I was so hot I could feel the sweat dribbling over my waist from my armpits. I knew that it would stain my silk shirt, so I was forced to keep my arms clamped to my sides. I was the most immobile object in the disco – even the glasses, stools and glitter ball moved more than I did. I had to get out of there.

Less than an hour after my arrival, I left.

There were Asian taxi drivers queued up in the rank outside, all in white Datsuns.

'Pssst,' one hissed at me. 'You need ride home?' He was about the same age as Dad. I stared at him in a way that he could only read as: 'You should be ashamed of yourself, *basharam*.' Inside I was feeling anxious. What if he knew Dad and told him that he'd seen me coming out of a nightclub? He turned round in his seat and called to the cabbies behind in Punjabi: 'Look at this one. Who does she think she is?' The others struck up a chorus of jeering laughter. I put my head down as I walked past them, feeling guilty and angry.

Bradford looked different at night. I'd walked around the city centre in daylight hundreds of times, past the Gothic-style City Hall, on the pedestrianised section of Broadway and in the eye-aching tube light of the Kirkgate Arndale Centre. It took just a few circuits of the centre for you to feel that all the life was being sapped out of you. That you were becoming as grey as the buildings around you. Walking and shopping here was always such a mundane experience. That's why Bill Bryson wrote that 'Bradford's role in life is to make every place else in the world look better in comparison' and why the city, described by visitors as 'ugly and boring' in a recent poll, was the number one place that they least wanted to visit.

Now, at nine p.m., I yearned for that safe boredom. In the dark, the city had lost its dependability. And I had lost my way. I couldn't get my bearings. British Home Stores and C&A were no longer the familiar shops I knew, where I stood patiently with Umejee as she thoroughly checked the quality of each item before she made a purchase, paying as much attention to a pair of socks as to a full dinner set. Even Littlewoods, where I'd bought so many tubs of potato salad and coleslaw, now felt strange. With no Pakistani mothers or OAPs out doing the shopping, and in the dim light, everything seemed less banal and much more dangerous.

Men, and boys pretending to be men, were behaving like dogs, using the shops as oversized lamp posts to piss against. The entrance ways of WHSmith and the Stead and Simpson shoe shop were like makeshift tattoo parlours, where young couples marked their lust for each other with a not-so-permanent mark, a love bite.

Even this early in the evening, men and women were staggering around. The sound of stilettos on the pavement was not a regular clickety-click so much as a long, high-pitched scrape followed by a quick succession of faltering clacks. Gone were the regular daytime noises of sensible Clarks shoes marching purposefully to work and lulled voices discussing family life and the weather. Come the night, the women's voices were now as shrill as Umejee's budgerigars and their conversations were as coarse as the grit the birds walked upon.

'I don't give a fuck about what he wants. I'm me own

fucking boss me. That cunt can right fuck off.'

'Too right, Jackie. Why should we wait on them bloody hand and foot? We're fucking free agents, you and me. Now let's see what other stupid cunts we can find for a'selves, shall we? Ha! Ha! Ha!'

Everybody I came across was part of a group. Apart from a homeless man begging and a young lad passed out on the ground, I was the only person on their own. I felt vulnerable with so many leery drunken people around. Asians didn't walk around Bradford city centre at night. The only non-whites in the city centre were safely positioned in their hackney carriages or behind their takeaway kebab counters.

I was desperately trying to find a telephone box that hadn't been vandalised or wasn't occupied by a urinating male so I could call Dad and ask him to pick me up. When did all this mess get cleared up? The pools of vomit, the shards of broken beer bottles that seemed to defile every corner I turned. I looked away every time a group walked towards me, petrified that the available glassware might be used to cut open my throat.

I'd only ever glimpsed drunken behaviour, scantily clad women and heavy petting on the television. Seeing it now, for real, it didn't feel or look like fun to me. I longed for home, where I knew how things worked, what was right and what was wrong, where I was safe. I was becoming more and more anxious. In the quiet side streets I could hear myself breathing harder and harder. It was fright, rather than the cold, that was making my hairs stand on end. I was too scared to approach anyone for help.

I headed up Darley Street, where I knew there was a

cluster of phone boxes. I put one of my five-pence coins in the slot. Dad picked up the phone.

'Daddy-jee, the party has finished. Can you come and get me?' I pleaded.

He didn't sense the desperation in my voice.

'Already? But I just dropped you off a while ago.'

'No, all the girls are going home now.' I thought he might be happy to hear this.

'Okay. I'm coming. Go to the post office and I'll pick you up from there.'

I was so relieved that I skipped down the hill past the Mappin and Webb jeweller's, past Greggs bakery. It took me about ten minutes to reach the post office.

We didn't live far from the city centre, so I thought Dad wouldn't be too long.

I waited and waited in the doorway, where I thought I couldn't be seen. Mistake.

'How much money do you want, pretty?' A Punjabi taxi driver was looking at me. Even though his moustache was so dense I couldn't see his lips, I could sense from his eyes that he was licking them.

'Get lost! My dad's on his way!' I screamed, as shrill as the inebriated women I'd encountered earlier.

'But darling, you are so nice.'

'I said get lost!'

He drove away. I started to weep. 'Please, God. Please, God. Please, God. Please, God.' Whenever I wanted something from God, I never needed to specify what it was I was after. It was God after all. He knew. I just needed to beg. To be at home.

It was more than obvious to me that I was being taught a lesson, for lying to Umejee and Dad about going to the disco. It was also obvious to me that my experience tonight was meant to put me off wanting to ever go to a night-club again.

When Dad rolled up in his car and I got in, I didn't mind that he didn't ask me if I'd enjoyed myself. I would have had to lie to him if he had. I was so relieved to be safe, away from the tarts and the drunks. I was happy to be in the car with the rosary beads hanging from the rear-view mirror and the quotation from the Koran stuck on the windscreen and the *qawali* blaring from the tape player.

I wanted to tell Dad that he was right.

And that I would never lie to him again.

Better to fib to the girls at school than deceive Umejee and Dad, even if it meant that I regularly strangled myself on my web of deceit.

Liar, liar, Zaiba liar.

I couldn't tell the girls that my life was so different to theirs. I couldn't tell them that I wanted to be nothing like them. I couldn't tell them that actually I wanted to be just like them.

Hence my second attempt at nightclubbing.

We queued for what seemed like hours outside the curved red-brick building on Whitworth Street in central Manchester. Apart from a line of people, there was nothing to indicate that this was a club – no flashing lights or candy-coloured neon. There was just a granite plaque on the wall that read FAC 51 HACIENDA. Apparently the digits were some kind of Factory Records catalogue reference.

In the cold wind I was grateful for my sweater. My mind focused not on what lay ahead in the forthcoming hours but a few days forward. Now I wouldn't have to lie to the girls at school about what I'd done over the weekend. Surely this would impress them, a night at the Hacienda signing a lucrative recording contract with Tony Wilson. I visualised myself in the classroom on Monday morning. I was sat in a chair in the centre of the room, an enthusiastic yet poised narrator surrounded by looks of envy and admiration. It didn't matter what I was saying, it was enough that I had the girls' attention.

What I'd seen of the Hacienda's exterior led me to assume that the inside would be a civilised affair, like the cocktail bars in *Miami Vice*. How wrong I was.

We entered through large metal doors with the numbers five and one punched through them. I felt the sound before I heard it. The thump-thump-thump entered my feet, travelled up my legs and found a home in my chest and head. It felt as though a defibrillator had been attached to my upper half. My body shook involuntarily. I could taste metal in my mouth, as if my fillings had become dislodged. My brain couldn't compute the sudden assault on all its senses. What I saw, heard, smelt, tasted and felt. It went into overload. I stood in one spot trying desperately to acclimatise.

'Where are the workmen?' I asked myself. 'The club hasn't even been finished and they're letting people in.' The entire place looked like a construction site, scaffolding supported the roof and steel girders were wrapped in yellow safety stripes. At the centre of the site was a raised stage, which was looked over by other floors. And in the centre of this was what looked like a huge paddling pool, partially filled with water and a few inflatable balls. Why would there be a pool in a nightclub?

Television screens broadcasting psychedelic patterns

were about the only source of colour. Pink, purple and orange globules appeared to expand and contract at the same time. The music continued to thud. I waited for the lyrics, but they came only fleetingly, and even then they were uninspired and repetitive. 'Are you happy? Are you fine? Are you happy? Dance! Dance!' It sounded as though a robot was singing. I'd never heard anything like it before. This was house music.

But there was nothing domesticated about this place. People on podiums dancing like monkeys. Boys in over-sized T-shirts with bright yellow smiley faces on them and manky woolly hats even Dad wouldn't be seen in. Women who were trying to look like girls by tying their hair in pigtails. Arms flailing everywhere. Nobody seemed to notice or care about the sweat patches that stained every armpit. The heat was suffocating.

I moved to the side of the room to find some air. The music bounced off the walls and into my body and my feet were lifted off the floor.

'Just enjoy it. Try and have fun. Just be like everyone else for a change,' I instructed myself. But there was something not quite right. I couldn't put my finger on it.

The white strobe light passed over hundreds of faces. As it flashed on and off you caught frozen snatches of the dancers' expressions, like photographs. Everyone was grinning inanely, with wide beams stretching from ear to ear, exposing their teeth. They weren't smiling. It was more sinister than that, more like the cartoon rictus of the Joker from *Batman*. They all looked mad.

Some were lost in their own world, concentrating on every beat of the thump-thump-thump. Others were inter-acting, hugging each other. Monotonous track after monotonous track, the black and white snapshots produced the same picture. Not one grin had dropped.

Suddenly I heard a wailing siren. I started to panic. Where was the fire? Probably near that paddling pool. Even I knew that water and electrics didn't mix. Why wasn't anyone moving? How were we all going to get out? Somebody had better phone Tony Wilson quick and tell him his business was about to go up in flames.

'We've got to go!' I screamed at the monkeys around me. 'There's a fire!'

Somebody hugged me. I was trapped. I was going to burn to death in a club, and a particularly immoral one at that, and Umejee and Dad were going to discover my deceit. What were they going to tell 'the community' at my *hutham*? 'Zaiba was studying very hard at Manchester Library when the building collapsed'?

Slowly I twigged. The siren was a sound the DJ used to punctuate the thump-thump-thump and get people whooping and blowing their whistles. This was tribal music, produced democratically and collectively. I hated it. I couldn't even generate a nodding head or a tapping foot. Couldn't they play something else? Some Fleetwood Mac or Simple Minds or Specials?

I had long since lost Melanie and Sara. My jumper was drenched, soaking up my sweat on the inside and the perspiration of other bodies on the outside. I needed to use the toilet at the same time that I needed a drink.

The bar was easily located. Scores of people scrambling to buy bottles of water. Why weren't they drinking alcohol? Didn't people go to clubs to get drunk? There were no signs pointing to the loos, only rooms labelled 'Gay Traitor' and 'Kim Philby'. I was too shy to ask anyone. I walked round and round, using the bollards and cats' eyes around the dance floor as a guide. Eventually I found the toilets at the back of the club.

Oh God!

What I saw in there made me forget that I urgently needed to use one of the cubicles. Men were doing things with men; women with women. In the harsh strip light I could see almost everything. Couples and trios were laid out on the floor, sat on the sinks and rammed against the walls. Usually I tried to be subtle with my stares, using a mirror or hiding behind my hair, but now my eyes were like saucers and my mouth formed a perfectly circular 'O'. I was aghast.

A bearded man in his early twenties was handing out the tiniest envelopes I had ever seen in exchange for cash. Inaudible words were murmured. Inside the see-through plastic was a single pill, which the buyer consumed on the spot with a swig of water.

These ecstasy tablets, the pink calis, white doves and rhubarb and custards as they were called by the clubbers, were the reason behind the hugs and the happiness. Everyone was off their faces. That was why they could so blatantly flaunt such depravity. And that was why they could spend hours not tiring of the tedious thump-thump-thump, applauding each tune as if it had something unique to offer. That was why this place became known as 'The Hashienda'. That was why this city became known as 'Madchester'.

I must have been one of the few clubbers who hadn't taken any illegal substances, but to any clean onlookers I now looked like the demented one. Oh God!

This was what Hell looked like – the toilets of the

Hacienda. I'd seen it in the cinema as a child. Films that showed what life was like before the Prophet Muhammad existed – hedonists who had no self-control or self-regard and who all too readily wrapped their limbs around other unrighteous bodies. In those films the skin tone was darker and more even than the blotchy pale flesh of the Manchester clubbers, and the setting was more exotic – a desert as opposed to latrines – but pretty much everything else was the same. The consumption of intoxicating substances, the surrender to ungodly passions, the groans and smirks and laughter.

What was wrong with these sinners? How could they submit to such debauchery? Didn't they know that they would have to pay for their deeds in the Afterlife? Did they want to dance for ever and ever in fiery flames, their skin dripping off them like hot candle wax?

God was trying to show me what Hell was like. Hot, noisy, crowded, mad. Just as on the way to Manchester, on the motorway, He had shown me what Heaven was like. Tranquil, glittering, magical. He had shown me a glimpse of both so I could choose where I wanted to end up.

I couldn't breathe. I cupped my hands over my mouth, inhaled and walked back into the club.

The paddling pool was full of bathers trying to cool down. They were fully dressed but their bodies were quite visible. The inflatable balls were being passed over the heads of the crowd. Many of the clubbers were now on their second or third E of the night. The whole building felt like it was jumping up and down to the beat of 808 State's 'Quadrastate'.

I felt sick.

I had to get out.

I used my elbows and my anger to work my way against the incoming crowd. 'Hey! Chill out!' warned the jigging revellers, just coming up on their pills. I was breaking every rule in the Hacienda Happy Handbook by looking so wrathful, leaving so early and on my own.

'Please, God. Please, God. Please, God. It's not easy being me. I don't know if You know how hard it is. But I'm doing the best I can. With this task, this burden that You have given me.'

The queue for the Hacienda was as long as when I'd arrived. The music was just audible enough outside that people could dance to it. I had no choice but to walk past them. I didn't want them to stare at me. Even off their faces, they couldn't mistake my tears for sweat.

I was having a bad trip.

In the top drawer of my filing cabinet, where I keep my most treasured possessions, underneath the *Roget's Thesaurus* and the signed autograph book I was given when I left middle school, there is a cream and white mottled envelope. Inside that envelope is a small square red and silver pin badge with a factory etched on it. Tony Wilson sent me this badge, bearing the logo of his record company, a couple of months before he died in 2008. There is also a letter that he typed, a reply to the one I sent to him telling him in some detail about the terrible experience I'd had at his nightclub twenty years earlier. In true Tony Wilson style, he wrote: 'Sorry about the Hacienda, but decadence is a lovely word, forgive me.'

When I read that now, I can't help but smile and think: God bless Tony Wilson, and God bless the Hacienda.

There was a trial fairly recently where five men were convicted and jailed for life following one of the biggest investigations ever carried out by the security services. You met one of those men, the ringleader, didn't you, about a year before you did what you did? Did he tell you about his plan to blow up a nightclub – the Ministry of Sound? Did he tell you that it was okay to do that, that it was justified because 'no one can even turn around and say "oh they were innocent", those slags dancing around and other things'?

But they *were* innocent, those nightclubbers, those 'slags'. They didn't deserve to die.

And neither did any of those people on that day when you did what you did.

So why did you do what you did?

7

The Lost City (1989)

'There's something going on in town. There are lots of men with *daris*, beards, in *shalwar kameez* outside the police station. I saw them just now when I was going past on the bus.' Adeeba had just returned from a trip to WHSmith in the city centre. 'I don't know what they were doing. It looked like they were protesting or something – I couldn't see what was written on their boards.'

It was Saturday 14 January, and the thousand or so men gathered on the Tyrls just outside the police headquarters, the town hall and the magistrates' court were carrying placards that demanded: 'Ban the Book'. They listened to speeches from various holy men and 'community leaders' and recited prayers from the Koran. And if they'd left it at that – banners, shouting, sermons – then things would have been quite different. For a start, Bradford wouldn't have been in the news that night and over the forthcoming months. But the protesters didn't stop there – they went further, much further. On that cold winter day, a member of the Council of Mosques, smartly dressed in a shirt, tie, wool coat and trilby hat – a vision of assimilation – attached a hardback copy of Salman Rushdie's *The Satanic Verses* to a stake, doused it in petrol and, in full view of the hundreds of Muslim demonstrators and newspaper photographers present, set it alight.

The crowd cheered as Rushdie's novel was finally destroyed. For many months the Council of Mosques, the guardian and voice of the city's Muslims, had called for a ban on the publication and distribution of the book on the basis that it 'contains distorted, unfounded, imaginary and despicable material about the Prophet of Islam' and that 'areas of Muslim religion, culture and history have been ridiculed with the sinister motive of portraying millions of Muslims all over the world as barbarians'. They had written to the publishers, Penguin, to Margaret Thatcher and even to the Queen. Such repeated requests had gone unheeded, so now it was time for action. Time to do something that would get noticed. In took only five minutes for the five hundred and sixty pages of 'the most filthy and abusive book ever to be written against Islam' to disintegrate into blackened ashes that rose up in to the grey sky, and consequently for the protestors to forcefully demonstrate just how aggrieved and insulted they were.

But the book-burning was a pyrrhic victory for Bradford's Muslims.

That day's front page of the *Telegraph & Argus* read: 'Fury as Book is Set Ablaze'; it was a headline that was to be repeated on the cover and in the editorials of national newspapers over the coming days. Journalists, writers, commentators and thinkers were appalled and shocked at what had happened at the Tyrls. Don't these Muslims understand that we believe in freedom of expression in this country, that free speech is a cornerstone of our democracy, that it is a right we have had to fight long and hard for and is one we will absolutely defend – even if it causes offence? After all, we are a civilised society. As Eric Pickles, then the leader of the Tory-controlled

Bradford council, who watched the incendiary incident from his office at the town hall on that Saturday, later told me: 'Of all the symbolic actions, setting fire to a book was probably the worst thing to do. It looked like something out of Nuremburg.' The Muslims of Bradford were now seen as the very barbarians they claimed they had been depicted as in *The Satanic Verses*.

Things didn't get any better. In fact, they got a whole lot worse when one month later, on Valentine's Day, Ayatollah Khomeini, Iran's spiritual leader, delivered a most unloving message on Tehran Radio – a fatwa against Rushdie: 'I inform the proud Muslim people of the world that the author of the book entitled *The Satanic Verses*, which has been compiled, printed and published in opposition to Islam, the Prophet and the Koran, and all those involved in its publication who were aware of its content, are sentenced to death. I call on all proud Muslims to execute them quickly, wherever they may be found, so that no one else will dare to insult the Muslim sanctities. God willing, whoever is killed on this path is a martyr.'

Although the concept of a fatwa, a religious edict, was not familiar to many people in Britain, there was no mistaking its content. Rushdie was immediately placed in a safe house and given round-the-clock protection by Special Branch officers. No doubt as he was shifted from house to house over the following months and years – it took almost a decade and the appointment of a more moderate Ayatollah for the fatwa to eventually be lifted – he contemplated the words he had uttered just before the publication of his novel: 'It would be absurd to think that a book can cause riots . . . That's a strange sort of view of the world.'

Rushdie didn't realise that the world had changed.

And so had Bradford.

When national and international focus returned to the city of the book-burners, post-fatwa, the debate was no longer about vague wishy-washy ideals such as freedom of speech and expression.

The question that was now being posed to Bradford's Muslims was this: given that the Ayatollah has declared that every Muslim around the world has a duty to carry out the fatwa – to kill Rushdie – would *you* obey such an order?

Meaning: where do your loyalties lie? With the country you live in or with a bearded holy man in Iran?

Meaning: what are you? British or Muslim?

Because you've got to choose. You can't be both. That much is obvious now. British people believe in democracy, debate, civilisation, the rule of law. Muslim people believe in suppression, the rule of religion, fatwas and death. So which is it to be, hey?

Well, the answer was there in black and white for all to see. At rallies in Bradford and around the country, placards that had previously called for a ban on *The Satanic Verses* and an extension of the blasphemy laws to cover offence to Muslims now advocated a much more violent strategy: 'Rushdie is a Mad Dog – He Must Die', 'DIE RUSH-DIE DIE', 'Kill the Pig', 'Rushdie, You are Dead'.

As effigies of the author were set on fire, there was a real fear that the warning laid down by the German writer Heinrich Heine over a hundred and fifty years earlier that 'Where they burn books, so too in the end they will burn human beings' was about to come true.

On the evening news, when middle-aged men in Bradford were asked what they thought about Rushdie, they shouted: 'He is the Devil! The true Devil himself come to life! We are true Muslims. If we get the chance we will definitely do what the Ayatollah says.' 'Rushdie should not be on this world. We cannot condemn the death threat because we agree with it. Every Muslim in the world agrees he should die.' And it wasn't just the Uncles who marched in support of the Ayatollah's order; there were also many young men in those crowds. Second-generation British-born Muslims who openly stated that 'Until he is dead, we won't leave him.' A new organisation, the Muslim Youth Movement, was set up to represent this increasingly vocal and active constituency. It blatantly warned that it would break the law in order to defend the honour of Islam. With a banner at one demo that declared: 'East or West – Islam is the Best', the Muslims – young and old – had very visibly tied their colours to the mast. 'We are Muslim. Our loyalty first and foremost is with God, our faith and the Ummah, not with you, Britain.'

The sight of Muslims protesting in Bradford was nothing new. They'd done it many times before on issues to do with halal meat, racism and education. Those gatherings had always been peaceful to the point of almost being like a jolly street party. But the organised events throughout 1989 were different. They were larger, angrier, more forceful. One rally in the city centre turned into a full-scale riot when around three hundred young lads broke away from the main group and ran through town smashing shop windows and cars and throwing bottles and cans at the police. It didn't have to be said – you could see it: it's them against us. And as the government continued to refuse to ban the book or change the blasphemy laws, so the unrest, the violence, the death threats and the divisions persisted.

Race relations had always been fairly fragile in the city, but whereas in the past there had been some support for the grievances of Muslims from community relations bodies, anti-racist organisations and politicians, this time there was very little. Right-wingers called for an end to immigration, newspapers offered to buy unpatriotic Muslims one-way tickets to Iran, councillors demanded to know why those who supported the fatwa weren't being arrested, and one MP argued that 'Those who wish to make their home in Britain cannot deny to others the very freedoms that drew them to this country in the first place.' As a concerned Bradfordian wrote in a letter to the *Telegraph & Argus*, 'Surely the leaders of our Muslim population must realise that, by their action, they have alienated thousands of citizens who could, and did, live in peace with their neighbours.' It didn't really help community cohesion when the Council of Mosques stated that the most important thing for them was getting the book banned and that 'everything else, including race relations, is secondary'. It wasn't long before white kids on estates had replaced the familiar yell of 'Paki!' with an altogether more eloquent insult: 'Salman Rushdie is our hero!' 'Rushdie rules!' they chanted. In any other circumstances the writer would no doubt have been chuffed to know that his appeal had spread way beyond London's literati, indeed all the way up to the working classes living in the Butterworth and Canterbury areas of Bradford. But not now. If he had seen the words 'Long live Rushdie' scrawled on an underpass just outside the city centre, I am sure he would have shuddered. By now there was a two-million-pound reward for his death.

There's no denying that 1989, the year of *The Satanic*

Verses affair, was a turning point for Bradford. More specifically, it was a pivotal time for the city's Muslims.

Previously, their main concerns had revolved around micro-matters such as how to raise funds for a new mosque or which Pakistani councillor to support. Now their absolute goal was to stand up for who they were. Servants of God, followers of Islam. Muslims. It was their duty to defend their faith against the Devil's words – Rushdie's sacrilegious assault – and against the West, the disseminator of that evil message.

This massive undertaking wasn't something they could do on their own – they needed to look beyond the Yorkshire valleys that surrounded them and out towards Islamic countries such as Iran and Pakistan, where there had also been huge and often violent protests against *The Satanic Verses*. Bradford's Muslims had to go global. They had to ally themselves with their brothers and sisters in those lands that made up the Ummah under the guidance of the Ayatollah, no matter that by doing so they were seen as turning their backs on the British government, British laws, British traditions and, indeed, British people.

Knowing that they now had the support of millions of their own around the world gave the city's fifty thousand or so Muslims a new confidence and vigour. As Ishtiaq Ahmed from the Council of Mosques told me: 'The Muslim community got together and said that, as far as we are concerned, this is our town and we are not going to be pushed around and be ignored by anyone. We are here to make a statement.'

Well, they certainly did that. Muslims were now openly and regularly described as 'fundamentalists, militants, fanatics, extremists and terrorists', a people prepared to kill for their beliefs, and Islam was now regarded as a religion that had come into Britain 'bearing gifts of fear and violence'. Being a Muslim in Bradford was no longer about wearing sparkly clothes on Eid or driving a Nissan; instead, it became about much bigger things – the global Ummah, international affairs and human rights. It became political.

This was an ideal opportunity for some young British-born Muslims to assert themselves, to create their own identity; one that was separate from the Council of Mosques, which they considered weak and ineffectual, and also distinct from that of their first-generation parents, who they often chastised for being far more interested in idle gossip than the words of the Prophet Muhammad. They joined organisations such as Hizb-ut-Tahrir, the controversial radical Islamic party, which has since been banned in many countries though not the UK. The goal of this movement is to establish an independent state, the caliphate, which will be governed by sharia law, pure Islamic doctrine. These youngsters were well educated, articulate and confident. They had seen anti-racist movements, left-leaning liberal policies, multiculturalism and integration-ism come and go; none of these secular approaches had worked. 'We're still treated and regarded as second-rate citizens. Look, we're not even protected under British law when our faith is attacked. Time for a change. Time for our own laws.' They argued that the most important rules they had to obey were those laid down in the Koran. They started to follow a more literal, more fundamental interpretation of the Holy Book, one that hadn't been diluted by the man-made traditions and customs of their parents, one that hadn't been warped by the power-hungry community representatives. They believed it was their duty to help their persecuted brothers and sisters in places such as Palestine, Kashmir and Afghanistan just as much, if not more, than to help an Aunty or Uncle in the next street.

These people had their own language – they used words such as jihad, *khilafah*, *kuffir*, intifada; they had their own concepts – they started to talk about oppression, martyrdom and ideological struggle. They were sure of who they were and what they wanted. They had no hesitation in providing an answer to the vital choice that Rushdie himself put forward in 1989: 'The battle lines are being drawn up . . . Secular versus religious, the light versus the dark. Better you choose which side you are on.'

Me – do I have to choose as well? Please don't make me. It's too hard. I don't know what to say. So, of course, I kept quiet. I watched the Uncles on the TV news, protesting against Rushdie's book – hundreds of men like Dad who wore traditional clothes and had beards. For them, Islam was the most important thing in their lives – it *was* their lives – but they were living in a country that didn't understand that, couldn't get it. And I thought what a bad man Rushdie was for hurting them like that. But then I was also angry with the Uncles and their sons for making us stand out, yet again. I didn't want to stand out any more. I didn't want to shout about my religion – I'd tried that and it hadn't got me anywhere. I wanted to blend in. This country had given us multiculturalism, and what were we giving it in return? Burnt books and death threats. I didn't want the newspapers to report to the rest of the world that 'Bradford is firmly established in the popular imagination as a citadel of Muslim radicalism, a hotbed of agitation by adherents of a cruel and intolerant faith.' I didn't want us to be described as 'fundamentalists, militants, fanatics, extremists and terrorists'.

'Better you choose which side you are on.'

After years of being asked to choose, to declare who I was, I'd had enough.

So I left Bradford.

I didn't go that far. Just seventy miles or so down the M1, to Nottingham University, to study law and politics. But for me it really was like entering another world. A world far, far away from Bradistan. Away from Umejee and Dad and the Aunties and Uncles. Away from mosques and madrasas and men with beards and book-burnings and demonstrations and fatwas. In 1989, as 'the community' stated its identity, I left home to find mine.

It's no wonder that Umejee wept uncontrollably the day that she and Dad dropped me off at my hall of residence. She knew what was coming; that the English translation of the Koran that she had packed in my suitcase would duly be placed in a drawer that was to remain closed over the coming years. I didn't need it where I was going – into the secular world, where, as I had seen on *East-Enders* and was about to discover for myself, there are no rules, no strictures. In the world beyond Bradistan, anything goes.

For me, going to university wasn't so much a learning curve as a sheer cliff drop. I came across students who were atheists, who injected drugs, who were borderline alcoholics, cross-dressers, rent boys and manic depressives. It was like being at the Hacienda every night – sin and

debauchery everywhere. If I was to survive in this godless-
ness, then I couldn't display the contempt and shock I had
done that time when I went nightclubbing. I had to realise
and accept that this was how things were in the real world
– people didn't say things like *Insh'Allah*, God willing, or
Maash'Allah, praise be to God, as they did on an almost
hourly basis in Bradford. In the real world, people never
mentioned God, and I was pretty certain they didn't think
about Him. Many of them didn't even believe in Him.
What was I supposed to do? Forewarn them of the flesh-
melting flames that would ravage them in Hell? Tell them
that unless they changed their ways, they would scream
and burn for Eternity? No, I couldn't do that. They would
think that I was mad. So I kept quiet and left my Koran
in its drawer. It stayed there even once I'd left university
to become a journalist. It was easier that way.

Umejee, Dad and me at my graduation.

I could still hear my father reading the Koran to me,
narrating stories about the Prophet Muhammad and his
life, reciting rules about how followers of Islam should
lead *their* lives and detailing the retribution they would

face if they digressed from this marked path. But whereas before Dad's voice had been clearly audible, now it was muffled. It was as though somebody had stuffed cotton wool into my ears. There were the odd times when this constant muted noise felt a bit uncomfortable, a bit unbalancing, but on the whole, I learnt to ignore it. And by doing so, I could get on with my life. I had a job working in television, plenty of friends and nobody to judge me.

Or at least that was what I thought, up until the time I was arrested and detained by the Bangladeshi government on a charge of sedition in 2002 whilst working on a Channel 4 documentary – where this story begins.

'You are not a true Muslim!'

That was what the Torturer shouted at me as I sat in front of him in the Torture Room. He didn't lay a single finger on me, as he had done with so many of the other prisoners being held in that compound, and yet I shook so hard I thought I was going to pass out.

So this is what happens when you neglect God, when you stop reading His Holy Book, when you no longer fast for Him or prostrate yourself in front of Him. When you think you can shove cotton wool into your ears to block Him out. You get punished. That was why I was in this Hell, lying on a sodden mattress on the floor of the police headquarters in Dhaka, trying to stop myself from having panic attacks – because I had failed the task God had given me on the day that I was born, that day when my father whispered the declaration of faith into my right ear. I had forsaken my duty to obey and surrender myself to Him.

'You are not a true Muslim.' It was a line that the

Bangladeshi interrogators often repeated at me when they ordered me into their office to be consecutively cross-examined and disgraced. After being accused of this one time too often, I snapped.

'Who do you think you are that you can accuse me of not being a true Muslim? Do you think that you are proper Muslims? When you treat people worse than dogs, when you electrocute them and break their bones, when you starve them? Where is the humanity in that? What way is that to treat your fellow Muslims? You are hypocrites. You talk about Islam but you do not practise it. It is you who are committing the sins.'

It must be something about being in an extreme situation that makes you behave in an extreme way, but I didn't care that it really wasn't a good idea to shout back at these men. I'd had enough. It was Muslims like them who had kidnapped my religion, distorted it, used it for their own purposes. I'd seen it at the Dhaka detention centre, where they tortured innocent people, and I would see it at the women's jail, where many of the women who were imprisoned had never even committed a crime; in fact they had been the victims of violent attacks. There were girls who had been gang-raped; teenagers who had been trafficked from rural areas to the big cities and then sold into prostitution rings, wives who had been beaten by their husbands over dowries; and women whose age you couldn't guess, their faces had been so grossly disfigured by sulphuric acid after they had rejected sexual advances. Weren't Muslims supposed to revere and protect their women, not degrade and cripple them? What interpretation of the Koran allowed such behaviour? Could they not read that:

Those who slander chaste women, indiscreet but believing, are cursed in this life and in the Hereafter; for them is a grievous Penalty. On the Day when their tongues, their hands, and their feet will bear witness against them as to their actions. On that Day Allah will pay them back their just dues, and they will realise that Allah is the Truth, that makes all things manifest. (Surah 24:23-25)

That time that I was held by the Bangladeshi authorities, almost three weeks, was the first time in my adult life that I removed those plugs I had packed tightly into my ears when I left Bradford many years earlier. Now not only could I hear properly, I could also think clearly.

I realised that I had distanced myself from my religion all this time because it didn't make sense to me any more. People around the world were saying that they were Muslims at the same time that they were killing innocent people or blowing themselves up. People were saying they were doing these things *because* they were Muslims. This wasn't something I'd just seen on the news; I'd witnessed it first-hand in Bradford when the Uncles and their sons had called for Salman Rushdie to be killed; some even seemed prepared to commit the act themselves. That wasn't what I had been taught as a child. I had been told that murder was a sin. Maybe I was wrong. Maybe I didn't understand. Maybe my religion was not what I thought it was or should be. I was too scared to ask questions in case I was accused of being an unbeliever. Besides, nobody else seemed to be querying what was going on, why some Muslims were doing things that seemed wrong. That was why I pressed the switch and put my religion on to mute.

It wasn't until I was in that Bangladeshi prison, where I saw for myself what inhumane acts were being carried out in the name of Islam, that I knew for certain that what these Muslims were doing *was* wrong. I could see it in the faces of the Torturer and the Interrogators. They had no tolerance, no mercy, no compassion.

They were the ones who were not true Muslims, not me.

And when I realised that, despite the predicament that I was in – locked up in a cell on a charge of sedition, which carried a life sentence or the death penalty – I breathed a sigh of relief, knowing now that actually I had never lost my faith since I had left Bradford all those years ago. It had been there all along.

The train pulls into Forster Square station. The carriage is empty bar one passenger, who alights clutching three pieces of luggage. He's wearing a long woollen coat underneath which is a smart tweed suit. On his head is a dark hat and in his mouth a glowing pipe. He has a jowly face that looks as though it doesn't regularly raise a smile.

'What brings you to Bradford today?' ask some journalists who are gathered on the platform with cameras and notepads.

The man replies, in an uncertain manner: 'I think I'm looking for something. I'm not sure what it is yet.'

Then he says: 'I haven't lived here properly for many years. I've lost touch with Bradford. To me, this is a lost city. Perhaps I've come here to find it.'

These words were uttered fifty years ago by J.B. Priestley for a BBC documentary entitled *The Lost City*. In it, the writer returned to the Bradford where he was born to find that the things he had cherished as a young man – the smell of freshly baked cakes every Thursday, the sound of military bands, variety performances at the theatre, vitality – had all disappeared and all that remained was 'just another English industrial city, not good enough for the people in it', a 'city entirely without charm'. Just as J.B. Priestley lamented the Bradford he had known when he was growing up half a century ago, I too mourn my old home every time I go back. The Lost City.

The train pulls into the station. Of course there are no hordes of journalists awaiting my arrival, pens keenly poised to make a note of some philosophical remark that I may make. I'm just like any of the other scores of passengers getting off at Bradford, with a particular nothingness displayed on my face.

It's always busy and noisy in the station. Regular tannoy announcements that remind fag-puffing passengers that a strict no-smoking policy operates within the area; scores of OAPs taking advantage of their bus passes that allow them to travel for free to the beautiful areas that surround the city – Haworth, Skipton and Ilkley; hijab-clad girls who know that they can hide at the top end of the platforms if they want to hold hands with their secret boyfriends; sodden alcoholics sleeping undisturbed on the steel benches in the concourse even as scores of buses start up their engines and hoot their horns. I head to the stop for the 617 bus, which will take me to my family on the outskirts of the city. I sit in my favourite seat – at the top of the bus at the front – from where I can see everything.

As the bus heads out of the station and up Sunbridge Road, one of the first things I see is coincidentally a statue of J.B. Priestley, cast in solid bronze, his coat permanently flapping in the wind and his pipe forever clutched in his hand. He looks out at us from one of the most cultured spots in the city – just outside the National Media Museum, where they show films in 3D and hold photographic exhibitions – and I wonder what this man who once said that: 'The England admired throughout the world is the England that keeps open house' and 'History shows us that the countries that have opened their doors have gained' would think of this place now, where just under 20 per cent of the population is Pakistani. The city that he once called Bruddesford and that is now known as Bradistan.

Maybe he would curse himself for ever publishing such words as he watched first with horror and then fury as those who had come through England's doors showed their hosts that they were no longer the placid guests they had once been but were now full-time residents who were entitled to entertain their own ideas – even if that meant doing something very un-English such as burning a book. From where he stands, at the top of a small hill, this esteemed man of words would have witnessed the torching of *The Satanic Verses* in 1989. Maybe that's why there's a look of disdain in his eye.

Just in front of the Tyrls, where the book was set alight, is Centenary Square – an open pedestrianised area with a semi-circumference of bars, restaurants and coffee shops. It never ceases to amaze me that even in Bradford, we now have a little bit of café culture. How wonderful. There's a large screen in the square that shows information films and sporting events, and there are always people sitting around here – council employees, the unemployed and young mums with their kids. I see a few Uncles – some of whom I recognise as Dad's friends. They never recognise me. I look very different to when they knew me as a child, as Hajjisa'ab's *bheti*. I never go and say hello – that's partly because Dad had always told the Uncles that I'm a successful barrister, and it would just be too complicated and uncomfortable to explain to them that actually I work as a journalist and have never practised law and so can't help them with their immigration or social security forms. But it's also because I know that if I spoke to them, asked them how they were, most of them would look at me with a sadness in their eyes and say: 'Things are so different now, *bheti*. Not how they were when we first came here. We have no control over our children. They don't care about us, they don't listen to us. They are doing what they want to do.'

If you go into the magistrates' court just behind Centenary Square and look at the lists that are pinned up every day detailing the names of the defendants appearing in front of the bench, and then sit in the public gallery and listen to the cases, you learn just what it is that some of these children are doing. Robbery, burglary, possession of Class A drugs, conspiracy to supply Class A drugs, possession with intent to supply Class A drugs. Time and time again there are Pakistani names on the court list; boys in their late teens and men in their early twenties – not the children of the elderly Uncles, but their grandchildren, the third generation. And when I look at the front page of the *Telegraph & Argus*, I see photographs of this third generation under headlines such as: 'Drugs Mr Big gets 12 years', 'Dealer kept drugs at sister's house', 'Drugs courier jailed for five years' and 'Drug trafficker gets 25 years'. It was never like this when I was growing up. In fact just recently I searched through the local newspaper archives going back about thirty years, and yes, there is the odd piece about men being sent to prison for smuggling cannabis resin or heroin from Pakistan into the UK, but the majority of stories that involve Pakistanis/Muslims are to do with planning permission of mosques or the closure of yet more textile mills. Not with drugs.

Five years ago, when I was writing a piece for the *Guardian* about Bradford, I came across Iqbal, a young crack and heroin addict who lived in Manningham. He'd been on drugs since he was a teenager, and the day before I spoke to him, he'd just got out of hospital after suffering a massive heart attack. He told me that drug use and dealing was rife amongst young Pakistani men. 'It's much worse than anybody knows. I tell you, what I see on the streets and in these houses, it would make you weep. Muslims are really getting themselves a bad reputation.' When I asked him why the problem was so bad, he replied: 'Well, we're always being told to fit in, aren't we, be like white people, so that's what we're doing. Some young lads, they do the religion thing like their parents. They're good and they go to the mosque and that and they look after their family. But for every one of those there's someone like me, someone who takes another way. Like the English way.'

A year later, when I tried to contact Iqbal for an article about the London bombings, I was told that he had died of an overdose a few months earlier; his body was found on the front doorstep of his flat. No doubt his parents wished he had done 'the religion thing'. Then at least he might still be alive. I've since met other drug addicts and dealers in Bradford – a father of three who lived in the attic of his house so his children couldn't see him when he was off his face on crack, a young lad who swapped his cocaine addiction for heroin when he was sent to Pakistan for rehabilitation, and a teenager who had run out of veins in his arm and was shooting up in his thighs. When I think about these people, and when I stare at those mugshots of lads sent to prison on the front page of the newspaper, I can hear them saying to me: 'Well you're the one who talks about blending in, about assimilating, about not being different. We're doing that, aren't we? What more do you want?'

I don't know.

The 617 bus heads up Westgate, past the grand Central Mosque, which has been under construction for as long as I can remember. That's because of either issues with planning permission or a lack of funds or both – I'm not sure. There isn't much money in Bradford – the statistics tell you that this part of the city is the eighth most deprived community in the country. All you have to do is look out from the top deck of the bus and you can see that – how the pound shops and bargain stores are always busy and how many other businesses have been boarded up. They've been empty for ages, long before the recession set in. Umejee doesn't go shopping in Bradford any more, she says there's no point. 'I can go round all the shops in ten minutes and never see anything that I want to buy.' She used to go every Tuesday without fail to the antiques market at the Midland Hotel, where she would expertly barter over a porcelain statue or some costume jewellery – 'It's fine, dahling. You give me for four pound. Special price. I come to you again' – but they even shut that down.

The double-decker trundles up White Abbey Road and we enter Manningham, the heart of Bradistan. Here you'll see Islamic bookshops that also sell hijabs and *jilbabs*;

jewellery shops displaying solid 24-carat gold necklaces and bangles that are bought for a bride by her in-laws to wear on her wedding day, and clothes shops that sell roll upon roll of printed, sequinned and beaded material as well as garish ready-to-wear party suits like the ones I used to wear to *shaadis*.

There have always been rumours that some of the Pakistani shops in Bradford are just fronts for washing dirty money, for moving large amounts of cash made through drug deals. I used to think that these tales were down to jealousy – in any tight-knit community it's easy to spread gossip if you're envious about the success or good fortune that a neighbour or family friend has had – but in the last few years there have in fact been a number of arrests in the city for money laundering, including one case where a travel agent was found to be part of a massive scam worth £500 million.

You just never know in Bradford what's happening behind closed doors. That's how it is. And I suppose that's how it's always been. Like that time when we were kids and we were watching *Crimewatch* and suddenly a photo of one of the Uncles appeared on the TV screen, this kind old man who came round to our house a few times for chit-chats and cups of tea. At first we thought he'd been the victim of some brutal attack. Turned out he'd gone on the run from the police for being involved in a kidnap plot. I wonder if they ever caught him.

Like they caught those other people – the ones who set Manningham on fire on the night of Saturday 7 July 2001, the night of the Bradford riot, when hundreds of boys and men, many of them Pakistani, fought against the police on White Abbey Road. The trouble had escalated throughout the day after allegations that a group of Asian lads had been attacked by members of the BNP in the city centre. By nightfall, Bradford 8 was the scene of the worst disturbances seen in Britain for twenty years. From the vantage point that the rioters held at the top of the hill, they were able to hurl petrol bombs, bricks, tyres, burning cars, anything they could get their hands on at the police officers, dressed in full riot gear, who lined the bottom of the road. Politicians and 'community leaders' were called in to try and calm the situation down. But the rioters weren't interested. They stole cars from a garage and used them to ram-raid and loot from local businesses. At one point, the Manningham Ward Labour Club was set on fire and a burning car was lodged against the fire escape so that its members were trapped helplessly inside. It was a miracle that nobody died that night.

Soon after the riot, Operation Wheel was launched. It was described as the biggest criminal investigation ever undertaken in the UK; its aim was to bring those responsible to justice, because, as one officer stated, 'the quicker we do that, the quicker Bradford can bounce back'. Over the following weeks and months, there were Wanted posters plastered all over the city, dawn raids, parents who informed on their sons, and the arrest of over three hundred people ranging from young teenage boys to men in their mid forties. It was revealed that scores of officers had been injured in the riots and that the cost of the damage had reached £27 million.

When sentences averaging four years in prison were handed down by the courts, the judges reminded the young rioters of a crucial point: 'Your family has been resident in this country for many years and this is the first occasion that any of them has troubled the courts. Today is a very sad day for them as they endure the shame which your irrational and irresponsible actions have inflicted on them.' When I went to White Abbey Road the day after the riots, as the buildings were still smouldering and the burnt tyre tracks scarred the tarmac and the stink of petrol in the air stung your nostrils, that shame was so evident. Uncles and Aunties didn't even have the strength to look at me when I asked them what had happened. They just shook their heads in silence. The Lost Generation living in the Lost City. I don't think Bradford has ever bounced back.

It came as no surprise, certainly not to me, when various reports into the riots pointed to long-standing problems of 'racial self-segregation and cultural lives. These lives often do not seem to touch at any point, let alone overlap and promote any meaningful interchanges' and suggested that 'the complete separation of communities based on religion, housing, education, culture and employment will lead to the growth of fear and conflict'. Too late. We've had segregation in this city for as long as I can remember – it was there when I was growing up and it's still there now, in fact, I reckon it's worse. I have no doubt that there are many Pakistani families in Bradford who do not live near, go to school with, work with or even ever speak to white people, and I'm sure that the reverse is also true. It's quite possible in this city. If you walk around Manningham, the only white faces you'll see are those of East Europeans, the new immigrants. The few non-Asian businesses that were in the area before the 2001 riot, such as the BMW garage, have moved out. And if you hang around at the gates of many of the schools here, you'll see that the vast majority of parents waiting for their children are Asian, more specifically Pakistani. As one education official observed: 'Few schools here could be described as multi-cultural; rather they serve mono-cultural populations of Muslim or white pupils'. There are some great initiatives in the city, such as the Interfaith Education Centre and the Schools Linking Project, which bring together kids from different races, religions and backgrounds, but we need to have sustained dialogue and communication – we need to mix much more than we do. It's the only way.

From my own experience of living in a Pakistani area and then being educated in a mainly English school, I know that segregation breeds distrust and fear. Of course it does. Pakistani families feel that everything is stacked against them – they live in overcrowded houses within the depleted inner city (they're too frightened to live on the predomi-nantly white council estates), they can't find work (in some parts of the city, where there is a high percentage of South Asians, one in four adults is out of work), they don't do well at school (Pakistani boys have GCSE pass rates that are half those of their white counterparts). They blame their bad situation on the racist policies of the white man. And the white man replies: 'Well you lot make no effort. You all live together, you don't learn our language and you keep to your own ways. You've made parts of Brad-ford no-go areas for us. This used to be our home.' That's why we've seen 'white flight' from some parts of the city – even working-class people who have lived in Manningham and the surrounding areas for generations have moved out. They've had enough.

It's difficult to see how things are going to get any better here; it's estimated that the ethnic minority population of Bradford will increase from 20 per cent to around 30 per cent by 2011 – does that mean even more segregation in the future? Probably. What will it be like for the fourth generation? Not much better than it has been for the preceding three. Probably even worse. So if you ever see me on the upper deck of the 617 bus on White Abbey Road and I look sad or fed up, as I often do, you know why.

The bus heads over the junction with Whetley Lane on to Toller Lane. The houses here are tall Victorian terraces that were once occupied by wealthy textile owners. Because there has been no substantial replacement for that once booming and prosperous industry, many of these properties have now been subdivided into flats, let out to foreign students, the unemployed and those on low incomes.

However, there is some enterprise here. Some resourceful Uncles and their offspring have set up their own businesses – halal fish and chip shops (no dripping, just vegetable oil) that seem to do quite well, shops that sell international phone cards so the Aunties can keep in regular and cheap contact with their families back home, and accident management companies that deal with your claim if you've been involved in a car crash.

These are Uncles who can now afford to send their daughters and grandaughters to the fee-paying grammar that I went to. As the bus goes past my old school, I see scores of Asian girls finishing their studies for the day. And all of them are trouser-less. It's a rare sight these days to see Muslim girls wearing trousers underneath their skirts as I had to. But certainly what you see more of today throughout the city is pupils and young women wearing the hijab. When I ask them why, they talk about Islamic identity and personal choice. 'It's to let everybody know that I am a Muslim. I'm not being forced to wear it by my parents; this is my own decision.'

I always thought that, given all the stories about drug-dealing and money-laundering in Bradford, there was little room for religion any more, that this third generation wasn't doing 'the religion thing' as Iqbal the crack addict put it, like their parents and grandparents had done, as I had seen twenty years earlier at the time of *The Satanic Verses* affair. Sure, you see boys going to the mosque for Friday prayers with their dads, but what are they up to the rest of the time? Well, according to Zaffar, there's more religion in Bradford than I realise. 'Young Muslim men here are moving away from the mosques. They see that many imams are illiterate so they are coming to us for information, for the truth. Our support is increasing; we have many professionals, students, people of all ages in our group.' The group that Zaffar is referring to is Hizb-ut-Tahrir (HT), the radical Islamic party that became popular amongst British-born Muslims after the publication of *The Satanic Verses*. He tells me that within HT there are many others like him, young Muslims who were born in this country to immigrant parents, who have graduated from university and now have good secure jobs that pay well – Zaffar is an engineer who lives in a large house just down the road from Umejee – but who feel that they are being attacked.

'Young Muslims in Bradford are aware of what is happening in this world and that is why they gather with us, so that we can become one body. They see how this government has demonised Muslims with its foreign policy in places like Iraq and Afghanistan. It is the Prime Minister who has brought terror to these shores,' he said, referring to the London bombings. 'There is huge anger and resentment by Muslims towards the treatment of Muslims. What we are calling for, a caliphate, an Islamic state – is not a fringe idea, it's in the mainstream.'

But elsewhere in the city there are concerns about the aims and operation of HT. Suleman, who works with young Muslims, some of whom have been HT members, accuses the organisation of 'breeding isolation'. He says that 'They put hatred into people, even hatred of other Muslims. They need to be outlawed. A lot of kids out there don't realise the dangers of these groups, that they teach a wrong Islam, one that causes alienation. There is a silent movement out there that wants to spread its word and cause chaos.'

Suleman may be working to dissuade Muslims from joining HT but it seems there may be a much more substantial, more deadly threat that is quietly operating in the city. In 2008, a twenty-three-year-old Bradford man called Aabid Khan was sentenced to twelve years for being part of a global network with links to al Qaeda that was planning a worldwide holy war against non-Muslims, 'to wipe out non-believers'. Khan used the Internet to recruit others into his cell, including a fifteen-year-old boy, and arranged for members to be given terrorism training in Pakistan. At his home police found 'the largest and most extensive material ever discovered, providing vast precise information and instruction as to how to carry out terrorist activity', including how to make a suicide bomber's vest. As I said before, you just never know in Bradford what's happening behind closed doors. It makes me shudder.

The only thing that gives me comfort is knowing that I'm now on the home run on the 617 bus, not far from

Umejee's door. Past the Royal Infirmary and up to the disused Seabrook's factory where they used to make the best plain crinkle crisps in the world. When I used to pass this stretch of Bradford when I was a kid, I knew that there was a point pretty much after the hospital on Duckworth Lane where the Asian faces would stop and the white faces would appear. This was a posh part of Bradford – where you were near the countryside, in particular Brontë country, where there were detached houses and plenty of space. But now, as some Pakistanis have left the working class that they were automatically part of in the 1960s and 1970s, and have escalated up into the middle class – either through education and qualification as a doctor, solicitor, accountant, etc., or through building up a solid business such as running a restaurant – they too have moved further out into the suburbs. The knock-on result of that is that 'white flight' has had to spread its wings even further afield out of the Bradford district to places such as Ilkley and Otley – the countryside proper. So when I get off the 617 bus and walk the two hundred or so metres to Umejee's, where there once were labradors and a Range Rover parked outside these houses, there are now three cars in the drive, one of which is a taxi (it's no exaggeration to say that the vast majority of taxis in Bradford are driven by Asian men), and a Koranic plaque in the window. Bradistan is expanding.

I don't want to sound like a misery guts when I describe my bus journey through Bradford, though no doubt I do. I can't help but feel that so many vital things have been lost in the two decades since I left – respect, tolerance, a certain level of acquiescence, a relatively peaceful co-existence. I'm not alone in thinking this. Ask any Aunty or Uncle.

Still there are some things that I love about the city – Salts Mill, where you can spend hours staring at David Hockney's still lifes, portraits, landscapes and pencil drawings and then have a delicious banana milkshake and a slice of lemon drizzle cake in the café; the chapatti shop off the Toller Lane roundabout, where you can stuff your face with fresh onion bhajis as you wait for your bread; the delicate Wool Exchange built in a Venetian Gothic style, with its carved portraits of notable men such as Titus Salt, King Edward III and Christopher Columbus, which has now been put to good use as a bookshop; the fact that pretty much throughout the year, somewhere in the city there will be festive lights wishing you a Merry Christmas, Eid, Vaisakhi or Diwali.

Most of all I love it when I ring the bell and Umejee opens her front door and kisses me on the forehead and asks me if I want a cup of tea and a handful of *baddam*, almonds, even before I've stepped into the hallway, and my six-year-old niece asks me if I want to travel with her on her magic carpet – 'We could go to Disneyland, you know, it doesn't take a long time' – and my two-year-old nephew looks at me suspiciously for a minute or two before he remembers that I'm the Aunty who blows big fat raspberries on his belly and he gives me the most amazing smile.

Once I've taken my shoes and coat off, I pay my *salaam*s to Dad. He looks very smart with his long jacket and shalwar bottoms and brown topi hat on his head and his trimmed beard. He looks just like an imam. Dad liked this photo. It was taken just a few weeks before he died.

8

Hutham (2002)

I've been dreading writing about this.

I can't cope with death at the best of times, but thinking about when Dad passed away and the days and weeks that followed sends me somewhere else – away from my desk in the Rare Books Reading Room at the British Library where I'm typing this, to a place where I really don't want to be.

I had that dream again last night that I used to have as a child – the one where the fat letter A floats in and out of darkness, in and out, and it's surreally enormous at the very same time that it is oh so tiny. Even after about thirty years of having this dream, I'm not sure whether it comforts or terrifies me. Just like I'm not sure whether thinking about where Dad is now, more than seven years after he died, brings me solace or scares the living daylights out of me.

Though of course, it's not Dad I'm worried about. Dad was devout. As I told you earlier, he never let anything get in the way of his religion. He prayed five times a day even if he had to do it at a friend's house, in their living room or bedroom, he read the Koran every day even if it meant going to sleep really late, he fasted every Ramadan even if it meant he became very ill; and he went on Hajj every year even when the doctor advised him not to.

It's me I'm worried about.

You see, for Muslims, death is what life is all about. Our virtues, our sins, our thoughts, our actions, our faith – the sum of our good weighed up against the sum of our bad on the Day of Judgement by the Angels Munkar and Nakir, using holy scales to calculate in a nanosecond everyone's individual divine balance. It's either positive – Heaven and Eternity in Paradise with rivers of milk and honey, trees bearing luscious fruit and silk garments; or negative – Hell and forever in damnation with boiling water poured over your head, fruit that burns your insides like molten brass and only one item of clothing, your own burning skin.

That's why I always feel sick and nervous when I think about death and the afterlife. It's so final and infinite and there's nowhere you can hide. Like you think you can on earth.

I went to Dad's grave at the Muslim cemetery in Bradford a couple of weeks ago. I stood there saying my prayers, possessing a bit more Islamic knowledge than I had at the previous visit. For example, I now knew that he was positioned on his right-hand side, not on his back. And that this period of him lying in the grave is called *barzakh*, which is like a period of sleep that started forty days after he died and will continue until the Day of Judgement. And that forty days before he had that fatal heart attack in his sleep, a leaf with his name on fell from the tree beneath the throne of God so that Izra'il, the Angel of Death, knew that Dad's appointed time had come.

There were some things I already knew: that Dad, like every other Muslim in this designated area of the cemetery, had his head pointing west, towards Mecca, and that although Islamic custom prefers to bury the dead shrouded only in a white cloth, for health reasons, everybody, no matter what faith, must be lowered into the ground in a coffin. (There was a time at the end of the 1970s when some Muslims buried their dead without coffins, arguing that such interments were more hygienic and were allowed in other towns such as Blackburn, Batley and Dewsbury. 'This sort of thing is just not on in Bradford,' said one appalled white councillor at the time.)

And there were some things that neither I nor anybody else seemed to know for sure. Like whether Dad's soul and body were together in his grave or if it was just his skeleton in there. Was he aware of the living around him, his family and friends, and could he contact them? The only information I can provide on this last point is that fairly recently my Auntie, Umejee's elder sister, who was suffering from bowel cancer, died for a few seconds whilst she was in hospital in Pakistan. In that short time, she says that she saw her dead mother, my maternal grandmother, and many of her dead siblings walking in a circle around her, and that her mother offered her a glass of water, which she refused. And then she came back to life.

It's these unresolved areas that were particularly difficult at the time of Dad's funeral, when we were already feeling vulnerable. Suddenly everyone – including Umejee's and Dad's friends – was a learned theologian with differing views as to what constituted the Islamically correct procedure.

'You must bring the body home so the soul can gain some peace before the *jannaza*, the burial.'

'You must take the body straight to the cemetery, otherwise you will disturb the soul.'

'Make sure that there is a small window in the coffin lid

so your father can know people have gathered for him.'

'Make sure that the coffin lid is solid wood. You don't want to upset your father with all the tears.'

And so it went on and on. Death is the time when you want and need to do everything properly so as not to cause the spirit any unnecessary woe, but it seems that it is also the time when Islamic practice, Pakistani culture and old wives' tales all get mixed up. I let Adeeba untangle them. I had no confidence in my own poor eschatological knowledge.

Dad's body was washed and shrouded at the morgue by my two brothers, Tassadaque and Ahsan, as prayers were recited – 'Oh Allah, forgive him.' His bier was brought to the house and laid in the garden. We, the family and scores of women, paid our respects and said our *salaam*s, even though I have since learnt that it should only be the close female members of the deceased's family, the *mahram*, who see the face of the dead.

And as Dad was taken out of the house for the final time and put into the hearse, I just remember crying: 'My dad's in there! My dad's in there!'

A thick heavy dark green cloth with Koranic scriptures embroidered in gold thread was placed over him. I can't remember if there were any flowers in the car, though I can recall how a tape was playing, a recording of somebody reading from the Holy Book, and I remember being impressed by how professional and dignified the funeral directors were. Compared to the pandemonium that I'd often witnessed at weddings as the bride and groom were trying to depart in their chauffeur-driven white stretch limo or silver Merc. Here, nobody had lost the keys to the hearse or blocked it in.

The women in the family – me, Umejee and Adeeba – weren't allowed to go to the burial itself.

'It's too distressing for females. They find it hard to contain their grief, which then makes it difficult for the soul to rest in peace.'

There was no opposing view to this edict. I don't think women had ever attended a Muslim funeral in Bradford.

However, there were many opinions on the issue of how long we should wait before we visited the grave.

'Forty days, no less.'

'You can go after one week.'

'There's no reason why you can't go after a couple of days. Just make sure you don't go after dusk. Then all the spirits rise from their tombs and they have the power to see a woman's naked body underneath her clothing.'

I think we went to the cemetery the very next morning. It was the first time I'd ever been there. My brothers told me that a few hundred men had turned up for Dad's funeral. Word had quickly got around Bradford, as word was prone to do, that Hajjisa'ab, Maliksa'ab had passed away.

All of Dad's friends, the Uncles, some of the men he used to work with at the textile mill, some of the men he'd helped out with their social security and immigration forms, the taxi drivers he knew, the Pakistani councillors he'd supported, the regulars at his mosque, they were all there. 'The community.'

I had no idea where they might all have stood. The graves were tightly packed in, a result of more and more families deciding to bury their dead in Bradford rather than transport them back to Pakistan. It was almost impossible not to step on the other fresh burial sites that surrounded Dad's. I found myself apologising many times to his new neighbours, a ninety-year-old man and a seventy-six-year-old woman.

And so the crucial forty-day period had started, where Dad gets a brief glimpse at the seven heavens and then, back at his grave, he's visited by the scary Angels Munkar and Nakir, with their black faces and eyes like lightning and voices like thunder, who ask him: 'Who is your Lord? Who is your Prophet? What is your Book?' and no doubt Dad replies with the same enthusiasm, passion and knowledge of his faith that he imparted to us when we were children as we sat around the kitchen table, so that his face lights up and he gets so excited that he does that Asian thing with his head, nodding it from front to back whilst at the same time shaking it from side to side so that overall his head looks like it's kind of rolling on his shoulders, and he quotes the Koran at length back at the Angels and he even tells them that his favourite bits are the story of Abraham sacrificing his son and the Prophet Muhammad's Night Journey, though he's also very keen on the bit where Moses parted the Red Sea in order to save the Hebrews. And the Angels, whose faces and voices no longer seem so frightening, just impatient, have to interrupt him and say: 'Okay, okay, thanks, Mr Malik, that's fine, that's plenty.'

And as he suffers some punishment in his grave, as does everybody, for no doubt having committed some sins in his life, we all start to pray, to make this period of discomfort as pleasant as possible for him.

For forty days we prayed for Dad, as we had prayed for his brother, Pajee. And nearly fifteen years after Pajee's *hutham*, pretty much the same group of women who turned up then to mourn were now present at the hall in Manningham where we said the final *duwah*, prayer, for Dad.

No matter that, according to the pamphlet 'Funeral Regulations in Islam', written by Muhammad Ali-Al Harakan, the General Secretary of the Muslim World League, 'The common customs of holding a gathering during which the Koran is recited for three nights following the death, and of arranging a mourning celebration and special gatherings on the day of the death, or on the third day after it, or on the fortieth day, or on the anniversary of the death are all abominable and heretical practices which people have introduced, and have no basis whatsoever in the Koran.'

Everybody else in 'the community' did it, held a wake. What would they say if we didn't?

I found it hard, that *hutham*. It was the first Islamic congregation I'd been part of for years, pretty much the first major one since I'd left Bradford in my early twenties. And it was for my dad.

I remembered all those *huthams* I used to go to as a child where I would moan and moan at Mum.

'But Umejee, why do I have to go? I don't even know who these people are, so why do I have to spend ages on a Saturday afternoon at their house when I could and should and want to be doing my homework?'

All those hours sat cross-legged and squeezed in on the floor, bored and unable to move, excruciating pins and needles in your legs. All that wailing, all those tears, all that *perishani*, all that sorrow.

Of course I never really got it then that one day we would need the favour returned from those Aunties whose homes we'd gone to to pray for their dead spouses or parents or children, people we had only occasionally met. But that's what we had to do – those prayers for deceased others, known or unknown, were the savings that we had deposited at the Muslim Bank of Jannaza, and now we were getting the interest back in the form of prayers for Dad; prayers that brought him peace in his grave.

As these *duwah* were being recited, I started to cry and cry.

'*Sabr kar.*' Have strength. No, please, not that phrase again. An Aunty sat next to me who I only vaguely knew had put her hand on my lap. 'You know, *bheti*, you should not weep so much. Your father is making the next step; this is the final step for him and it is the most important one. Yes, cry. Of course you are only an *insa'an*, a human being, but your religion tells you that this is the destiny for us all, for all Muslims. He is going to a good place, *insha'Allah*, a place unlike this earth, where he will see his family again and he will meet his Maker. And you will all see him again. This is not a thing to be tormenting about.'

'It's not that easy to find comfort in a transcendental Paradise when you're trying to come to terms with the very real loss of a father.' That was what I wanted to tell Auntie but didn't. I didn't have the gall.

'Your father was a religious man,' she continued. 'God will look upon him kindly that he performed his Hajj many times and said his *namaz* regularly, even just before he died. That is a beautiful thing.'

'Yes, you're right, Aunty.' This time I did speak out loud. 'You're right.'

You see, that Monday morning when Dad passed away, he had woken up at dawn to say his prayers, as he did every morning. Then he went back to bed, and that was when it happened. He died peacefully in his sleep, minutes after he'd bowed down to God.

That gave me comfort.

I knew that Dad would be fine on this, his final journey. He never doubted or neglected his faith and was as well versed in it as many of the imams he knew.

Unlike me. As I'm writing this, sat at Desk 377 in the British Library, the books I have in front of me are: *Koran for Dummies* by Sohaib Sultan; *Islam for Dummies* by Malcolm Clark; *Teach Yourself Islam* by Ruqaiyyah Waris Maqsood.

I've tried to recall from memory the things that Dad taught me from the Koran when I was growing up, but to be honest, it's been so long since his in-depth lessons that I'm struggling to remember the details, like what the Holy Book says about the birth of Jesus: he was born to the Virgin Mary, who 'Allah hath chosen and purified' (Surah 3:42), or about the rights of women: 'I will deny no man or woman among you the reward of their labours. You are the offspring of one another' (Surah 3:195).

So I'm now referring to study aid books, like the ones listed above, which incidentally are very good. I've glanced at other more detailed books from the vast collection that the British Library holds, with titles such as *The Empowerment of Women in Islam* and *Democracy: the rule of Law and Islam*, but I just get confused and can't fathom what they're going on about.

As I leave the Reading Room and the two guards sitting at the desk ask to check my bags (as they do with all visitors), one of them picks up my Koran, translated by Abdullah Yusuf Ali, and asks me: 'Do you mind if I look at this?'

Instantly I reply: 'Of course not. I'm sure God would be very happy.'

Where did that come from? That's the kind of thing Dad would say, not me.

The guard flicks through it and then picks up another book, a thin book with a black and red cover that I bought in a bookshop in Notting Hill. It is called *The Inhabitants of Hell*, and so far I've only ever opened it once, because I've been too petrified to read it, having glanced at chapter headings like 'Hell is Real' and 'The People who will be in the Fire Forever'. I'm sure it's meant to make me feel very nervous, to literally scare the hell into me, so for the time being, I'm leaving it unread.

He then picks up *Jihad: The Trail of Political Islam* by Gilles Kepel and *From Muhammad to Bin Laden* by David Bukay. He looks up slowly at me from behind his desk.

'I think I know what you're thinking,' I think to myself.

Then out loud I say: 'I'm just researching a book. These reference books are brilliant. They explain the religion in easy, basic terms so even someone like me can understand.' I shift my . . . *for Dummies* collection towards him in the hope that he might realise I am one.

'Are you a Muslim?' asks his Asian colleague.

'Yes, I am.'

'Have you seen the Koran that they have in the library here? It's beautiful.'

'Yes, I have seen it. It's lovely, isn't it?' I lie, because I'm relieved that they don't think I'm a fundamentalist and aren't going to confiscate my library pass, which is crucial for my research.

Two days later, I do go and look at the Holy Book that the guard was referring to. In fact there are three Korans on display in the library's John Ritblat Gallery, and they really are beautiful.

There's one – Sultan Baybar's Qur'an – that was made in Cairo in 1304 AD with all seven volumes written in gold; another, the Mamluk Qur'an, which looks like a tapestry in gold, white and blue; and another from Arabia that is one of the earliest Islamic codices in the world, so I don't recognise any of the script.

In part I go and see them because they're right here, in the very same building where I'm working, in part because I've been thinking a lot about the sacred text; but in the main I go because this is how I will always remember Dad. With the Koran.

Untying that loose knot he tied the day before in the ivory-coloured silk sling that is wrapped around his favourite copy with its dark green cover that you only saw when Umejee decided to handwash the luxurious dust jacket, which was maybe once every couple of months. Slowly and respectfully unravelling the silk, entwining it around his left hand, ensuring all the time as he does so that it never touches the floor. Then he slips the neat bundle off his hand and places it on the table. Holding the hard-back Koran in his right hand, he kisses its spine and then touches it with his forehead and gently lays it down on its latticed wooden lectern, always so that it is resting on the left-hand side of the V-shaped holder and the cover, with the words 'The Holy Qur'an' embellished in gold, is visible. He opens the front, searching for the little red silk thread that is just poking out of the bottom of the pages to mark which *surah* he is up to (Dad never folded down any of the page corners out of reverence, though other copies of the Koran we had at home did have creases – probably down to me and my siblings), then finds the correct chapter and starts to recite from it: '*Alaf, lam, min . . .*'

'*Bismillah hirahman niraheem*, Ya' Sin . . .'

Just as I am reading from the Holy Book now, standing by Dad's grave in Bradford. From Surah 36, which is called the Ya'Sin, also known as the Throbbing Heart of the Koran. The one you recite to ease the pain of the dead and to receive blessings for yourself.

I read slowly in unfamiliar Arabic, using my finger to guide me through the scripture. I should be reciting out loud so that Dad and/or the Angels can hear me, but I'm embarrassed and I don't want a nearby family who are in mourning to hear how clunky my speech is, so I compromise and mutter under my breath.

Even though there's a busy road and a primary school nearby, the cemetery is quiet, and even though my head-scarf is tied tightly around my ears, I can hear myself in my head mumbling words that I don't understand. It takes me about half an hour to finish the chapter, twice as long as most regular readers.

There are three pink flowers, petunias, I think, that are still thriving, a few weeks after we planted them to commemorate the sixth year since Dad's death.

I am feeling much better now than I did on that terrible day. I had a dream recently – well, it wasn't really a dream, more like a snapshot. And I only saw it the once, but it was such a beautiful thing that I will never forget it.

I'm standing on the edge of a diving board that is so high in the sky that I can touch the sun. I'm wearing a white gown and a white swimming cap, one of those old-fashioned plastic ones that straps underneath your chin.

I'm about to jump off either into the bright blue sea in front of me or the bright blue pool below me. It's not clear. As I bend my knees, I wave down at Dad, who is lying beside the bright blue pool, listening to music through some headphones. He can see me even though I am so far away. Umejee is next to him reading a *Hello!* magazine and my three siblings are relaxing, stretched out on white chaises longues. Everybody is dressed in pristine white – the men in white T-shirts and shorts and the women in long flowing dresses. Everything is beautiful. Everything is calm. Paradise.

'You will live in our hearts and minds for ever' is what is inscribed in English on Dad's black marble tombstone. And in Arabic: 'In the name of Allah, the Compassionate, the Merciful'. The very first words Dad taught me from the Koran.

It's quite a size, the Islamic section of Scholemoor Cemetery. I suppose it needs to be, to cater for Bradford's growing Muslim community. Since we buried Dad, there have been scores of other graves dug. Quite a few of his friends are in here, like Uncle who used to own a halal meat factory and Uncle who used to work as a taxi driver. I wonder if Dad gets them all round to his every night for a bit of *gap-shap*, chit-chat, and a cup of *chai*, kindly brewed by the woman in her fifties three rows up from him who probably does a much better job of making Pakistani tea than I ever did, whilst a group of young lads congregate at the main gate and watch speeding Subarus and Mitsubishis zoom past, and up in the top right-hand corner of the necropolis, babies and children play quietly with their cuddly teddy bears. As dawn breaks, everyone retires and all that is left for us humans to see is the fur-less, sun-bleached teddies, now perched on the tiny graves. They don't look loved or hugged. But they are really.

Infants' Corner at the cemetery is very sparkly. Garlands of green, red and blue tinsel, silver bells and gold foil flags, incongruously cheerful, are wrapped around the melancholy headstones, and those brightly coloured hand-held windmills that I thought you could only buy at the seaside are either whizzing around so fast that their collective tik-tik-tik is annoying, like a broken extractor fan, or they're twirling calmly, humming like a yogi. Neither sound can distract you, however, from what you see. It's got to be one of the saddest sights – the tomb that reads: 'Born and died on 5th August' or 'Lived for 2 hours on November 18th'. And when you see one after another, it's impossible not to weep.

I can't imagine how much strength God gives the parents of these babies.

'It's got to be one of the hardest things, hasn't it? There was one man, Pakistani I think, who couldn't find a bone marrow for his eleven-year-old and he died. It's tragic.'

Graham Swain is a gravedigger whose name is known to any Bradfordian Muslim who has ever lost a loved one. He dug Dad's grave and pretty much every single other hole that holds a Muslim at the Scholemoor and Bowling Cemeteries. You can spot him there most days, in his tractor, with his brother and son who work with him. Graham's a very talkative fellow, and by his own admission has a loud voice.

'You've got to, with my job. It can be very chaotic, a funeral, with one person saying we should do this and another person saying no, that's not right. Tensions can run high. There's one that comes to mind – there'd been a road traffic accident and the police had got involved and the coroner withheld the body for four days. People stop sleeping then, don't they, because all they can think is that we've got to get this person buried as soon as possible as Islam says. So something was said at the funeral by one of the young lads: "What's a white man doing here?" and the elders had to calm him down.

'It's not a job, this, it's a responsibility. When I was a kid, I used to live near a cemetery and I used to think that gravediggers were the lowest of the low. But I take this very seriously – I went to night classes to learn Urdu, and then I started to study the Islamic way, talking to imams and reading books. That's why people take me seriously – because I know what I'm doing. Sometimes I get imams and mullanas coming to me for advice. Did you know that?'

'No, I didn't. So what is the proper way to bury a Muslim?' I ask. 'You hear so many conflicting things. What did you do with my father?'

Graham spends the next twenty minutes or so explaining in meticulous detail what happens. That you don't need to have an imam present; that mourners stand inside the grave to pack soil tightly around the cadaver; that everyone throws three handfuls of earth into the hole; that once everyone has done that, he uses his digger to fill it up. And he puts me right on a few things.

'Oh no, you don't have to be buried in a coffin. A lot of the Bengalis, Somalis and Iraqis go in just in a white shroud. And you do sometimes get women at the funeral; I think it's mainly the Mirpuris that do that, but Pathans are seriously against it. I expect you wanted to be at your father's funeral.'

Actually, I'm not sure I did. Too upsetting.

Graham obviously talks with a Bradford accent, but his sentences are peppered with Urdu words, like *mittee*, soil, *pehr*, feet, and *sihr*, head. It's really sweet to hear him speak, the fact that he's making such an effort, and no doubt that's what endears him to the Muslims he comes across.

'They do like it when I speak their language. They feel as if they're in safe hands.'

That plus the fact that he's prepared to dig graves any time of the day or night, twenty-four hours a day, three hundred and sixty-five days a year. No matter that he also works as a builder and is fifty years old.

'I've done them at midnight, sometimes even later. I understand the Islamic way of burying as close to death as possible, and every one of them has to be dug a fresh grave, there and then. Your grave shouldn't be waiting for you. Muslims have to do their *ʐakat*, and so I also have to do my bit of charity.'

I ask him the inevitable question. Does he ever get frightened?

'To be honest, the only time I was scared was the night of the Bradford riots and I was burying an eleven-year-old girl. We thought the trouble was going to come in to us. But no, this is a peaceful place, isn't it? You become friends with them. It's like a community. Mind you, I can tell you some dreadful stories. There was a family of three – mum, dad and their kid – and they were on their way to a funeral in London and their car crashed into the central reservation on the motorway and they all died. And there was a twelve-year-old girl whose mum had converted to Islam. Her parents weren't getting on and the kid took an overdose. She didn't mean to kill herself; she told her sister:

'I've taken some pills, just wake me up in an hour,' but the sister fell asleep. The young girl never woke up, and when her mum tried to bury her in this part of the cemetery, the dad was trying to stop the funeral, saying, 'I want her in the Christian section.' I just said to him: 'We're all going into the ground. It really doesn't matter where.' There are quite a few converts buried, you can tell from their names.' I spot Joselyne, Charlie and Sarah. 'There was another one where they had to exhume a body because it turned out this bloke's mistress had poisoned him with arsenic. And then there's the grave of the very first Muslim to be buried in Bradford.'

I can see why Graham gets invited to so many meals by the families he meets – an intriguing, if chilling, dinner guest.

It turns out that there's a bizarre story behind this first Islamic interment. Back in 1904, when Bradford held its Great Exhibition, a whole Somali tribe of around a hundred warriors and their women were invited to the city to live in a specially reconstructed village in Lister Park. There they entertained and educated Bradfordians with daily demonstrations of dancing, spear-throwing and arrow-shooting. Unfortunately one of the women, Halimo Abdi Batel, contracted tuberculosis and was put into isolation for five months but then died. As her body was transported from the park to Scholemoor Cemetery along Manningham Lane, accompanied by scores of mourning Somalis, this extraordinary spectacle 'drew the gaze of shopkeepers and pedestrians alike' and the police were called to keep these observers a 'respectful distance' from the funeral cortege. Up until a century after Halimo's burial, her grave was unmarked. In 2004, a new headstone was erected with a Koranic inscription.

So that was the first Islamic burial. The latest one, Graham tells me, was a young lad, 'and they say that about five thousand people turned up for his funeral'.

The young lad he mentioned was called Qasim. It wasn't difficult to locate his grave in the cemetery. Although there was yet no headstone (these are set in after forty days), only a small marker with his name on, there were five or six plastic chairs around the mound of soil. The only other bits of furniture in the whole graveyard were small inconspicuous stools that looked as though they would only seat children. It was apparent that mourners were coming regularly, in large groups and for long periods, to pray for Qasim and so needed somewhere more comfortable to sit.

By coincidence, a few days earlier I'd seen a full-page tribute to Qasim in the classified section of the *Telegraph & Argus*.

In the name of God, the most gracious, the most merciful,

Qasim tragically passed away on May 11, 2008.

Dearly loved by his mother, father, brother, uncles, aunties, his girlfriend and all his friends.

His father would like to sincerely thank everyone for attending his son's funeral.

Qasim was just twenty-two when he died. His photo in the *T&A* showed a fit and smiling young man who'd certainly been popular and much loved. I saw that a website had been set up in his memory where family and friends had posted their condolences, something I'd never seen before.

'U were jus the best, cheeky smile :) top lad had sum

gud tymz t'getha may ALLAH grant peace on your body and soul till the DAY of JUDGEMENT! Inshallah bro. AMEEN!'

'studio on a Friday/Saturday isn't d same u used to get sum sik haircuts rip cant get over it we will meet again jannat inshallah' – a language that was part religion, part street.

There was even a message from Amir Khan, the boxer: 'QASIM TAKE CARE MY BROVER INSHALLAH SEE U IN HEAVEN TAKE CARE HUDAFIS X'

There were quite a few tributes to Qasim on the website from his mates at the gym, and some photos of sporty Audis. It seems that he was like many other young men in Bradford I'd come across – into looking good, weight-lifting and fast cars.

Maybe I'd seen him driving around the city or at the many halal takeaways in Manningham, or even maybe at a *shaadi*.

Though his face didn't look that familiar.

Not like yours. I'll never forget your face for as long as I live.

Epilogue

A Letter (2009)

To Shehzad Tanweer:

I think about you a lot. Most of the time you're just in my head, but at other times there's something in the news and then I see your face on the television and in the papers.

Like a few days ago when it was announced that the inquest into your death is going to be held at the same time as the inquests of the fifty-two people who died when you did what you did.

And the time last year when they showed Mohammed Siddique Khan's video with his baby daughter, where he says to her: 'Sweetheart, not long to go now. And I'm going to really really miss you a lot . . . Be strong. Learn to fight. Fighting is good.'

And then on the third anniversary, precisely three years after you did what you did, there was a story about how your family held a 'party' at your grave in Pakistan, where apparently they said prayers for you and gave out food – salted and sweet rice – to the villagers.

I didn't know that your grave is in Pakistan. They say that it's got the biggest headstone in the whole cemetery.

What's in there? Surely there can't be much?

Some people say that when a person dies, the soul and body remain together in the grave until the Day of Judgement, and others say that the soul leaves the body after burial and wanders the earth.

Where are you? Where's your soul?

Anniversaries are, of course, supposed to be a time when you remember. The first thing that always comes into my head isn't really a memory – it's an image, an aerial shot of London. Everything is gridlocked, stuck, apart from a few emergency vehicles with flashing blue sirens that jerk forward. Stop, start, stop, start. Even the pavements are congested with pedestrians. It's all very busy, noisy and agitated. Then there's a whoosh of silence and I see your face.

On the cover of all the newspapers.

And they've got your birth certificate. To prove that you're British. It says that you were born at St Luke's Hospital in Bradford on 15 December 1982. You lived at Waverley Road. That's just a couple of streets away from where I grew up in Great Horton. I bet I passed your mum on the street as she pushed you in your pushchair – I was on my way back from the grammar school and she'd been to the fruit and veg shops near the junction with Horton Park Avenue to get some *thunya*, *gobi*, *aloo* and *mirch*. She probably looked as stressed as Umejee did back then, when they had to do everything themselves, no car, hardly any money. Trying to get the most for her cash – inspecting every bit of produce, every vegetable, every herb, every spice, making sure it wasn't going off.

What were you thinking about then as your mum wheeled you around those shops? What did you see that made you do what you did?

I was trying to work out what it was about you that drew my attention to your face more than to the other three photos on the front page of all those newspapers.

Two things, I think. That you were born in Bradford 7 and that you looked so much fresher, younger than the other three. I know that Hasib Hussain and Germaine Lindsay were actually younger than you, but it was just that picture the press got hold of. You looked like you had a school uniform on, a white shirt and a black sweater, and you had a half-smile on your face, whereas the other three looked older and harsher. You didn't look like you belonged to that group. Though that isn't the right word, is it? I'm sure you were all much tighter than 'a group'. You had to be.

I went back to Bradford three days after you did what you did, back to the street where you were born. I'd been asked to do a piece for the *Guardian* newspaper about what Muslims felt about it. It was the first time in years that I'd been down Waverley Road. I wrote about what the area was like back then when I was a kid:

It was an unremarkable, even dull place. Most of the Pakistani families were traditional, so adolescent girls were not allowed to play on the streets. My playground was the landing in our terraced house. Our mothers-cum-housewives would entertain themselves by gossiping – Bradford's Asian community was tight-knit to the point of being claustrophobic. Everybody knew everybody else's business. Two decades on and you now see young girls on their bikes, dressed in *shalwar kameez* (traditional dress) on Waverley Road. The gossipmongers are still there. But this time they genuinely have something to talk about. 'How could a boy do this to his own mother? That poor woman. She must feel like it's *kemat* [Judgement Day].' A bearded man, a halal butcher, tells me what he thinks will happen to the boys in the Afterlife. 'They will not go to Heaven. That is a myth. Their bodies will be eaten by scorpions and snakes and they will burn in Hell.'

I remember how angry the butcher was. He spoke in that half Yorkshire, half Pakistani accent that makes you think at first that he's taking the mickey, but he was so angry he was spitting as he talked so that he had to wipe the saliva from his mouth and beard, exclaiming that what you had done was 'bang out of order!' and that you 'won't have to wait until Judgement Day to be punished; his Hell will start in his grave'.

What's happening inside your grave right now?

When you did what you did on that Thursday morning, I was at a conference in a hotel on Piccadilly in the centre of London. I was bored senseless, listening to the speakers going on and on. At first there were all these reports of electrical surges on the Underground causing problems. The conference organisers advised people not to travel on the Tube. No worries. I haven't stepped foot on the Underground for years. I'm claustrophobic, you see. The last time I was on the Tube, it stopped in the tunnel between South Kensington and Gloucester Road for about twenty minutes and I had such a bad panic attack that I had to ask the passenger sitting next to me, who happened to be a Buddhist monk, to calm me down by chatting to me.

So I was planning to get the bus home, or even better, walk through St James's and Hyde Park.

But then I received three phone calls in quick succession. One from the editor of the *Guardian*, asking me if I could file a piece about the bombings; one from my sister, who was at King's Cross, scared and confused; and one from a Pakistani news organisation who wanted to see if I could do some live reports for them from central London.

The sum total of these three brief conversations was devastating – my legs started to shake and my head felt giddy and I had to sit down. I started to cry. And once I'd started, I couldn't stop. People were staring at me. A woman, one of the event organisers, came up to me and put her hand gently on my arm.

'Are you all right? Have you had some bad news?'

I nodded slowly.

You must have heard those women weeping at *huthams* when you were growing up. So maybe you know what I mean when I say that it's not like a noise humans make. At first you can't catch your breath and you end up braying like a donkey – eeorr, eeorr – and then as realisation kicks in, the stuttering stops and you whimper like a shot deer.

Your parents must have told you how bloody petrifying the end of the world would be, that sense of the absolute end approaching when the earth quakes and spins and everything is on fire. Well, when you did what you did, that's the sound I made and that's what I felt had happened.

I was exhausted all day, and it wasn't down to the six miles I had to walk home.

I knew that from now on, it would all be so different.

The very next day happened to be a Friday. Like many other journalists, I went to the East London Mosque on Whitechapel Road, a short walk away from Aldgate, where you did what you did. But unlike all the other journalists there, I didn't end up in the main prayer hall (which was packed, by the way). I found myself in the women's room. Well, the temporary women's room. There was so much media interest that their regular prayer area was being used to accommodate the press pack, and so the ladies found themselves in a strange room. And I found myself in a strange position. You won't like this but on 8 July 2005, I prayed in a mosque for the first time in over twenty years. It had been as long as that. Or maybe you will like it. Maybe you'll think that it was only because of what you did that I ended up doing *jummah* that day, that your action triggered my reaction and made me 'a better Muslim'. I don't know.

I have to say that I didn't enjoy the mosque experience when I was a kid. I had to sit with loads of old women in a dank, dark room. It wasn't a fancy purpose-built mosque, like the ones you see in Bradford these days. It was just a room in a house, a makeshift mosque. A bit like the one I saw on the TV news, the Shahjalal mosque in Merseyside that was petrol-bombed two days after you did what you did, and like the one I visited on Mile End Road in London, the Mazahirul Uloom, that had its windows put through a few days after you did what you did.

I don't know what it was like for you over at the men's section in the mosque, but watching these old women carry out their ablutions wasn't a pretty sight. All that spit and mucus being hawked from mouths and noses. And that stink of sweaty shoes that wafted in from the corridor. It's not very trusting, I know, particularly in a holy place, but I got into the habit of hiding my shoes behind a shelf. I'd heard so many stories of footwear going missing, and there was no way I was going to suffer the embarrassment of going home barefoot.

Given the option of being surrounded by elderly women reciting their prayers in Arabic (a language I didn't understand) and chatting away in Urdu (a language I didn't understand) or being at home watching *Top of the Pops*, I knew which one I'd always opt for. Not that I had the choice. If Dad said: 'Go to the mosque', I went to the mosque.

And I suppose I didn't have any choice twenty-odd years later, when a young girl at the East London Mosque asked me if I was going to join the kneeled congregation that Friday afternoon. I immediately replied yes. Partly out of respect and partly out of embarrassment – I couldn't justify being in a mosque and not praying. Not after what had just happened.

What should have been a profound moment was brought to a premature end when a woman exclaimed: 'Sisters! You're all praying in the wrong direction! You need to move to the right!' It turned out that in this new room, and without a compass to point us to Mecca, we'd unwittingly been praying to China. We shuffled round on our knees. I smiled. It was comforting to know that even after all this time, there was still disarray in mosques.

When prayers finally began, I was scared that the women would spot that I wasn't a regular worshipper. My memory of the *duwah* was hazy and my attire wasn't appropriate – I was wearing a shirt that rode up my back every time I bowed to the floor, exposing my flesh.

But even after all this time, after all these years, I could still recall the Arabic that Dad had taught me. All those times he'd woken us up in what seemed to be the middle of the night so we could learn our prayers. When we would rather have had an extra hour of sleep. When we couldn't understand why we were learning this foreign language. Now it made sense. I did have to really concentrate, though. I expected silence once *jummah* had begun, but the room resonated with the laughter of children playing at the back of the room and the sound of coins being dropped into plastic charity buckets. And, of course, the now constant police sirens outside.

You know it's said that prayer is a time of private meditation, a one-to-one with God. Well, only He can tell you what was going on in the heads of the other women in that room. Why they were all dry-eyed. Me, I can tell you that I was sobbing so hard my lap was soaked with tears. At first I thought it was guilt, remorse at not having stepped inside a mosque for so long. Then I realised. It was sadness. I was crying for my faith.

And for Muslims.

For the women in that room.

For the men downstairs.

For the Aunties and Uncles.

For Umejee and Dad.

For myself.

You must know that our parents – your parents and mine – did what they could to bring us up in a country that was alien, indeed sometimes hostile to them. I read that your dad used to work as a police officer and then he started up his own fish and chip shop. Mine worked in the textile mills. I'm not sure if your mother had a job. Mine didn't. She brought up four children. Mum always says that she brought us up pretty much on her own – Dad was always working or at the mosque. He taught us about Islam and Mum did everything else. She never learnt to speak or read English, and so life was really tough for her, even in a Pakistani area like Bradford 7. Simple stuff, like going to the doctor's or getting on the right bus, was difficult. Sure, language is an essential tool for living, but I have a gut feeling that even if Mum was fluent in English, things would still have been hard. You see, for her and many others, it was about more than communicating with others, fitting in and getting on with things. It was about her, who she was. She suffered the most fundamental loss when she came to the UK. She lost herself, her very being. That person who had been born and grown up with an untainted identity of culture, customs, family, nationality and religion.

When she left Pakistan, she left behind that life and her real self. It's easy for people to say, 'Well, she came here for a better life, of her own free will.' But it's not that straightforward. Her life here has always been foreign. This is why you hear so many Aunties, maybe even your own mother, talking about *perishani*. It's a word that I always thought meant 'sorrow', but I've slowly realised as I've got older that it really means 'bereavement'.

You know, when I was younger, I used to get really annoyed with the Aunties in Bradford, 'the community'. I thought that they just moaned and gossiped all the time, were full-time pessimists, only ever saw their cup as completely empty. I used to avoid them at weddings or when they came round to our house. But now I see them as my Ummah, my community. Sure, I know there are Muslims suffering all around the world because of war or famine or disease, people who need our help, but you can't just forget about the Ummah on your own doorstep. Your family, the Aunties, the Uncles, *apnay lokhi*, our people, 'the community'. They need us too.

There's a whole generation of women out there who are in mourning for themselves, for the loss of their true lives, and you might have witnessed that, even in your short life.

So why did you have to add so to your mother's grief?

I don't know how familiar you are with the Koran, but you probably know what it says about parents:

> Thy Lord hath decreed that . . . ye be kind to parents . . . Say not to them a word of contempt, nor repel them, but address them in terms of honour. And out of kindness, lower to them the wing of humility and say: 'My Lord! Bestow on them thy Mercy, even as they cherished me in childhood.' (Surah 17:23–24)

You must have heard that saying: 'Paradise lies under the feet of the mother', and that story when the Prophet Muhammad advises a would-be soldier that his primary duty isn't fighting on the battlefield, it's staying behind to look after his mum.

I wonder how your mother is these days. Without her Kaka, her little one. I wonder if she has that same mournful lost look that I once saw on the face of a woman whose two sons had been murdered in a gang fight in Tooting, or whether she threw herself against the walls like an Aunty in Bradford did after her son died in a road traffic accident.

Your poor mother.

We sometimes forget how bloody hard things have been for our parents, how they still are so difficult.

We never forget what they're like for us, though, do we?

The next generations on, the 'British Muslims'.

It would take too long to go through it in detail now, and I'm pretty sure you already know what I'm talking about, but briefly what I mean is:

Being pulled in opposite directions (a bit like that woman in the religious film I saw at the Liberty cinema in Bradford with Dad when I was little, the woman whose arms are tethered with rope that two men heave on, one to the left, the other to the right).

Being cut in half (a bit like that story Dad told me when I was little, about two women squabbling about who was the true mother of a baby boy and the wise King Solomon advising: 'Well, cut him in two so you shall both have a part of him').

Never feeling that you belong anywhere.

Not being sure/confident of yourself, your thoughts, actions and beliefs, one week feeling proud of your Pakistani heritage, maybe because you went out with your friends for a curry and they really enjoyed themselves, and the next feeling ashamed, maybe because there's been a story on the news about an honour killing in a Pakistani family.

Never feeling that your parents understand how difficult it all is, even when they say that they do.

Never feeling that your friends understand how difficult it all is, because, according to them, 'You were born here, weren't you? Why should it be difficult?'

Getting utterly fed up with the number of times some idiot asks you: 'Do you class yourself as Muslim first or British first?' Then privately asking yourself, actually just how compatible are those two things in practice, and is it humanly possible to strike some working agreeable balance between them, agreeable to you, to those around you and to God?

Always contemplating and never knowing what it means to 'do the right thing'.

Wondering why you spend so much time thinking about all this stuff, and whether other people do too.

It's not easy, is it? Did you find it hard?

I can't tell you precisely how long I've spent thinking about who I am, but I'm talking years, not months. Long before you did what you did. I don't know if I'm a particularly sensitive person, not very robust, but at one stage, it got to the point where I was looking at normal people – ones on the bus, on the streets, in shops, in cars, in their homes – thinking to myself: 'I should be like you', then seeing somebody else: 'No, I should be more like you.' 'No, you seem quite happy and sorted. I should be like you. Tell me how you run your life.' It really did my head in but I couldn't stop myself. Once I'd started, that was it.

Basically what I was doing was trying to find somebody who could tell me who I was. Because I didn't know.

I still don't really.

Which is why I can never listen to songs like 'Losing My Religion' by REM or 'Faith' by George Michael. They make me nervous.

I remember once having to interview a family in Stoke-on-Trent for an ITV current affairs programme. It was a really sensitive subject; the mother or the daughter, I can't recall which one, had been sexually abused by a doctor. It was a Sunday afternoon, and even though the family had taken this big decision to talk to me about this horrific thing that had happened in their lives, I really struggled to pay attention to what they were telling me. I was too busy looking at what furniture they had in their living room, what they were wearing, what biscuits they had put on a plate for me, if they allowed their Yorkshire terrier to sit on the sofa, what car they had parked in their driveway, how many photographs they had on their mantelpiece, if they had fresh or dried flowers in the hall, whether they had lots of fragrant toiletries in the bathroom.

I'd become obsessed with the physical minutiae of people's lives, the objects that they surrounded themselves with, what their lives looked like at a glance from the outside, because it might provide me with some crucial information, an authoritative picture of how to live, albeit a two-dimensional record, but one that I could take away and then duplicate. And then I would be sorted. Then I could relax and not fret any more about who I was.

So if I lived in a semi in the Midlands with a dog and three kids and an estate car and ate custard creams and drank tea from a floral teapot and kept lavender soap in the bathroom and a rocking horse in the hallway and grew yellow hyacinths in the garden, that would be it, that would be who I was.

Me. Simple. I would be defined by these straightforward basic criteria. No need to delve any deeper than that. No need to analyse how they lived or how I should live. No need for a third dimension. And for those brief joyous moments when I thought like that, I could breathe.

But for the rest of the time, I thought about it too long and too hard and it made me feel ill. Who I was.

And then all I could do was try to breathe.

It's not a good idea, believe me, to think about some things too much. They just screw up your head.

So what was going on in your head when you did what you did? You were just twenty-two years old. Did you ever struggle, or were you so sure of yourself and of who you were by that age? When did you start staring at normal people on the bus, on the streets, in shops, in cars, in their homes, thinking to yourself: 'I don't want to be like you. I never ever want to be like you'? Did you hate normal people? Like the ones you played cricket against, or the ones who came to your fish and chip shop.

I was trying to find out if you'd had a lot of hassle at the shop. Whether that was what made you angry at normal people, white people – racism.

For quite a while I was angry at white people. In the summer of 2001, I was doing an undercover film for Channel 4 in a town in the Midlands that had a history of far-right activity. This man called Ian Stuart Donaldson who had been the head of a neo-Nazi band had lived and died around there and he still had many supporters in the area who gathered for gigs and meetings. The place used to be a thriving coal-mining town, but when I was there, there was hardly anything left, apart from a train station, a few shops and some terraced houses. And there were hardly any non-whites, just a Chinese takeaway and a curry house.

I spent three months running a corner shop in the town, and all the time, hidden cameras recorded everything that went on – day and night, inside and outside. In that short time, they filmed the young man who smashed eggs against my window; the man who threw gravy at the shop; the car passenger who lobbed a brick through the window; the young child who walked past and said, 'Hey, Paki, come and get me'; the two men who tried to break in, justifying it by stating that 'I don't mind black people. You know what I mean, black people, fair enough, but Pakis, man. Fuckin' asylum seekers'; the middle-aged skinhead who stuck his finger up at me when he walked past and uttered the words: 'Shoot you, Paki bastard'; the lad who asked for twenty Superking Blacks and then added: 'If you want to fuck, fuck off back home. You dirty-mouthed bitch;' and the skinny man who warned me he was going to 'call the NF, know what I mean? You shouldn't be allowed over here, you should fuck off back.'

I'm not kidding, in the entire time I was in this place, I only walked down the high street about five times. I was too scared.

And do you know what hurt me the most? That I'd assumed

I was only going to get hassle from the members of the far right that lived in the area, but in fact pretty much all the abuse I got was from the normal white people in the town – men, women and children. So then I stopped liking or trusting white people. Because I thought they all thought that I was a piece of shit.

Even though I had a security man with me, I was petrified the whole time. You can't relax in a situation like that, let your guard down. You never know when something's going to happen or who's going to do what. I was living above the shop, which made it so much worse. I could never sleep at night.

After I'd finished those three months, I was really poorly. The muscles in my back seized up because of all the tension, and I got stress-related eczema all over my face and neck – I looked like I'd aged about twenty years and I lost a lot of weight. I had to go and see a doctor. And I was angry all the time, so angry. It was like a rage that these people thought that they could treat me like that. Like I was nothing. Like I had no right to be there. Like they were so much better than me. Like they could judge me.

I think if I'd been in the shop for more than three months and if the TV cameras weren't recording, I would have tried to get my own back somehow. Maybe by selling out-of-date Peperami and chicken and mushroom pies. Make those racists sick as they had made me sick.

The only thing I can say is thank God I got out of there just a few weeks before 9/11. It makes me shudder to think what might have happened then.

So I could understand why you might have been angry if you'd had a lot of trouble at your fish and chip shop. But from what I can gather, you didn't. And there didn't seem to be economic factors that drove you to do what you did. Apparently you left over £100,000 in your account.

Of course, that's been the big question, hasn't it?

Why did they do it? What made them like that? Home-grown terrorists. British Muslim bombers.

There have been all kinds of things said about you.

By your dad: 'My son was more British in his orientation than anything else.'

By your cousin: 'He felt completely integrated and never showed any signs of disaffection.'

By your friend: 'He was always praying. He'd even get up at four a.m. to pray. He's a very religious lad but a lot of his friends are white. He never put a white man down.'

By your Uncle: 'He was a very kind boy, intelligent and well respected by everyone. This is not the boy I know. He must have had forces behind him. There is no explanation I can come up with for why he did this. Our lives have been shattered.'

By your dad's friend: 'With Shehzad, there was no indication. It's not as if he was growing up in a home where there was a radical outlook. His father loves England. He's built up businesses here, made some money, and Shehzad was also on the way up. His parents both speak English. Theirs is truly a British Muslim household.'

By your tutor: 'It didn't feel like you got to know him in any way. You could classify [his nature] as private. He didn't appear to be all that outgoing or bubbly.'

They even printed what you wrote down on your university application form to get some sense of you:

> I have many interests and would like to keep my options open regarding my future career. I know that I am still curious about human behaviour and the scientific study of the human mind. I also have a keen interest in the way we grow physically as well as cognitively. I believe the 3 A levels that I am studying at present will

enable me to continue my studies and hopefully help me find answers to some of my questions on human behaviour.

All this conjecture and theorising. And then you come out and say it in your own words. In the videotape that you filmed before you did what you did, the one that was released in July 2006, entitled 'The Final Message of the Knights of the London Raid'.

I was just watching it and thinking how old you look. Quite haggard, like you haven't slept for days. Maybe that's down to the beard, the red and white checked keffiyeh wrapped around your head and the bad lighting. And the anger.

'To the non-Muslims of Britain, you may wonder what you have done to deserve this. You are those who have voted in your government, who in turn have, and still continue to this day, continue to oppress our mothers, children, brothers and sisters, from the east to the west, in Palestine, Afghanistan, Iraq and Chechnya. Your government has openly supported the genocide of over 150,000 innocent Muslims in Fallujah ... You have openly declared war on Islam and are the fore-runners in the crusade against Muslims ... Our blood flows across the earth. Muslim blood has become cheap ... We are one hundred per cent committed to the cause of Islam. We love death the way you love life. I tell you all British citizens to stop your support to your lying British government and to the so-called "war on terror" and ask yourselves why thousands of men be willing to give their lives for the cause of Muslims.'

And then you have a message for me:

'Oh Muslims of Britain, you, day in and day out on your TV sets, watch and hear about the oppression of the Muslims, from the east to the west. But yet you turn a blind eye, and carry on with your lives as if you never heard anything, as if it does not concern you. What is the matter with you that you turn back not to the religion that Allah has chosen for you? You have preferred the *dunya* (world) to Allah, His messenger and the Hereafter. Fight against the disbelievers, for it is but an obligation made on you by Allah . . . Fight against the oppressors, the oppressive British regime.'

When I heard you speak, do you know how I felt? Like I did when I was running that corner shop in the Midlands, like I've already just told you: 'I was angry all the time, so angry. It was like a rage that these people thought that they could treat me like that. Like I was nothing. Like I had no right to be there. Like they were so much better than me. Like they could judge me.'

What you have said and what you did has made me angry.

What you have said and what you did was wrong.

What you have said and what you did were not the things my dad taught me.

I am by no means an Islamic scholar, but I do know that suicide is a cardinal sin in Islam, punished by eternal damnation and the endless repetition of the act by which the person killed himself. According to the Hadith, 'Whoever kills himself in any way will be tormented in that way in Hell. Whoever kills himself with a blade will be tormented with that blade in the fires of Hell. Whoever kills himself with a piece of iron will be punished with that same piece of iron in the Hellfire.' Life is the ultimate gift of God, and only He can decide when to take it back.

You say: 'Fight against the disbelievers, for it is but an obligation made on you by Allah.' But the people you killed weren't disbelievers, *kuffirs*, as you call them – they were also born of the Abrahamic faiths, they were People of the Book, and as Surah 2:62 states: 'Those who believe in the Koran, and those who follow the Jewish scriptures, and the Christians and the Sabians – any who believe in Allah and the Last Day and work righteousness, shall have their reward with their Lord; on them shall be no fear, nor shall they grieve.' The Holy Book includes quotes from the Bible and the Torah – stories of Adam and Eve, Moses, the Golden Calf, David and Solomon, Jesus and the Virgin Mary. Dad was always telling us stories about Moses and Jesus and Abraham.

There's also Surah 109:6: 'To you be your religion, and to me, mine' and Surah 2:256: 'Let there be no compulsion in religion.' Surah 5:32 states: 'We ordained for the Children of Israel that if anyone slew a person it would be as if he slew the whole people.' This was quoted quite a lot by Muslims after you did what you did, to show that killing one person is like killing all of humanity.

You state that: 'Muslim blood has become cheap. Our blood flows across the earth.' Did your actions not just add to that flow? Muslims died on that day when you did what you did. Were you not thinking about your Muslim brothers, sisters, mothers and children then? And how can you talk about the oppressed in Iraq, Palestine and Afghanistan when it is also Muslim killing Muslim there? Didn't Saddam Hussein as a Sunni Muslim torture and kill the Shia Muslims in Iraq? And you neglect to mention the genocide in Darfur, where thousands of African Muslims have been killed by Arab Muslims. Where is the Ummah, the Islamic brotherhood there?

The Prophet Muhammad's orders to fighters forbid direct and intentional attacks on civilian targets, on non-combatants, even under conditions of necessity. Surah 2:190 says: 'Fight in the cause of Allah those who fight you, but do not transgress limits; for Allah loveth not transgressors.' Isn't that what you did, use disproportionate force against people who had caused you no harm? Islam doesn't accept the idea of collateral damage, holding innocents responsible for the wrongs of others. That isn't honourable combat.

You have an Islamic obligation to the country where you

live, a contract as a British citizen to obey its laws and respect its government and to participate in its systems, including its political processes, to promote justice and fairness and to maintain peace and stability.

Jihad is the struggle for righteousness, to do God's will and yes, it can be violent or non-violent, but the Prophet Muhammad said that the greater jihads were the jihad of the heart – one's internal spiritual struggle against the whispered temptations of Satan and for the sake of God, the jihad of the tongue – to peacefully spread the teachings of Islam and the jihad of the hand – to carry out those actions that lead to justice. Fighting against others, jihad of the sword, is the one you gave precedence to, but this is the minor jihad.

This list is by no means conclusive. I know that there are some things that I've left off – for example, that surprise attacks are forbidden; that only the leader of an Islamic state, not individuals, can declare war; that armed struggle must not create a sense of fear, terror and helplessness in society; that any part of the Koran must be read within the context of its historical setting and the writings as a whole. But there is one other vital point I want to add, which isn't from any academic or scholarly text, just from what I know.

The God I read about in the Koran, the God my dad taught me about, the God I was brought up to understand, is not the same God that you seem to believe in. How many times does it say in the Koran: 'In the name of Allah, Most Gracious, Most Merciful'? How many times does it say: 'For Allah is Oft-Forgiving, Most Merciful'? 'Allah is He that careth for all'? 'For Allah doth blot out sins and forgive again and again'?

I don't recognise your god, who is violent, vengeful and malicious.

My God is kind, loving, compassionate. He knows that we are *insa'an*, human beings who sometimes make mistakes.

After all, He made each and every one of us. It is up to Him and nobody else to judge us and our deeds.

Where did you learn all that stuff you talk about in the video? Who taught you it? It wasn't your father.

Strange. I can see you now, sitting at your kitchen table, wearing a white embroidered topi on your head. You must be about six or seven years old. You're reading the Holy Book with your dad, as I did with my dad. Did yours do that thing that mine did? As he was reading, if he came across a bit he really liked, he would stop and say out loud: 'Vah bay vah, such beautiful words' and smile.

I can see that you're really concentrating. You're trying hard to get it right.

When did you start getting it so wrong?

I recently interviewed a young Sri Lankan man who had been a member of the terrorist organisation the Tamil Tigers (LTTE) for many years, first as a child soldier and then as an officer. He told me that he had been taken away from his parents and siblings at an early age and placed in a camp, where the LTTE announced that they were now his family. He was trained to fight, to kill, to become a suicide bomber, to die for their cause. They taught him different morals where wrong was right and right was wrong. 'We had no choice but to do what they asked. Including killing ourselves and others. We had no choice.'

Did you have a choice?

I wonder if things are ever going to get better for us, after you did what you did.

If all this can ever be salvaged.

I know there's a lot of work going on in our communities, a lot of people trying to educate, inform and guide, like Sheikh Musa Admani at the London Metropolitan University, the Naisha project in Bradford and the Muslim Youth Helpline. All striving to separate haqq, truth, from batil, falsehood.

But maybe it is too late.

You say in your video: 'What you have witnessed now is only the beginning of a series of attacks, which, *insh'Allah*, will intensify and continue until you pull all your troops out of Afghanistan and Iraq, until you stop all financial and military support to the US and Israel, and until you release all Muslim prisoners from Belmarsh and your other concentration camps. And know that if you fail to comply with this, then know that this war will never stop, and that we are ready to give our lives, one hundred times over, for the cause of Islam.'

When I was much younger, it must have been around the period of the National Front marches in the late 1970s and the 1981 Brixton and Toxteth riots, I remember Mum used to watch the news, trying to concentrate on the words as well as the pictures. She heard 'Defend Rights for Whites' and petrol bombs smashing and saw angry men, some in suits with Brylcreemed hair and some in braces and bovver boots with shaved heads, overturned police vans, riot shields, flames and black and white faces streaming with blood.

She turned round to us and gave us her own translation.

'One day, you will see, they will send us all back home. They won't want us here any more.'

And we used to laugh openly in her face.

'Mum, don't be so silly. We were born here. We've got British passports. They can't just throw us out like that.'

'You'll see. Maybe not now. But some time. When the situation gets really bad.'

The situation has got really bad. And it makes me wonder.

There are always stories of arrests and trials; so many that it's hard to keep up. Plans to behead a British Muslim soldier, to blow up the Ministry of Sound nightclub, to detonate bombs on transatlantic flights, to kill travellers at Glasgow airport, to cause explosions at the Bluewater shopping centre. Sometimes the defendants plead guilty and sometimes they plead not guilty. Nobody knows for sure what's coming, what is being planned, but what's obvious is that you weren't the only ones.

Maybe you know this, but a lot of people have been arrested in relation to terrorism and then released without charge. They say that of around twelve hundred arrests, only about forty people have been convicted.

I met a young man who lives in east London. He was detained by the police for six days. They asked him what his views were on 9/11 and on what you did, they questioned him about a text message on his phone to his wife asking her to get some garlic, cake and masala, which they thought was some secret code, they raided his home, took away his car, computer and passport and interviewed his neighbours. He told me he was 'boiling inside with anger for ages'. There was another man I met in Birmingham who ran an Islamic bookshop. He said that when he was detained, his business suffered and he had real difficulty getting some of his property back from the police. He described the UK as a 'police state for Muslims'.

There was a report recently that stated that British Muslims 'suffer disproportionately more from discrimination, racial abuse and racial attacks than any other faith group, and the more openly devout they are, the more likely they are to experience harassment and abuse'. There have been reports of women's hijabs being torn off, arson attempts on mosques and pigs' body parts being nailed to their doors, a man being force-fed bacon and an imam being blinded after an attack.

I've covered a lot of 'Muslim stories', and in the last four or so years, things have changed. People are tired, fed up, furious, scared. They talk about Islamaphobia, foreign policy, Guantanamo, torture, unlawful detention. And they talk about you.

'Islam is all about peace, its direct translation is peace. Those boys were brainwashed. They were not Muslims. They have brought a very bad reputation to us. They have caused us much trouble. This is our home and we don't want to cause any trouble with anyone.' That was what an old man told me when I spent a couple of weeks in your part of Leeds for a story for the BBC on the second anniversary of what you did.

Another man who sent his two kids to the local madrasa said: 'We're not hiding anything in there. We're not teaching anything out of the ordinary. We have to live in this society, by its laws and regulations. I want to get to Heaven when I die.'

You could feel the weariness in people – it reminded me of Bradford after the 2001 riots. They didn't want to feel that they had to justify themselves, apologise for their faith, for their existence. Some of them had lived there for years, had settled with their families, were working in offices and shops, running small businesses, going to the local schools, and yes, praying at local mosques. They did all this just like many other Muslims around the country. They'd found a practical compromise between following their faith and living in Leeds 11. Islam and Beeston. They had tried for ages to fit in as best they could. And now they were the objects of scrutiny. Their way of life was being analysed, debated, criticised and even distorted. And still it goes on.

Because of you. Because of what you did.

No surprise really then that more than one person told me to fuck off when I was there.

During the time I was in Beeston, I visited all those places you know so well – your home on Colwyn Road, your fish and chip shop on Tempest Road, the mosques on Hardy Street and Stratford Street, the Iqra Learning Centre and the Hamara Youth Access Point.

As I walked round Leeds 11, I couldn't help but wonder.

What did you do on Eid? Did anyone keep a goat in their back yard, like they did in Bradford 7?

Did you have to go to loads of weddings like I did and be brutally assessed by the Aunties to see if you made the grade as future spouse material for their precious offspring?

Were you banned from watching *EastEnders* like we were?

Did you dance in private like I did?

Did your mum love the royal family as much as mine did?

Did your dad drive a clapped-out Nissan like mine did?

Were you a quiet child, like I was?

Did you think a lot, like I did?

Did you talk to God as often as I did?

What did you pray for in your *duwah*?

What thoughts did you have during Ramadan?

Did you ever stay up during the Night of Power? Did you ever see the Angels? What did you ask them for? Did you ever get it?

Why did you do what you did?

All these questions and hardly any answers.

I didn't really find out much about you when I went to Beeston. Apart from a story someone told me about how you'd been involved in something called 'the Mullah Crew', where they claimed you basically kidnapped young Pakistani drug addicts, locked them in a room for a few days and put them through cold turkey. I don't know if that was true, though.

Actually, there was one other thing. Most people I met described Leeds 11 as 'a peaceful, integrated community', but it seems that wasn't the complete picture.

A few others, Asian and white, told me that there'd been racial tension between a couple of the local schools for some time – Matthew Murray High (with a significant number of Asian pupils, where your friends Mohammed Siddique Khan and Hasib Hussain went) and Merlyn Rees High (in the white area of Belle Isle) – and that there'd been ongoing fights between the kids, some of them so bad the riot police had been called out. People talked about the murder of a sixteen-year-old, Tyrone Clark, by four Asian lads in April 2004. They laid into him with baseball bats, poles and bits of wood before he was fatally stabbed. The trial judge said it hadn't been a racial attack, but some in Beeston that I spoke to said it had.

What you did hasn't helped the situation. I was just looking at a report for those two schools I mentioned, which were merged into one school fairly recently. It says: 'The links of the London bombers with the Beeston and Holbeck areas have heightened tensions and concerns, as have the activities of the extreme right wing.' I went to see the headmaster when I was in Leeds, and the poor man was trying to do what he could to calm the situation. But they're now planning to shut that school down.

On the whole, Beeston struck me as not massively different to Bradford 7, where I grew up. Various nationalities, a lot of Pakistanis, some students, a few fancy cars, the odd boarded-up building and increasingly a lot of drugs. I found out the other day that not far from our old home in Great Horton, a group of Vietnamese men had turned one of the houses into a cannabis farm and that there'd been some trouble with a rival Pakistani gang. There are always things going on behind closed doors. And in people's heads. Things that we have no idea about.

Maybe you kept a lot of stuff in your head. Did you talk to anyone about it, about what you wanted to do and why you wanted to do it?

In your video, 'The Final Message of the Knights of the London Raid', there are many mentions of 'martyrdom' and the Afterlife: 'The love of martyrdom for the sake of Allah was not motivated by poverty, unemployment and emptiness . . .

It was motivated by the love of Allah and his messenger . . .
Oh Allah, grant us martyrdom in Your cause, and accept us
among the righteous on the day we shall return to You . . .
Little is the enjoyment of this world compared to the Hereafter.'

Was that what it was about for you? Being a jihadi and
martyr, to get into Heaven? Did you know that you don't have
to die with such violence in order to be classed as a martyr?
A mother who dies in childbirth also achieves that status –
all her sins are forgiven and she enters Paradise for ever.

I'm sure that those people you met before you did what
you did told you all about Paradise, about the beautiful gardens,
the velvet couches, the silver bracelets, the crystal goblets,
the flowing rivers and the valleys of pearl, but how much
information did they provide you with about the Day of Judgement, when that trumpet blows and:

> When the sun with its spacious light is folded up,
> When the stars fall, losing their lustre,
> When the mountains vanish like a mirage,
> When the oceans boil over with a swell,
> When the World on High is unveiled,
> When the Blazing Fire is kindled to fierce heat,
> And when the Garden is brought near,
> Then whither go ye?
> (Surah 81)

And what did they tell you about Hell?

Were you frightened by Hell and Satan when you were
growing up?

About three months ago, I bought a book called *The
Inhabitants of Hell* by the late Shaykh Muhammad Mitwalli
al-Sha'rawi, an Egyptian scholar and teacher. It's only seventy-
seven pages long, and has a black cover with an orange-red

panel set in the middle. I've been carrying it around all this time and I've never dared open it. You see, Hell gives me a cold chill – makes me shiver.

I've only read the back, which states the book's mission.

Shaykh al-Sha'rawi compellingly shows that the eternal destiny awaiting every human being, in the grave and after resurrection, is the fruit and the embodiment of his or her own actions, intentions and beliefs in this fleeting world.

But now I've finally plucked up the courage to open up this book. I know it's right there in the Koran, but when I see it all together, all those details, all those descriptions, page after page in *The Inhabitants of Hell*, it petrifies me.

As for those who reject Our signs, We will roast them in a Fire. Every time their skins are burned off, We will replace them with new skins so that they can taste the punishment. (Surah 4:56)

And when those burning call for help, they will be helped with water like seething molten brass, frying their faces (Surah 18:29).

Verily the tree of *zaqqum* will be the food of the sinful. For it is a tree that springs out of the bottom of Hell-fire; the shoots of its fruit-stalks are like the heads of devils. Truly they will eat from it and fill their bellies therewith. Then on top of that they will be given a mixture of boiling water. (Surah 37:64–67)

And so it goes on – garments made of fire, sinners bound together in chains and yokes, punishment with red-hot iron maces, burning sparks as huge as a palace arising from a fire made of men and stones, a thorny plant for food, a boiling mixture of blood and pus for liquid, much screaming and weeping.

Shaykh al-Sha'rawi concludes that 'This book must be taken quite literally for what it is: a practical manual, describing terrible aspects of the fate awaiting those who fail to get the point of what it is to be a human being.'

Not equal are the Companions of the Fire and the Companions of the Garden. It is the Companions of the Garden who are the victors. (Surah 59:20)

What made you think that killing so many people would make you a Companion of the Garden?

I haven't mentioned this to you, but I'm writing a book about growing up in Bradford. I was born in Leeds but we moved to Bradford soon after. It struck me that I'd never visited the street where I was born, so one Tuesday evening last summer – in fact it was just a few days before the third anniversary of what you did – I drove down the A647, past the Yorkshire Television studios where I once worked, to LS6. It was one of those evenings where there are streaks of pink in the sky and everything seems just warm and fine. The area was a bit familiar to me – a few years back, I'd driven to a friend's house there, and when I got back to my car, I found footprints on the driver's window. Somebody had tried to break in. So now I parked on a main road and walked to my old address.

The area wasn't that different to Beeston – red-brick houses and a main road with loads of streets, cul-de-sacs, branching off it. It was poorer than Beeston, though – these were proper two-up, two-down houses, rather than Victorian terraces. And there seemed to be more young people around, who looked like students to me. But it was quiet.

As I turned off the main road, I couldn't see a road sign for my street, so I asked a young African couple who were walking towards me.

'What, you want to see the bombers, do you?' the man laughed.

My mind couldn't make sense of his question, and before I had the chance to pursue it any further, he pointed up the next side street and said: 'Yeah, this is it.'

It was a short climb. Number 13. Number 13. No number 13. There was a 1, 3, 5, 7, 9 and 11. But no 13. I knocked on one of the doors.

'Excuse me, I'm sorry to disturb you, but I'm looking for number 13. Maybe I'm being a total idiot, but I don't seem to be able to find it.'

'Number 13? No, it doesn't exist. Who is it that you're wanting?'

'Nobody. I'm just researching my family history and that was my first home.'

'I've been here for nearly thirty years in this house and I can't recall a number 13. Mind you, they did build lots of new houses just before I moved in. I was one of the first to live here.'

'Do you know if there were other houses here before?'

'There were, yes. Do you want to come in? Better than standing at the door.'

I walked into a large kitchen and introduced myself to Gary. We sat at the dining table, where there was an ashtray, the *Racing Post* and *The Plays of Oscar Wilde*.

'We have to stick up for our own,' he commented, glancing at the book. Gary was born in Northern Ireland, but moved to Leeds when he was a teenager. 'When I came here, Paddy wasn't welcome. I've seen a lot of prejudice in my time, even now. So where are you from?'

I wasn't in the mood for all the toing and froing that

normally accompanies this question, and which goes a bit like this:

'So where are you from?'

'Bradford.'

'No, where are you really from?'

'Really Bradford.'

'No, I mean where do you come from?'

'I just told you. Bradford.'

So I just came straight out with it.

'My parents are from Pakistan.'

'What did your dad do?' asked Gary.

'Well, he used to work in the mills.'

'There used to be a factory up on Kirkstall Road. He might've worked there. There used to be a lot of Asians round there and not so many here when I moved in first. Now it's all mixed. Do you see that white building there?' He pointed out of the window at what looked like a derelict house. 'That was a pub where the English, Irish, Scottish, Indians and Jamaicans used to go. There was never any trouble until people started selling drugs, and then the police closed it down. Now people don't mix as much. My next-door neighbour was an Indian woman and we used to chat. This is mainly a student area now.'

'So do you think my old house was pulled down?' I asked.

'I think it was. Though I dare say that the old foundations, you know, the cellars, are still here, underneath. They're still at it, building new properties. Those flats there, they're for students. Done by some developer. They only went up two or three years ago. And that's quite new too.' This time he pointed at an ugly block of brown flats opposite his house.

'Can I ask you something?'

'Yeah.'

'Just a minute ago, when I was walking up here, this bloke said something about bombers. Was he joking or something?'

'Oh that. I nearly forgot about that. It's funny how you forget about these things with a bit of time. Well, I'm not sure if it was a Tuesday, or a Thursday, but my daughter came to pick me up to go shopping. I was coming back, along Kirkstall Road and there was a helicopter just going round and round. The woman at the shop said to me: "You won't get home now, Gary. The whole place is surrounded by police." I had to get in, to feed my dogs. When I got here, they'd cordoned off the area, quite large it was, from the church. A lot of people just ended up going to the bookies. The police had to give my dogs some water. There were all kinds of rumours being spread at the time. Chemicals and bombs. Where I come from in Northern Ireland, bombs is bombs, not chemicals. But then I saw it on the news – a bomb factory, right here, on my doorstep, and I didn't know it.'

You know though, don't you?

Alexandra Grove, Leeds, LS6.

You know that address, don't you?

The street where I was born.

The street my dad walked down to work a triple shift at the mill.

The street my mum pushed me up as I slept or chuckled or cried in my pram.

The street you and your friends marched along determinedly, all the while staring straight ahead as though you were wearing blinkers, to enter the block of flats that weren't there when I lived there. Or have I got that wrong? Were you nervous? You and the others.

Because this wasn't a normal flat, was it?

There were no comfy sofas, no wide-screen TV blasting out the latest Bollywood feature, no proud family photos, no overly decorated tissue box holders, no vases stuffed with silk flowers, no fridge stocked with full-fat milk and *matai*, no curries on the hob.

No. Your flat contained triacetone triperoxide, hydrogen peroxide, citric acid and bicarbonate of soda, bulbs, ice packs, wires, batteries, respirators, masking tape and filter paper. And a list that reminded you to buy: Cooler Box, Fire Extinguisher, Cig Lighters, Blinds 4 the Car, *Zam Zam* and to 'Memorise *duas*'.

Why did you want to drink Holy Water before you did what you did? To purify your soul?

Why did you want to remember your prayers by heart? Which god were you praying to before you did what you did?

The flat on Alexandra Grove, with its curtains taped down, a gas mask on the cooker beside a bright yellow saucepan, plastic containers floating in a bath full of filthy water, dying plants on the shelves, a protective suit and heavy-duty gloves in the bedroom, a pedestal fan standing in the corner of the living room amongst plastic bottles and boxes and funnels and glass jars and electric hot plates and all sorts of powders: this is the flat where you made your bombs to do what you did.

The flat that you and the others left at 3.30 a.m. on 7 July 2005 with your black rucksacks in your Nissan Micra. To do what you did.

To drive down the M1 motorway. To stop at Woodall Services for petrol and snacks. To carry on to Luton station. To get the Thameslink train to King's Cross. To hug your friends at the station. To board an eastbound Circle Line tube train. To sit on the second carriage of the train. To detonate the rucksack next to you on the floor at 8.50 a.m.

To kill innocent people.

To injure innocent people.

The very street that you and your friends left to kill yourselves and fifty-two other people in the name of your god was the very street where I was born, thirty-nine years ago, in the name of my God.

When the words '*La illaha ill Allah, Muhammad ur rasul Allah*' – 'I bear witness that there is no God but Allah and that Muhammad is the Messenger of Allah' – were whispered into my right ear.

When I was born a British Muslim.

Then there were no suicide bombers, no inflammatory clerics, no jihadis, no *kuffirs*, no war on terror, no extremists or fundamentalists, no radicalism or fanaticism, no Islamism, no Islamaphobia.

Then there was just my father and his four children sat at the kitchen table quietly reading the Koran.

Zaiba Malik

Acknowledgements

My heartfelt thanks to my family for their love and support – to Adeeba, Tassadaque, Ahsan, Ammarah, Rayan, Kamran and Yasmin.

I am grateful to Jason Arthur for his good advice and diplomacy and to the rest of the team at William Heinemann, in particular Emma Finnigan and Laurie Ip Fung Chun. Thanks also to Claire Paterson.

My gratitude to three people who have encouraged me to write at different times of my life – Shirley Elliot at Great Horton Middle School, Dr JS McClelland at Nottingham University and Ian Katz at the *Guardian*.

Thanks to Emma, Deena and Suzy for their wonderful friendship and to Nancy for her wisdom.

And for ensuring that the task of writing a book never became a lonely ordeal, I am indebted to the brilliant British Library and the security guards there who always welcomed me with a smile. Thanks also to the helpful staff at the Local Studies section of the Bradford Central Library.

My utmost admiration to all those who work and volunteer in the various day centres of Bradford; what you do is invaluable.

To all the Aunties and Uncles, our mothers and fathers

who have given us so much, I can only offer my sincere respect.

Much love to SRS.

In memory of Maliksa'ab, Hajjisa'ab; my Dad.